THE GREAT BIG GLORIOUS BOOK FOR GIRLS

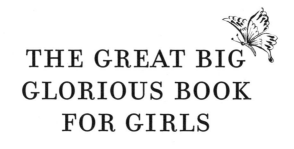

ROSEMARY DAVIDSON *was brought up in County Down, Northern Ireland, along with her three sisters, many dogs, a pet sheep and several cows and horses. From her seamstress grandmother, she learnt to sew, and from her Great-aunt Dolly, to knit and to bake. From her father, she discovered the recipe for itching powder and where to always find tadpoles in spring and wild strawberries in summer. And from her sisters, amongst many other skills, the fine art of leg-wrestling.*

She now lives in London with her daughter Florence, eleven, and son Spike, eight, and works as an editor and translator of children's books.

SARAH VINE *was born in Wales and grew up in Italy. As a child she showed very little talent for sporting activities and an almost infinite capacity for sitting around reading silly comics, gossiping, trying on her mother's shoes, eating and high theatrics, all of which have stood her in excellent stead as an adult. She has been a journalist all her working life, and now writes for* The Times. *Sarah is married with two children.*

THE GREAT BIG GLORIOUS BOOK FOR GIRLS

Rosemary Davidson and Sarah Vine

Illustrations by Natacha Ledwidge

VIKING
an imprint of
PENGUIN BOOKS

This book is dedicated to
Florence and Spike
Bea and Will

VIKING

Published by the Penguin Group

Penguin Books Ltd, 80 Strand, London WC2R 0RL,
England

Penguin Group (USA) Inc., 375 Hudson Street,
New York, New York 10014, USA

Penguin Group (Canada), 90 Eglinton Avenue East,
Suite 700, Toronto, Ontario, Canada M4P 2Y3
(a division of Pearson Penguin Canada Inc.)

Penguin Ireland, 25 St Stephen's Green, Dublin 2,
Ireland (a division of Penguin Books Ltd)

Penguin Group (Australia), 250 Camberwell Road,
Camberwell, Victoria 3124, Australia (a division of
Pearson Australia Group Pty Ltd)

Penguin Books India Pvt Ltd, 11 Community Centre,
Panchsheel Park, New Delhi – 110 017, India

Penguin Group (NZ), 67 Apollo Drive, Rosedale,
North Shore 0632, New Zealand (a division of
Pearson New Zealand Ltd)

Penguin Books (South Africa) (Pty) Ltd, 24 Sturdee
Avenue, Rosebank, Johannesburg 2196, South Africa

Penguin Books Ltd, Registered Offices: 80 Strand,
London WC2R 0RL, England

www.penguin.com

First published 2007
1

Copyright © Rosemary Davidson and Sarah Vine, 2007

The moral right of the authors has been asserted

All Illustrations by Natacha Ledwidge unless otherwise
stated below. Copyright © Natacha Ledwidge, 2007

Silhouettes and other illustrations by Dover Books
used on the following pages: 14, 26, 27, 38, 50, 54, 55,
58, 66, 67, 128, 129, 135, 154, 169, 170, 172, 192, 194,
201, 230, 240, 249, 252, 257, 273 and 296.

**Grateful acknowledgement is made to the following
for kind permission to reprint copyright material:**

for the syrup recipes, *Darina Allen's Ballymaloe Cookery
Course* by Darina Allen © Darina Allen 2001, Kyle
Cathie Ltd

for the lemon barley water recipe, *The Times Cookbook* by
Frances Bissell © Frances Bissell 1993, Chatto & Windus

for the jokes, *You Must be Joking* © Ladybird Books Ltd 1986

for the Hungarian Water recipe, *Herbs for Natural Beauty*
by Rosemary Gladstar © Rosemary Gladstar 1999,
used by permission of Storey Publishing Inc.
All rights reserved. www.storey.com

Set in Filosofia and Wingdings

Printed in Great Britain by Clays Ltd, St Ives plc

A CIP catalogue record for this book is available from
the British Library

ISBN: 978-0-670-91710-5

This book contains information on health-related
matters. Neither the authors nor the publisher intend
this to be a substitute for professional medical advice,
or accept any legal responsibility for the use or misuse
of such information in this book.

CONTENTS

INTRODUCTION

Boredom, as a wise man once almost said, is the mother of invention. Precisely when the earliest cave girl got together with the cave girl next door for that first, pioneering game of Knock Down Ginger we shall never know, but one thing you can be sure of: those two little girls never looked back. Perhaps they went on to devise hopscotch, or to make the first face mask out of some mud and a handful of bog weed. They might even have grown up and invented language — you know, so they could get together and gossip about her in cave number 63.

All the best things in life — theatre, painting, music, books, fashion — came about partly through a need to make life more interesting. Millennia later, and girls haven't changed — well, not that much anyway. Obviously today's women know all about the Internet and computer games, and most can text 100 words a minute while programming the DVD player — but they all still thrill at the sight of a pony, and will spend hours experimenting with glitter paint. The modern world may be a superhighway of technological invention, but sometimes you just have to spend a week making a papier mâché piggy bank, or a special tie-dye T-shirt.

In this book you will find hundreds of things to do — some of them old, some of them new, some of them familiar but forgotten. There are games, recipes, tricks, old wives' tales and home truths. Some of it is tremendously practical and useful, some of it more flighty. Some of it your mothers will approve of — in fact they might even want to join in (if this happens, don't be too hard on them: it can be very traumatic for mothers when they discover they can't skip like they used to). Other stuff (e.g. the sugar sandwiches) might raise a frown, but they won't be able to tell you off too much since you can bet your last button they did the same when they were girls.

This book is also packed with tips of the sort no girl can afford to overlook (or so we like to think), from how to pluck your eyebrows to dealing with a boy to knowing how to tell if an egg is fresh. There are films, books, quotes and jokes to inspire you – and some excellent diagrams and drawings to show you the way.

As for us, the authors, well: Rosemary's the outdoorsy type – grew up in rural Ireland, one of four sisters. She spent many happy years in the elevated world of book publishing before leaving to pursue her own muse. Sarah, on the other hand, is an urban girl through and through (hardly surprising since she grew up in Turin, an industrial town in the north of Italy) and writes for *The Times*. Rosemary likes gardening and knows which way is up on a sheep. Sarah, on the other hand, is so hopeless when it comes to nature that she has AstroTurf in her garden. She does, however, make excellent fairy cakes, even if she does say so herself. Between the both of us, we hope we've covered all the bases. Enjoy!

NEEDLECRAFT

Time was, most girls knew how to sew, embroider and generally do a range of fiddly things with yarn, thread and needles. Then came equality and feminism, and needlecraft somehow seemed dull and demeaning. After centuries of sitting at home embroidering while men did all the strutting about, shouting and starting wars, women put away their sewing boxes and joined in. Out went home economics. In came really useful stuff, like . . . er . . . learning to use a lathe.

It's a shame, really, because sewing isn't just about taking up hems and darning socks; you can make lots of fun and beautiful things. And besides, being able to sew a button back on your coat doesn't mean you can't also become prime minister.

EQUIPMENT

Our grandmothers all had sewing boxes, marvellous treasure troves of useful little bits. Typically, a sewing box would contain:

* pin cushion and needles
* tape measure
* small scissors
* different kinds of thread
* safety pins
* elastic
* seam unpicker
* dressmaker's chalk
* thimbles

They would also collect beads and buttons (often in jars or old biscuit tins) and keep bits of string or pretty ribbon. You should do the same. Next time you get a new pair of shoes or someone gives you a present in a nice box, keep it. Then start collecting items for your sewing box — you'd be surprised how much stuff you can save or scavenge from everyday life. Ribbons, spare buttons, beads, safety pins — stow them all away. Most haberdashery stores have a fabric remnant box, where you can pick up pretty pieces of material for a few pennies. In charity shops, look out for old clothes that can be cut up and made into new things such as bags or outfits for your dolls.

Sewing

There are many different types of stitches in sewing, but you only need a few basic ones to get started. Choose a medium-sized needle, some pretty-coloured cotton thread and a napkin-sized piece of material — a basic cotton or linen is best. Finally, make sure you have somewhere comfortable to sit, with good lighting and a surface to spread your things out on.

The following basic stitches may seem a little dull at first, but practising them will give you a good foundation from which to expand your repertoire.

RUNNING STITCH

* Easy-peasy-lemon-squeezy. Thread the needle and tie a knot at the end of the thread. Pass the needle in and out of the material, picking up roughly ½ centimetre at a time (diagram A). Try to keep the stitches as even as possible. Do this until you're feeling confident (or bored). It helps to set a goal: sewing round all the edges for instance. You can use this stitch to tack two pieces of material together; and if you pull the end of the thread it will gather the material, for example round the top of a doll's skirt or to make a little bag.

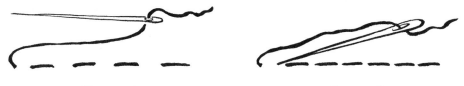

diagram A   diagram B

BACK STITCH

* This is an incredibly practical stitch. It's strong, reliable and you can use it for almost anything. Pass your needle through the material from back to front. Then put the needle through the fabric about ½ centimetre away to the right. Bring the needle up through the fabric about ½ centimetre away to the left of the first top stitch. Now push the needle back through the fabric as close to the left-hand end of the first stitch as you can manage (diagram B). Continue.

diagram C

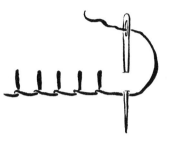

diagram D

BLANKET STITCH

This is a very useful stitch for edging and joining two pieces of material together (as it sort of hems as it goes) or for securing appliqué. When you get good at it you can also use it to make buttonholes.

* Have the edge of the material towards you. Working from left to right, put the needle through the two pieces of material at the distance from the edges that you want the stitch to be, probably slightly less than ½ centimetre.

  Bring the thread up, around the pieces you want to join together. Bring the needle up through the same hole, feed it underneath the loop of thread that you've made (diagram C). You should end up with one stitch with the thread coming out of the top. Now bring the needle around and thread it through the two pieces of fabric at the point where your want the bottom of the next stitch to be. Bring the needle up around the back of the fabric, through the loop of thread that you're pulling through and gently pull it tight (diagram D). You should be left with a nice little boxy stitch which will make your great-aunt think you are a very clever and nicely brought up young lady.

FINISHING OFF

* When you've finished sewing (or when your length of cotton runs out) you need to tie off your work securely, so that the stitches don't unravel. The easiest way of doing this is to go back and repeat the last stitch, then, before you pull it tight, pass your needle a couple of times through the loop you've made. When you pull the thread tight, you're left with a neat knot. Any loose ends can simply be cut short, although you should be sure to leave at least a centimetre or so of thread so the knot doesn't come undone.

Making Dolls

PEG DOLLS

The easiest type of doll to make is a peg doll. To do this, you'll need:

* a pipe cleaner
* some old-fashioned wooden clothes pegs
* coloured pencils or felt-tipped pens
* some glue
* scraps of wool, fake fur, embroidery thread, fabric
* needle and thread

Fold the pipe cleaner in half and wrap it a few times around the 'neck' of the clothes peg so that the two 'arms' are an equal length, then fold the ends of the pipe cleaner over to form 'hands'.

This gives you the basic body to work with. From now on, it's all up to you. Draw on some eyes and a mouth using coloured pencils or felt-tipped pens, then glue on lengths of fine wool to give your doll long hair (you can even plait it, once you're done) or stick on a little circle of fake fur to give her short, spiky hair. You can use fuzzy wool, and pile it up on top of your peg doll's head, or you can use embroidery thread and give her a fringe.

Once you're happy with the hairstyle, fold a scrap of material in half and cut out shirts or dresses, with the long folded edge along the top. Sew up the side seams using back stitch, cut a small hole for the head and you can dress your doll however you choose. To make a skirt, cut out two small rectangles of material, sew up the side seams using back stitch, then tack along the top using running stitch and pull on the end of the thread to gather it tight (you might need a couple of spots of glue to hold it in place – peg dolls don't have much of a waist). Colour in the 'feet' to give your doll shoes; use ribbon or embroidery thread to make an outfit special; make a little pair of wings out of gauze or feathers and your doll can be a fairy!

RAG DOLLS

One up from a peg doll is a rag doll, made from — well, rags and scraps of fabric! A rag doll isn't hard to make, but she will take a bit of time and effort; it's worth it, though, when you end up with your very own doll, which you can dress exactly as you choose. To make the doll, you will need:

* small pieces of skin-coloured cotton fabric
* needle and thread
* stuffing (old cut-up tights will do,
  but the white fibrous stuffing you can buy is better)
* embroidery thread or fabric paint
* fake fur or wool for hair

Here is a basic pattern.

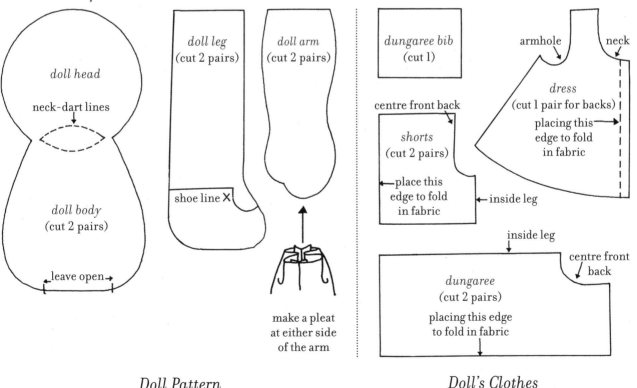

Doll Pattern   *Doll's Clothes*

Join all the pieces together using back stitch with the right sides of the fabric facing, allowing about ½ centimetre for the seams. Cut two body pieces from the fabric. Fold each over at the neck, right sides of the fabric facing, and sew along the leaf shape to make a dart. Then join the body pieces round the edges, leaving a gap of about 4 centimetres in the bottom seam. Turn the body right side out and fill it with stuffing. Close the seam at the bottom using blanket stitch.

Cut out two pairs of leg pieces (one toe facing forward, one facing back) and join each pair together, turn them right side out and stuff, leaving about 2 centimetres empty at the top. Fold in the raw edges so the seam is at right angles to the toe, then sew the legs shut using blanket stitch. Now, sew the legs onto the front of the body about a centimetre away from the bottom seam.

Cut out two pairs of arm pieces and join each pair together, leaving the top seams open. Turn right side out and stuff, leaving about 3 centimetres empty at the top. Now turn in the raw edges, bring the two side seams together, and make a pleat at each side. Sew the pleated arms shut using blanket stitch, then sew them onto the body, about a centimetre down from the neck.

This gives you the basic body: now it's time to customize your doll. First, she needs a face. The traditional method is to sew eyes, nose and mouth with embroidery thread, but you might prefer to paint them on using fabric pens or paint (it's always best to practise on a piece of paper first, then carefully mark where your doll's features are going to go using pins or chalk, so you're sure you're happy). If you want your doll to have a really old-fashioned look, you could use little black buttons for eyes. Beads can look good, too.

Now for the hair. One of the easiest ways of making hair is to use fake fur. Using the basic doll pattern, cut out two head shapes, cut out a face shape from one, join them together (fur-side facing) to make a little 'hat', then turn it the right way round and sew it over your doll's head to make hair. Experiment with different kinds of fake fur. You could give your doll sleek short black hair, fluffy yellow hair, or even bright pink shaggy hair.

Once you have made your doll, it's time to dress her. You can have lots of fun with your new sewing skills and make her new outfits to suit every season.

MAKING A DOLL'S DRESS AND SHOES

To make her clothes, you'll need:

* felt
* scraps of fabric
* needle and thread
* ribbon, beads, buttons, etc.
* snap fasteners or hooks and eyes
* narrow elastic
* darning needle

To make shoes for your doll, cut two pairs of shoe shapes out of felt, join them round the outer edge then turn them inside out so the seam is on the inside. Then, cut out a narrow strip of felt ½ x 2 centimetres long, to make the strap. Join the strap to the inside edge of the shoe (where the X is on the pattern – remember to make one right shoe and one left), make a tiny slit at the other end of the strap to make a buttonhole, then sew on a bead or a button to fix the strap in place.

For the dress, cut two back pieces and one front piece from your main material. Join the back pieces to the front at the side seams but don't join them at the shoulders. Hem the bottom. Repeat with some lining material, to give you two dress shapes. Place the two dresses together, right sides facing, and sew around the neck, the armholes and down the seams at the back. Turn the dress right side out, then join the shoulder seams. Fix snap fasteners or hook and eye fasteners to the two back edges, and you have a basic dress! Try adding pockets, or putting ribbon or lace around the bottom.

Remember, this is just a basic pattern – once you've mastered it, you can start designing your own clothes for your dolls. If you've been saving scraps of fabric, you should have plenty to choose from. Because everything you're making is so small, it's best to use quite thin fabrics like cotton or jersey; small patterns generally look better than large prints, but it's entirely up to you. Why not sew your doll a dress to match your own? Or, you could make a doll with the same skin and hair colour as one of your friends, and dress her in your friend's favourite outfit as a special present.

Making a Bag

The easiest bag of all to make is a draw-string bag. It's a very simple design and you can make it as big or as small as you like. It's best to use quite sturdy fabric, or else it'll just rip whenever you put anything heavy in it. For a gym-kit-sized bag, you will need:

* a rectangle of fabric 45 x 70cm
* pins
* needle and cotton
* scissors
* 1 metre of thick cord (about ½ cm in diameter)
* large safety pin

Put the fabric right side up on the table, fold it in half lengthways, pin the bottom and the side edges together and, using back stitch, sew these seams up. Ten centimetres before the end of the long seam, tie off your thread, leave a gap of 4 centimetres, then sew the remaining 6 centimetres of the seam. Now, make a hem for the top of the bag: make a 2 centimetre fold, then a 4 centimetre fold. Stitch along the bottom of the hem. Next, tie a knot in one end of the cord, fasten the safety pin through the knot, and feed it through the gap in the side seam into the hem you've made, which is like a tube or a pocket.

From the outside, push and pull the safety pin all the way round the inside of the hem, feeding the fabric along the cord as you go. Once the cord emerges at the other end, cut off the knot and safety pin and pull the cord through until you've got two equal lengths. Tie the ends together, pull on the cord, and the fabric will gather up, leaving you with a bag!

You can make your bag out of any material, and decorate it any way you like – it's so easy to do, you could even have a different bag for every day of the week! By varying the size of the piece of cloth and the thickness of the cord, you can make smaller shoulder bags or draw-string purses for your beads and buttons.

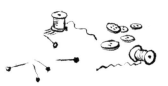

Useful but Boring Sewing

SEWING ON A BUTTON

Most clothes you buy have machine-sewn buttons on them, which inevitably means they fall off after the third or fourth wear. A safety pin will do in an emergency, but it's quick and easy to sew the button back on.

* Knot a length of thread and trim the end. If you like you can use double thread, but it can be fiddly for beginners. Draw the thread through the fabric from back to front at the point where you want the button to sit. Thread your button on. Pass your needle back down through the next hole. Bring the needle back up through the material and the other hole. Continue four or five times until your button is firmly in place. If you've got a two-hole button, you can just go from side to side; if you've got four holes it's nice to make a criss-cross pattern with the thread. Pass the thread up through the fabric one last time but do not pass it through the buttonholes, but wind it around the button, effectively bunching all the stitches up into one neat bundle. Then pass the thread through to the underside of the fabric, do a couple of straight stitches, make a knot, and trim off.

TAKING UP/REPAIRING A HEM

* In order to stop a cut piece of fabric from fraying, it's necessary to hem it. To do this, carefully fold the material over, about ½ to 2 centimetres from the edge depending upon the thickness of the hem you want to make (as a rule of thumb, use narrow hems for light fabrics like cotton or jersey, and wide hems for heavy fabrics like denim or fake fur). Then, make a second fold about ½ to 2 centimetres wider than the first, so that the raw edge is rolled inside.

You'll need to pin or tack the material as you go along, to stop it from unfolding. Using back stitch, sew along the top of the hem you've made, making sure that the neat stitches are on the outside of your work, and the folded up hem is on the inside. When you iron this, you should end up with a clean, flat edge which won't fray.

Knitting

FRENCH KNITTING

This is much less complicated than real knitting, and a good place to begin. You can buy knitting spools, or dollies as they are sometimes called, in most craft shops. Essentially, they consist of a piece of wood with a central hole and four pins stuck into the top. You can only knit a tube with them, and this feeds out through the hole in the middle, but it's amazing how many things you can make with your long tube of knitting, including doll's socks and scarves.

To begin, pull the wool up through the hole in the middle and loop it around the pegs, going from right to left (diagram A). Pass the wool round the outside of all four pegs and hold it in place with your finger. Take a slim knitting needle and slip the first loop round the first peg (diagram B) and over the yarn you're holding (diagram C). Repeat for all three other pegs, and then go around again. When you've done enough, finish (this is called casting-off in knitting) by cutting the yarn and threading it through each loop. Pull tight to fasten off.

diagram A   diagram B   diagram C

GROWN-UP KNITTING

Grown-up knitting requires two basic virtues: patience and perseverance. Having a relative who can actually knit is also invaluable, since all the diagrams in the world are no substitute for hands-on teaching. Still, there's no harm in trying.

Feeling confident? Then equip yourself with the following:

* A pair of medium-sized knitting needles. Size 5 or 6 should do. The size relates to the circumference of the needle in millimetres.

* Some yarn. Again, it's best to start with a medium weight, say 4-ply. Ply refers to the number of strands that, when twisted together, make up the yarn — so 4-ply is a yarn made up of four strands. Choose a nice bright colour to keep your spirits up. Early knitting attempts can be quite frustrating.

diagram D   *diagram E*

* To start, you'll need to cast on. This involves setting up a row of stitches on one needle. Aim to begin with 15 to 20 stitches: this is a manageable number for a beginner. There are various ways of casting on, but the easiest is using both needles.

Begin by making a slip knot (diagram D). Make a loop in the yarn and slip the tip of a needle under the short end. Draw the thread up and through and pull both ends tight to secure the knot on the needle (diagram E).

Transfer that needle to your left hand (if you are right-handed; if you are left-handed, please reverse all these instructions). Pass the right-hand needle through the loop of the slip knot. Hook the yarn round and under the tip of the right needle. Draw the hooked yarn through the slip knot. This forms your first new stitch. Now slide the new stitch on to the left-hand needle, next to the original slip knot. Slip the right-hand needle through the front of your new stitch, and underneath the left-hand needle. Hook the yarn under and over the right-hand tip. Continue to form new stitches.

Once you've mastered this basic set-up, you're ready to move on to knitting proper. The two fundamental stitches to learn are knit and purl.

KNIT

* Hold the needle with your cast-on stitches in your left hand. On the other hand wind the yarn over the top of your index finger, round the inside of your two middle fingers, and loop it round your little finger (diagram F). The idea is to keep the yarn moving, but also to retain control of the tension. The tension of the yarn is very important in knitting. So much of the skill of a good knitter is in not allowing the yarn to get too loose or, worse, too tight. But that's all about practice.

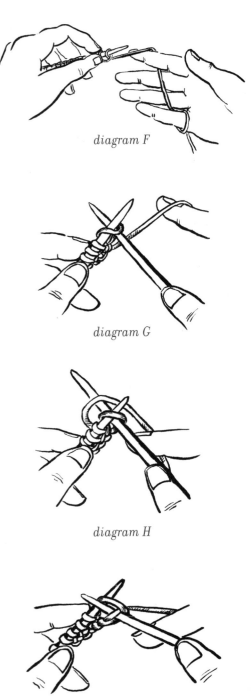

diagram F

diagram G

Now pick up your right-hand needle. Keeping the yarn behind your work, insert the needle into the front of the first stitch, passing the right-hand needle behind the left-hand one (diagram G). With your right forefinger, loop the yarn under and over the right-hand needle (diagram H). Draw it through the loop, sort of hooking it towards you. Gently slip the new stitch off the left-hand needle and on to the right-hand one (diagram I). This last bit can be quite fiddly, and if you do it too quickly or jerk the yarn you can accidentally undo the stitch next to it. This is called dropping a stitch.

diagram H

The idea is to transfer all the stitches from the left-hand needle onto the right-hand one, creating a new row of stitches as you go. Then you swap hands and start again, building row upon row.

diagram I

PURL

Purl is slightly different from knit: knit produces a horizontal semicircular stitch; purl a flat, vertical stitch.

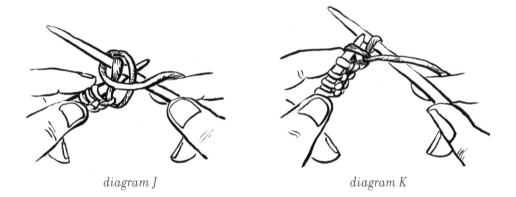

diagram J   *diagram K*

* Hold the yarn as before, with the stitches on the left-hand needle. This time you want to keep the yarn in front of your work. Insert the right-hand needle into the front of the first stitch, so that your left-hand needle is behind the tip. Using your right index finger, loop the yarn over and under the point of the right-hand needle (diagram J). Finally, draw the resulting loop through and off, slipping it onto the right-hand needle (diagram K).

  And that, girls, is basic knitting. If you want to make something simple, like a doll's scarf, for example, you knit one row, purl one row until it's long enough, and then you cast off.

CASTING OFF

* Knit two stitches. Then slip the tip of your left-hand needle through the first stitch and pull it over the second one, dropping it, so that only one remains on the needle. Knit the next stitch, pull the following one over it – and so on, until the whole row has been cast off. You will be left (hopefully!) with a single stitch. Slip this off your knitting needle and loop the yarn through it, pulling tight to close.

IN THE GARDEN

Not everyone is a natural gardener. Sarah has made many valiant attempts over the years to become at one with nature and, after much agonizing, has finally given up. She now has AstroTurf (you know, that fake plastic grass they sometimes use on tennis courts) in her back garden instead of the real thing and everyone is much the happier for it. The AstroTurf requires nothing more than a little gentle hoovering now and again, and the few hardy trees and shrubs that remain are mercifully low maintenance.

But you don't really need green fingers to have fun growing things – just some soil, water and sunlight. Many of these ideas incorporate good, basic techniques that can easily be adapted for other botanical purposes.

Kitchen Gardening – Easy Things to Grow Indoors

MUSTARD AND CRESS

One of the easiest and most satisfying things to grow from seed is mustard and cress. It will grow in pots on the most cramped windowsill as long as you have light and water, and best of all you can feast on delicious sandwiches when it's ready – and it grows really quickly, so you won't have long to wait.

* empty clean yoghurt pots
* kitchen paper
* cotton wool
* mustard and cress seeds

Wet some kitchen paper and scrunch it into each pot. Put a thin layer of damp cotton wool on top leaving a gap of about 2 centimetres between it and the top of the pot. Sprinkle the seeds onto the cotton wool and press them down gently. Place the pots in a warm position with plenty of light – a windowsill in the kitchen is ideal. Check them each day for signs of sprouting (this should happen after about a week) and add a little more water to keep the cotton wool damp if you need to. After 10 to 14 days the mustard and cress should be tall and green and ready for harvesting.

To make your sandwiches cut the sprouts close to the root with scissors and rinse gently. Butter some fresh bread, place the mustard and cress on top – and, hey presto! You have grown your very first meal.

AVOCADO PLANT

Next time you have an avocado for supper, don't throw away the large stone in the middle – try growing it instead. Alas, your avocado plant won't bear its own fruit, but it will grow into a lovely houseplant with glossy leaves that could reach almost 2 metres in height.

* clean jam jar or glass
* 3 toothpicks
* avocado seed

Soak the avocado seed in lukewarm water overnight. The next day, push the toothpicks at equal distances a little way into the stone. Fill the jam jar to the top with water and suspend the seed over the jar, balanced by the toothpicks, with the pointed end up and the broader, flat end just covered with water. Keep the jar in a warm, dark place – an airing cupboard for example – but don't forget about it! Check it regularly and top up the water so that the base is always just below the water. When the seed germinates it will crack, roots will start to grow out of the bottom and the stem will rise from the top. As soon as this happens move the young plant to a windowsill in the light.

When the stem has grown to about 15 centimetres tall, cut it back with some sharp scissors to roughly half its size. Cut at a point on the stem just above a bud.

This helps strengthen the plant and encourages bushier growth.

Now it is time to plant the sprouted avocado in a pot with soil. Put a little gravel or sand at the bottom of a 12 centimetre pot – this helps excess water to drain – then half fill it with potting compost. Make a hole deep enough for the young roots and, holding the plant carefully by the stone, lift it from the jar and pull out the toothpicks. Put the plant in the pot and backfill with soil leaving the top 2 to 3 centimetres of the tip above the surface. Put the pot on a saucer and water the plant well, always with lukewarm water.

cut

* The plant will grow new leaves at the top of stems. Pinch off the top two and each time four will grow in their place. (If you don't, the plant will grow straight and tall like a beanstalk rather than thick and bushy and glorious.)

When you notice roots growing out of the bottom of the pot it is time to replant it in a bigger pot with fresh compost.

Water your avocado plant well, but don't over-water. Allow the compost to dry out between watering. After watering it, the compost at the top of the pot should feel just moist to the touch, not soaking wet with puddles on top!

TIP: *Stones from very ripe avocados are most likely to germinate.*

SPROUTING LENTILS

If you turn pale at the idea of ham and lentil soup, you can try growing lentils and eating them in a tasty salad instead. All you need is some water and a jam jar.

* large clean jam jar
* piece of muslin, cheesecloth or clean tights
* rubber band
* packet dried lentils – brown, green, pink or yellow.

* Put three tablespoons of lentils in the jam jar, fill with cold water and leave overnight. The lentils will swell and double in size. Place the clean cloth over the top of the jar and fasten it in place with the rubber band. Pour the water out of the jar. The lentils should be rinsed with clean water every evening and morning. Make sure the water drains thoroughly.

After a couple of days the lentils will germinate and a tiny white sprout will appear from a crack in each one.

Once sprouted, place the jar in the sunlight on a windowsill for half an hour before eating. This boosts their mineral and vitamin content.

PRICKLY PINEAPPLE

Like the avocado, you can grow an unusual houseplant from the part of the pineapple you would normally throw away.

* ripe pineapple with leaves
* wide plant pot
* seed and cutting compost
* pebbles or crocks
* large, clear plastic bag
* rubber band

Slice off the top of the pineapple with its prickly leaves, leaving about 2.5 centimetres of the fruit attached. Leave this pineapple crown to dry out flesh upwards for 2 days.

Prepare the pot by placing some pebbles or crocks (broken-up pieces of old clay plant pots or dishes) at the bottom, then fill nearly to the top with seed and cutting compost. Place the pineapple top in the pot and add more compost to cover the fleshy base leaving only the green leaves exposed. Water the plant well with lukewarm water, then place the pot inside the large plastic bag making sure it has lots of room to breathe. This helps keep the plant warm and moist, and encourages the pineapple to take root. Keep it in a warm, sunny place. When you notice new leaves appearing from the centre of the crown, remove the bag.

The growing pineapple plant will thrive best in a warm and sunny position. Water the plant regularly to keep the soil moist for best growth.

Preparing Your Garden

If you've caught the gardening bug and your windowsills are full to bursting with plant life you might like to turn your green fingers to the garden. Ask your mum or dad if you can mark out an area in the garden as your plot. You don't need a huge space to grow things, but the position of the plot is important.

The ideal spot is one that faces south/south-west so it gets plenty of sun. A good way to work this out is to observe where the sun is in the sky at midday and choose a patch facing that direction.

Once you have chosen where you are going to have your garden, mark out your patch so everyone knows it's yours. You can make a pretty border with pebbles, broken tiles, bits of wood and bricks or whatever there is to hand.

Now for the hard work – it's time to get digging with a garden fork. As you dig the earth, you'll notice what type of soil you have to work with. The best soil to have in your garden is a nice crumbly peat or 'loam' which is easy to dig. If you have a thick, sticky clay soil, you will need to work a lot harder, but don't despair – you can improve any soil by digging in lots of compost each year before planting.

Dig over the soil in your plot in rows. Work from the back to the front and, as you turn the earth over, pull out any weeds and large stones. Fork over the patch once more, then add some compost or well-rotted manure to your garden. This provides food for your plants and will help them grow. Spread it evenly and then use the fork to mix it loosely into the soil. Walk over your freshly dug patch in your wellies from the back to the front to gently even out any lumps and bumps. Finally, use a rake to make the surface of the soil nice and even.

Your garden is now ready for planting. You might like to grow some of your favourite vegetables, or make a flower garden, or both. This is your garden, so you can decide. And remember, gardening is largely a case of trial and error, so if you don't succeed in growing a prize marrow first time round, don't despair.

Vegetables

CHERRY TOMATOES

* Some things naturally go well together – strawberries and cream, Fred Astaire and Ginger Rogers, tomato and basil. Not only do they taste delicious together, but growing basil alongside tomatoes helps keep them healthy by keeping greenfly away. This is called companion planting. Tomatoes need to be planted in full sun and they need to be watered regularly so they will grow well and the fruit will swell.

Buy small tomato plants in early summer. Plant 40 centimetres apart in your prepared garden. Spread a little general compost around each plant, but make sure it doesn't touch the stem, and water well. Push a bamboo cane in the earth just behind each young tomato plant, and as the stem grows tie it to the cane.

Side shoots will start to grow out between the leaf stems and the main stem – pinch them off as they appear. This encourages the plants to bear lots of tomatoes rather than make lots of leaf. Water regularly and feed with liquid tomato feed once a week throughout the summer. Pick your tomatoes when they have turned a nice glossy red colour.

Tomatoes can also be grown in pots and do particularly well planted in growbags. You can buy these at your garden centre.

TIP: *Gardeners often grow French marigolds alongside their tomatoes to repel whitefly – they swear their tomato plants produce more fruit when marigolds are planted nearby.*

BASIL

* Basil can be grown from seed in spring, ready for planting outside in May once the danger of frost has passed. It loves lots of sunlight and water.

Fill a flower pot (or several) almost full with seed compost and press down a little with your palm to make the surface level. Basil seeds are very small, so just sprinkle a small amount into each pot, keeping the seeds well spaced.

*   Scatter just enough compost on top to cover the seeds – don't drown them! Place the pot in a bowl of water so that the compost draws the water up and becomes moist.

Put the basil on a warm windowsill. When the seedlings appear, place the pot on a windowsill which gets lots of sunlight. If you have sown too many seeds and the pot is crowded with seedlings, pull some out so the remaining ones are at least 3 centimetres apart. If any seedlings seem small and weak, pull them out as well. Do this gently so as not to disturb the roots of the seedlings that are left.

In May, plant the basil out in your garden, putting the plants 35 centimetres apart, ideally close to your tomatoes.

From May onwards, basil seeds can be sown directly outdoors in the garden or in pots, but starting them off indoors gives you fresh basil earlier.

GARLIC

*   Take a look in the vegetable rack and the likelihood is that you'll find a rogue bulb of old garlic. The garlic bulb is made up of individual cloves, which can be separated and planted to grow garlic greens which you can cut and chop up to add to salads, scrambled eggs and sauces for pasta. Cutting the garlic greens encourages more growth, so snip them often. Plant in October for garlic greens in the spring.

Carefully remove the garlic cloves from the bulb one at a time and push each clove into the soil so that the pointed end is just covered. Plant the cloves 15 centimetres apart. Water well.

If you want to grow new garlic bulbs, allow the shoots to grow throughout spring, wait until the leaves have all dried out and died down in June/July, and then harvest your home-grown garlic.

Grow garlic indoors in pots in winter – you will have greens for eating within a couple of weeks.

TIP: *Grow garlic alongside roses to keep greenfly away.*

RADISHES

* Radishes are one of the easiest and fastest vegetables to grow. Eat them dipped in a little sea salt with fresh French bread and lots of butter.

  Sow the seeds at regular intervals from March to August to ensure a regular supply. Use a stick or hoe to make shallow drills, or grooves in the soil. Sprinkle the seeds along the row thinly and cover lightly with soil. Remember to mark the row so you know what you've sown and where the row is!

  When the seedlings appear, you will have to thin them out a little bit to leave 3 to 5 centimetres between each plant. Pull out small and weak seedlings, leaving the stronger plants to grow. Water well during dry weather.

  Harvest your radishes as soon as they reach a good size – leave them too long in the ground and they will get tough and too strong-tasting.

Flowers

SUNFLOWERS

* Start to grow your sunflower seeds in May. Fill small 10 centimetre plant pots with potting compost and push a single sunflower seed about 2 centimetres into the compost. Fill the hole with more compost. Water each pot well and leave in a warm sunny place to germinate. Water regularly so the pots do not dry out.

  You should see the first sprouts after about two weeks. When the plants are about 30 centimetres tall they are ready for planting outdoors in large pots. Place the pots in a position where they will get full sunlight.

  If you would like to plant them straight into your garden, choose a position in full sun, preferably against a wall where they will not shade other smaller plants. Plant the sunflowers about 30 centimetres apart. Water them well and continue to water them regularly during the hot summer days – sunflowers are thirsty plants. As they grow taller, you may need to support the stems with a long bamboo stick. Push the stick into the soil about 5 centimetres from the plant and loosely tie the plant to the stick about halfway up the stem.

BULBS

* Most of the flowers which appear very early in spring – daffodils, snowdrops, tulips, crocuses and hyacinths – are grown from bulbs and planted in the autumn. The fleshy bulb contains all the nutrients and energy the plants need to grow. When your daffodils or tulips stop flowering, it is important to let the leaves and flowers die down completely rather than cutting them down – the dying leaves provide the fuel to feed next year's flowers stored in the bulb deep in the earth.

When buying bulbs at the garden centre, always choose carefully and pick only those which feel firm when gently squeezed and are free from bruises. The bigger bulbs are usually the best. A handy general rule with bulbs is that they should be planted in a hole three times as deep as the length of the bulb, and they are planted nose, or pointed end, up.

Crocuses, daffodils and snowdrops will cheer up any garden after the long, dark winter months and look nice planted at the base of trees or among the grass in the lawn. Daffodils and tulips can be grown in large pots or containers in a sunny spot in the garden or on a balcony or windowsill.

Wildflower Garden

One of the nicest things you can do with your little patch of earth is to create a wildflower garden which will attract birds, butterflies and bees.

Packets of wildflower seeds can be bought at the garden centre and the flowers are very easy to grow as long as you follow the instructions on the packet about when to sow the seeds. Start the seedlings off indoors in pots, following the steps above for growing basil from seed. Once the plants are big enough and there's no danger of frost, plant them outside.

There are masses of wildflowers to choose from – cornflowers, bluebells, primroses, wild pansies, foxgloves, corn marigolds, poppies, toadflax and ragged robin, to name a few – and they look really pretty growing together in a border or in large terracotta pots.

If you have a lawn, why not ask your parents if you could let a small section of it grow wild to make a miniature wildflower meadow? Cut holes in the earth and plant the wildflowers, then allow the grass and flowers in your 'meadow' to grow wild. When the flowers die, don't cut them down but allow them to scatter the seeds in your meadow, or gather some of the seed heads and keep them in an envelope ready to sow the following spring. Cut the grass in your wildflower meadow down in late summer once all the flowers have died, leave them to dry out for a couple of days before raking the debris away; cut the grass again in early spring if necessary.

Container Herb Garden

Herbs are great things to grow — they give off a wonderful scent as you brush past them in summer, they are useful year round for cooking and you can grow them in a window box or in pots even if you don't have a garden.

* You can create a herb garden in any large container as long as it has holes in the bottom to allow water to drain — you could use an old sink or a chimney pot, for example. Or, if you want to splash out, you could invest in one of those lovely big terracotta strawberry pots which have openings around the sides into which you can plant different herbs.

  It's easiest to buy a selection of your favourite herbs in small pots from the garden centre; it's more expensive to buy packets of seed and you usually only want one or two of each plant. Choose ones you like to eat or use for making herb teas, or wonderfully scented ones — mint, basil, camomile, parsley, coriander, sage and spearmint, for example.

  Prepare your container. Line the bottom with some pieces of broken clay pots or some pebbles to help the soil drain. Put a little compost in the bottom of the container and take the herbs out of their pots (keep mint in its pot, as it tends to take over the whole garden if you allow it to) and arrange them. Now infill with enough compost to completely cover the roots of the plants. Water well and put in a sunny place.

Plants for Scent

* lilac
* honeysuckle
* lavender
* scented geraniums
* jasmine
* roses

Plants to Attract Butterflies and Bees

* buddleia (butterfly bush)
* wallflowers
* sedum (ice plant)
* viburnum
* sweet william
* cornflowers

FOOD, GLORIOUS FOOD

You don't have to be a master chef to have fun in the kitchen, and a lot of
recipes are surprisingly easy. The most important thing to remember
is that cooking is about trial and error so don't give up if it goes wrong.
Above all, don't be afraid to ask a grown-up for help – and before you do
anything, make sure you read all the rules.

Random and interesting facts about food:

* Honey is the only food that does not spoil. Archaeologists have found
  honey that is still edible in the tombs of Egyptian pharaohs.

* It is said that cheese was invented by accident over 5,000 years ago. An
  Arabian merchant rode across the desert on his camel with some milk
  stored in a pouch made of a sheep's stomach. The motion of the camel, the
  hot sun and the residual rennet in the sheep's stomach caused the milk to
  separate into curds and whey, and so cheese was born.

* The tropical fruit durian is banned from the entire Singapore public
  transport system because it smells so horrid.

Top Kitchen Rules

* Never run in the kitchen.

* Keep handles of pots and pans on the stove turned to the side. If they are sticking out at the front, you may knock them and have a horrid accident.

* Never touch anything electrical with wet hands.

* Wash your hands after handling meat and particularly poultry.

* Be careful with knives. A sharp knife is actually safer than a blunt one; blunt knives are more likely to slip and hurt you.

* Never use a blender, naked flame or knife without adult supervision.

* Always use oven gloves for hot items: pans, baking trays, opening the oven, etc.

* Make sure you turn everything off once you have finished.

* Clear up as you go along. A mess is distracting. Also, you do not want to be slipping on a dirty floor or puddling about in a muddled work surface.

* Do not, obviously, put your face near the oven when opening it, as the heat will blast out and make you flustered and pink.

* The greatest rule of the kitchen – PAY ATTENTION. Bad cooking is not about ignorance or lack of talent, but is all about the slapdash, the careless and the lazy.

Starting Out

* First, wash your hands.

* Clear plenty of space, making sure all worktops are sparkling clean.

* Put on your apron and tie your hair back (chef's hat optional).

* Read the recipe you have chosen all the way through, and then read it again just to make sure.

* Assemble all the implements you are going to need.

* Measure all the ingredients. Put them in small glass bowls or on pretty saucers, like they do on the cooking programmes.

Now you are ready to cook . . .

Weekends

Weekend breakfasts are the most fun. There is no rushing off to school, and it is a time when treats might be allowed, instead of the usual cereal, yoghurt and fruit of weekdays.

Eggs can be eaten at any meal, but they are ideal for breakfast, since they're full of goodness and will easily see you through to lunch. If you can, try to use free-range eggs, since factory farms are places of cruelty and nasty chemicals.

SOFT-BOILED EGG AND SOLDIERS (DIPPY EGGS) SERVES 1

Follow the same cooking method as for hard-boiled eggs (see page 38), only time it for 3½ to 4 minutes from the rolling boil. Plunge it into cold water to stop it cooking and to make it easier to open the egg without scalding your fingers. Put the egg in an egg cup and slice off the top about three-quarters of the way up. To do this, tap firmly with the edge of a knife. Then use a teaspoon to lever off the rest. Pick out any stray bits of eggshell. The white should be firm and the yolk runny. If the white is transparent and gelatinous, your egg is undercooked and you should NOT eat it.

For the soldiers, toast two slices of bread, spread them with butter and cut them into finger-sized strips. Dip into your egg and eat.

SCRAMBLED EGGS SERVES 1

* 2 eggs per person
* dash of milk
* dollop of butter
* salt and pepper

* Break the eggs into a bowl and beat them together with the milk with a fork until they are frothy. Put a large dollop of butter in a small saucepan and let it melt over a medium heat. Add the eggs. As they start to cook, make wide, gentle stirring movements with a wooden spoon.

The minute there are no runny bits visible, get the eggs off the stove and onto a warm plate. Bear in mind that they will go on cooking for a moment or two, so the trick is to take them off the heat when they are almost, but not entirely, cooked. What you are looking for is something soft but not too runny. What you are avoiding at all costs is anything hard or watery.

EGGY BREAD SERVES 2

In America, this is called French toast, although we have never, ever seen a French person cooking or eating it.

* 4 slices of white bread
* 2 eggs, beaten
* salt
* olive oil
* butter

* You need good quality white bread, sliced quite thickly. Beat the eggs with a pinch of salt in a wide shallow bowl. Lay two slices of bread at a time in the mixture. Turn the bread over and make sure it is fully covered by the egg.

Put a big non-stick frying pan on a medium to high heat, add a gloop of olive oil and swish it about a bit. Put in the bread, two slices at a time, and cook for 2 to 3 minutes each side until golden. Spread some butter on each slice while they're still hot, so the butter melts. Mmm.

CODDLED EGGS SERVES 1

These require an egg coddler, which is a ceramic container like a small cup, with a screw-top lid, often decorated with pictures of flowers or herbs.

* Put a pan of water on to boil. Butter the inside of the coddler by dipping your finger in some soft butter and smearing it all round the inside. Break one large egg (or two small ones) into the coddler. If you like, you can add a small dollop of cream and seasoning. Screw on the lid (not too tightly, or else you won't be able to get it off again) and put it in the boiling water for about 10 minutes (it takes a few goes to get the timing exactly right). The water should reach halfway up the sides of the coddler.

  Remove the coddler from the water by hooking the handle of a wooden spoon through the ring on the lid. Stand it on a plate and allow it to cool for a few minutes (you can get your toast ready during this interval). Remove the lid and eat. Coddled eggs are a bit like boiled eggs, only even more delicious since there's no fiddling about with eggshell.

HARD-BOILED EGGS SERVES 1 EGG PER PERSON

Excellent for lunchboxes or picnics. Remember, picnic lunches do not only have to take place outside on balmy summer days. You can have a perfectly delightful carpet picnic in February when you need cheering up.

* Put your eggs in a pan and just cover with cold water. Bring the water to what's known as a rolling boil (i.e. it's bubbling away like a witches' cauldron) and start timing. Medium-sized eggs need about 6 minutes; larger ones will take a minute or two more. When they're done, drain and leave them to sit in a bowl of cold water for a few minutes before taking them out. When you're ready, peel an egg and eat it with your fingers and some salt.

  Hard-boiled eggs make excellent egg mayonnaise. To eat them on their own, peel and halve the eggs and lay them on a dish. In a cup, put one tablespoon of mayonnaise for every two eggs. Mix in a teaspoon of water at a time, until you have something that can be poured. Pour over the eggs.

SAUSAGE SANDWICH SERVES 1

* The easiest and safest way to cook sausages is to put them on a baking tray and pop them in the oven. Good fat sausages will take about 40 minutes at 190°C/gas mark 5; smaller ones take about 25 minutes.

While you're waiting, butter the bread and add some ketchup. When the sausages are cooked, cut them in half lengthways and arrange them on the bread; add the second slice to make your sandwich. Eat while still hot.

BACON SANDWICH SERVES 1

* Put two rashers of back bacon under a grill, and cook under a high heat for 2 to 3 minutes each side. Spread soft butter on thick-sliced bread. Place the bacon on one slice of bread, put the other on top, cut in half or quarters. Eat.

POTATO CAKES MAKES APPROX. 4

* 2 cups potato, mashed
* ½ cup of plain white flour
* salt
* 1 egg, beaten
* olive oil
* butter

* These are delicious and very easy, particularly if you have some left-over mashed potato in the fridge. (If not, take two large floury potatoes, King Edwards are best, cut into quarters, boil in salted water for twenty minutes, drain and leave to dry thoroughly, and then mash with a pat of butter.) Mix all the ingredients together with a wooden spoon. Flour a wooden board and roll out the dough until it is about a centimetre thick and cut it into squares or triangles. Add a little more flour to the wooden board and press both sides of the cakes into it, so they have a thin coating of flour each side. Fry in a little olive oil over a medium heat for 2 minutes each side, or until golden. Serve with butter.

HUMMOUS SERVES 4

* tin chickpeas
* 2 generous gloops olive oil
* handful parsley
* 1 clove garlic
* juice ½ lemon
* sea salt

* Put all the ingredients in a blender and blitz for about 30 seconds. You want it to look rough and not over-processed. This is delicious with toasted pitta bread, or as a dip with tortilla chips.

CHEAT'S GUACAMOLE
SERVES 2

* 2 ripe avocados
* sea salt
* juice ½ lemon or lime
* glug of olive oil

* Chop the avocados roughly (you can tell if they're ripe by squeezing: they should just give) and put them in a deep bowl. Don't leave the avocado long before adding the rest of the ingredients, otherwise it will blacken in the air. Add a pinch of sea salt, the lemon or lime juice, and a good glug of olive oil. Mash it all up with a fork. That's it.

BLUEBERRY SMOOTHIE SERVES 2

* 1 medium glass of apple juice
* 5 tbsps natural yoghurt
* 1 banana
* 1 medium glass of blueberries
* 1 tsp honey (optional)

* Healthy and delicious for breakfast; this has a particularly lovely colour.

Put all the ingredients except the honey in a blender and blitz until smooth. You can add a teaspoon of runny honey if you like, for extra sweetness. To make it super chilled, add a couple of ice cubes, or freeze the blueberries beforehand.

Tea

A proper English tea is one of the great pleasures of life. There should be sandwiches, biscuits and cake. If you do not like tea as a drink, you can have home-made lemonade or hot Ribena instead.

CUPCAKES (FAIRY CAKES) MAKES APPROX. 10

* cupcake cases
* 125g butter
* 125g caster sugar
* 2 medium-sized eggs
* 125g self-raising flour
* 1 tsp vanilla extract

* Before you start cooking, preheat the oven to 180°C/gas mark 4. Line a cupcake tin with the cupcake cases.

Cream the butter and sugar with a wooden spoon until they are smooth and light. Add the eggs, one at a time, and beat them into the mixture. Add a couple of tablespoons of flour as you do this to stop the mixture curdling. Add the vanilla extract. Fold in the flour using a metal spoon. Using a tablespoon, put a dollop of the mixture into each of the cupcake cases, leaving room for it to rise.

Bake for 18 to 20 minutes. They are ready when they are risen, golden and firm to the touch. Allow to cool on a wire rack.

If you like, you can ice them (see page 42) . . .

BIG SPONGE CAKE SERVES APPROX. 10

* To make one big sponge cake, just follow the recipe for cupcakes but pour the mixture into a 20 centimetre cake tin rather than the cupcake cases. Once you have mastered the basic recipe, you can add different flavourings – lemon juice and zest for lemon cake, cocoa for chocolate cake, peeled apple chopped very small for apple cake, and so on.

BUTTER CREAM ICING

MAKES ENOUGH FOR APPROX. 10 CUPCAKES

* 140g butter
* 280g icing sugar
* food colouring (optional)

* Cream the butter and icing sugar until smooth. Add a few drops of food colouring of your choice. Use a spatula or a flat knife to spread the icing on the cupcakes.

If you don't like butter icing (and there are those who don't), you can make a sugar drizzle. Put 150 grams of icing sugar in a pan with 50 millilitres of water (or lemon juice) and allow the sugar to dissolve over a low heat. Let the mixture cool a little (but not solidify) and pour over the cakes.

Decorate the cupcakes with hundreds and thousands, mini marshmallows, sprinkles or any other tempting treat you can think of.

CHOCOLATE FRIDGE CAKE SERVES 8–10

* 200g dark cooking chocolate
* 200g milk chocolate
* 50g plain digestive biscuits

* 100g chopped pecan nuts (optional); if you don't like nuts double the quantity of biscuit
* 10 glacé cherries, halved (or dried cherries or raisins)

* Melt all the chocolate using the bain-marie method (see page 67). Line a baking tray with greaseproof paper. Leave a good couple of inches of paper over the sides; you'll need this to lift the cake out later.

* Smash up the biscuits by putting them in a plastic bag and bashing with a rolling pin. You want pieces rather than crumbs, so go easy. Mix the digestives, nuts and cherries in a bowl, and then distribute them evenly over the bottom of the baking tray. Pour the chocolate over the top and smooth it out with a spatula so all the dry ingredients are covered. Chill in the fridge for at least an hour.

When set, use the greaseproof paper to lift the cake out of the tray and cut it into pieces. Store in foil or an airtight container in the fridge.

SANDWICHES SERVES 1

* Sandwiches for a polite tea should be made with good bread, neatly sliced (not too thick). Favourite ones are jam and Marmite, both self-explanatory. If you want to be very grand, you can remove the crusts and cut them into dainty triangles. A plain tomato sandwich sounds dull as ditchwater, but made well, it is hard to beat. Slice the tomatoes very thinly. Arrange them on the bread in two layers and season with salt and pepper. Add the top slice of bread. Cut into quarters.

DELICIOUS CHEESY BISCUITS SERVES 8

It's always nice to have something good and savoury among all the sweet things that you find at teatime.

* 100g self-raising flour
* 100g Cheddar cheese, grated
* ½ cup olive oil

* Pre-heat the oven to 180°C/gas mark 4.

Put all the ingredients in a deep bowl and mix with a fork. Flour your hands and a wooden board and press the mixture out until it is a centimetre thick (you can be quite rough with it; it's not a delicate operation like the scones on page 44). Cut it into rounds. Bake them for 8 to 10 minutes, until golden.

SCONES MAKES 8

This is the most simple recipe as made by our mothers, who learnt it from Constance Spry.

* 200g self-raising flour
* pinch sea salt
* 50g softened butter, cut into small cubes
* 1 tsp soured cream
* ⅓ cup whole milk

Preheat oven to 200°C/gas mark 6.

Place the flour, salt and butter in a large mixing bowl, and, with the fingertips of both hands, pick up the mixture and rub it gently. At first, not much will happen, but keep picking up and rubbing, softly, softly, and after a couple of minutes you will see the butter and flour becoming one. As you pick up and rub, lift the mixture up above the bowl and let it fall back each time – the scones will be light.

After five minutes, the mixture should look like soft breadcrumbs. Add the soured cream and then the milk a little at a time, mixing gently with a metal knife until they come together and form a ball. It should be damp but firm. Cover a wooden board (or work surface) with a handful of flour, and flour your hands too. Lift the dough onto the board and, using only the tips of your fingers, press it very lightly all over until it is about a centimetre thick. No rolling pins, please. Flour a round cutter (or use a jam jar or, for baby scones, an egg cup) and cut the dough into rounds and put them on a floured baking tray (you do not need to grease it).

Gather up the left-over pieces of dough and cut them out again, or, if you only have enough for one scone, shape it with your fingers. All cooks find that they have one knobbly scone in each batch.

Bake in the middle of the oven for 10 minutes or until golden and risen. Cool them on a wire rack. If you find your scones don't rise as much as you would like, add a teaspoon of baking powder to the recipe next time you make them.

Scones are best eaten warm with butter and jam, or thick cream and jam. Debate rages as to which you should spread first, the jam or the cream; we're too busy stuffing our faces with them to care. You could also have them with . . .

CHEAT'S JAM

MAKES ONE JAR

* 750g mixed summer fruits (strawberries, raspberries, blueberries, blackberries)
* 100ml water
* 400g caster sugar

* Put the summer fruits and water into a stainless-steel saucepan. Bring to the boil and simmer for 15 minutes, stirring all the time. Add the sugar, keep stirring it, and simmer for another 20 minutes.

Rinse out two or three glass jars with hot water from the kettle.

Allow the jam to cool, pour it into the jars and chill in the fridge. It will thicken up and become almost exactly like actual jam. But it won't last like real jam, so eat it quickly, and chuck it out when it goes furry.

HOME-MADE LEMONADE

MAKES 1 LITRE

* juice of 4 lemons
* 1 litre water
* handful fresh mint
* 2 tsps honey
* zest of 1 lemon
* ice cubes

* Put all the ingredients in a blender and blitz until smooth. It will go a bit frothy, but this will die down. The zest and the mint will sink to the bottom, but if you do not like any bits at all in your lemonade, put it through a fine sieve when you transfer it to a jug. Add more ice and a sprig of mint for decoration.

HOT RIBENA

* If you do not like tea, but want something hot, this is perfect. Just make up the Ribena as normal, but with boiling water from the kettle instead of cold from the tap. You might like to make it a little stronger than usual. It's also heaven when you're feeling a little bit poorly, for some reason.

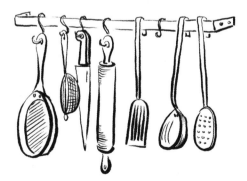

High Tea

High tea is a combination of tea and supper, when you want to eat early and have a bit of a treat. It is particularly good if eaten while wearing pyjamas and a cosy dressing gown. You can take any element of the tea above, but you need to add something a little more substantial. We like . . .

CHEESE ON TOAST SERVES 1

* Take a slice of good bread, and toast very lightly in the toaster. Cover it with about half a cup of grated cheese. Make sure you spread the cheese right up to the edges. Cook for 2 to 3 minutes under a medium grill until bubbling.

BAKED BEANS ON TOAST SERVES 1

* Heat the beans gently in a small pan. You can add a tiny pat of butter for extra deliciousness. Pour over buttered toast.

BAKED POTATO SERVES 1

* Choose a good floury potato. Wash and dry it, rub a little olive oil into the skin and stab it a couple of times with a knife to stop it exploding in the oven. Cook in a pre-heated oven at 200°C/gas mark 7 for an hour and a quarter. When it's done, cut it in half and top it with whatever you like – cream cheese, butter, crème fraiche, cottage cheese, grated Cheddar, little crispy shreds of bacon, etc.

FOR SOMETHING MORE EXCITING . . .

* Once the potato is not too hot to handle, scoop out the flesh, leaving the skin intact, and mix the potato with half a cup of grated Cheddar and a beaten egg. Then carefully put this mixture back in the skin, and cook under a medium grill for 5 minutes, until golden and crispy.

Midnight Feasts

SUGAR SANDWICHES SERVES 1

* Delicious and highly toxic, and to be kept to a strict limit of once a year on a very special occasion. Butter a slice of white bread and sprinkle on a teaspoon of sugar (the temptation here is to get carried away with the sugar, but don't: you'll feel sick). Fold the bread in half. Eat. You can of course do the same with crisps or condensed milk – just keep the tin in the fridge for a while beforehand so you can spread it like butter. Clean your teeth afterwards.

POPCORN SERVES 1

* In a deep, non-stick pan, put a gloop of sunflower oil. Let it warm for a couple of minutes over a medium heat, then add two handfuls of popping corn. Put the lid on the saucepan.

For a while nothing will happen. You begin to think the whole popcorn-making thing is a myth. And then, just as you are about to give up, you'll hear a solitary ping. As if all the other corn kernels think this a tremendous idea, they'll follow suit, as the heat makes them go from hard inedible little nubs of nothing to heavenly fluffy crunchy popcorn.

Keep shaking the pan over the heat so there is no burning or sticking. Make sure the lid is heavy enough not to be lifted by the exploding corn. Once the mad pinging dies down, listen for the last two or three pops, shaking all the time.

Take off the heat, remove the lid using an oven glove, and pour the popcorn into a big bowl. Some people like to add a little melted butter at this stage. If you like sweet popcorn, add a sprinkle of sugar; if you prefer it savoury, add salt.

BANANA TOAST SERVES 1

* Take one banana and some wholemeal bread. While you are making the toast, mash the banana with a little fresh lime or lemon juice. When the bread is toasted, butter and spread with your home-made banana 'jam'. Irresistible.

SPRING

Traditionally spring begins with the flowering of the first snowdrops – usually around the beginning of February. After that, it's a free-for-all of flowers, leaves, blossom, frisky little lambs, bunnies, baby birds and just about any cute creature Mother Nature can dream up. The air smells different, the wind is less biting and the days slowly begin to get longer.

Things to Look out for in Spring

THE CUCKOO

One of the first signs that spring has well and truly sprung is the sound of the cuckoo's distinctive and unmistakable call, usually from early March.

Legend has it that the first time you hear a cuckoo you should run round three times in a circle in the direction of the sun and you will have good luck all the rest of the year. If you hear the cuckoo to your right, you will have good luck; but if you hear the call to your left you may not be so fortunate.

Others believe that on hearing your first cuckoo, you should run to the nearest gate, and sit on the top bar – if you don't you will become a terrible lazybones for the rest of the year. This probably has a lot to do with the fact that the cuckoo is a notoriously indolent bird. It lays its eggs in other birds' nests, and then scarpers, leaving the unsuspecting nest-owners to sit on the cuckoo's egg until it hatches – so not only lazy, but rude too, and a bad mother to boot.

It's not surprising, then, given their general anti-social behaviour, that cuckoos are evasive birds, and you are far more likely to hear one than see one. But if you do catch sight of one – they are grey, with white and grey striped tummies and pointed tails, about the same size as a dove – this is what you should do. Put a stone on your head, and start running as fast as you can. When the stone falls off your head, mark the spot. Next day when you come back, money will be found under the stone. Supposedly.

LAMBS

Sheep themselves are pretty uninspiring creatures, being on the whole quite stupid and rather smelly. But baby sheep – i.e. lambs – are something else, the essence of sweetness and one of the most cheering aspects of springtime.

* Watching a lamb being born is a mind-boggling experience. One minute they are in their mother's womb; then within literally minutes, the lamb will be on its feet, admittedly shaky, but nevertheless feeding and generally raring to go.

If you're out for a walk in the country you'll often see tufts of white lambs' wool caught on hedges or fences. If you find some, take it home. It makes good bedding material for dolls' and fairy houses. You can also put it outside in the garden – birds will come and collect it to line their nests.

Here's a little ditty to sing to yourself as you watch the spring lambs frolic about the fields:

> *Mairzy doats and dozy doats and liddle lamzy divey*
> *A kiddley divey too, wouldn't you?*

BIRDS' NESTS

* If you observe the garden closely in early springtime, you'll spot all kinds of little birds going busily about the place collecting twigs, straw, moss and even bits of string. They're building nests in which to lay their eggs.

You can help them. You know how when you don't brush your hair you get a 'bird's nest' at the back of it? Well, brush it properly, then pull out all the hairs that have gathered in the hairbrush and lay them on a bush or in the grass for the birds to find.

TADPOLES

* From early February, you might see frogspawn, aka frogs' eggs, in ponds, ditches and slow-moving streams. Look out for a thick, jelly-like mass in the water, with little black spots inside it. It can sometimes look like bubbles.

If you want to collect some and rear some tadpoles at home, take only a small amount. Wear your wellies and bring a clean jam jar (with holes punched in the lid) and a bucket. Transfer about 8 to 10 eggs to the jar along with some of the pond water. Fill the bucket with pond water and a few of the pond's weeds.

You will need to prepare a home for the baby frogs as they won't survive long in a jam jar. A fish bowl or tank is ideal – it's best NOT to use the bath. Fill your container with the pond water. You can also use rainwater (or a mixture of pond and rainwater), but NEVER put the frogspawn into tap water unless you have let it stand outside for at least three days. Change the water every three days.

The frogspawn will need to be kept in a cool place (between 15 and 20 degrees centigrade is ideal, so away from any radiators) since the eggs will die if you subject them to extremes of temperature. Keep them in the shade too.

When the tadpoles hatch from the eggs, feed them with some fresh lettuce leaf, torn into little pieces. Each time you change the water, remember to add some fresh pond weed to the tank.

When the tadpoles start to grow legs, they become carnivorous. That means they need meat – and if they can't find any they will simply start eating each other (eek!). Suspend a little liver on some string into the water, or pop some fishing worms (these are known as bloodworms, and you can get them from pet and fishing shops) in with them. Remember to change the food every day to stop it going off and polluting the water.

Your froglets (not strictly a technical term but perfect, we feel, for describing that difficult in-between stage) now also need to come up to the surface of the water frequently to breathe air, so they will need something to rest on. Provide them with flat pieces of wood or twigs that can float on the surface of the water.

When the tadpoles have grown into tiny frogs (usually about 6-12 weeks), it is time to say goodbye. If you can, put them back in the pond where they were born.

CHEWING ON FRESH GRASS

* No – it's not just rabbits and sheep that eat grass. In spring, when the sap is rising, the tender shoots of new, tall grass are delicious to suck and nibble on when you're out on walks. Pull the grass right out by the stalk and put it in your mouth, the tender shoot first.

WHISTLING ON A BLADE OF GRASS

* Find a good, long and wide blade of grass. Place it down the outer side of one thumb all the way down to the wrist and hold it taut and in place with a finger, or lick the edge of your thumb from the top down to the wrist, so the grass sticks to it. Put your two thumbs together, nails facing you, as if you are praying. There should be a little hollow between your thumbs with the blade of grass showing – press your lips to the hollow and blow as hard as you can, to, hopefully, produce a high-pitched, though not terribly tuneful, whistle.

HAWTHORN BUDS AND LEAVES

* Hawthorn buds and leaves are so delicious that the plant is sometimes called the bread and cheese tree. The small, thorny hawthorn bush is often found in hedges and in woods and its tiny, green buds have a fresh, nutty taste.

   Later in spring when the buds have opened, snack on the glossy green leaves straight from the bush, or pick some to take home and chop to add to spring potato salads or cheese sandwiches. NEVER eat anything if you're not sure what it is. A lot of leaves, flowers and berries are poisonous.

WOOD SORREL

* If you're out for a walk in the woods, look out for wood sorrel. The leaves look a little like shamrock leaves and it has white bell-shaped flowers. Sorrel leaves have a tart, zingy taste – a quick pick-me-up to revive flagging spirits on a long trek. You can collect them and use them at home in salads.

NETTLE SOUP SERVES 6

You might think of nettles as just that hateful weed that stings, but in fact nettles have many health-giving properties – including clearing the lungs and treating eczema. You can boil the leaves in water for 10 to 15 minutes to make a restorative infusion; or you can even cook them – they taste just like spinach and are full of vitamins. They're very good in a soup.

Put on some long trousers and gardening gloves and pick the tender young nettle leaves from the top of the plant. Do not take the leaves from plants that have already flowered – they can sometimes damage your kidneys. If you do get stung, find a dock leaf (they often grow in the vicinity of nettles) and rub it vigorously over the sting – the idea is to get the juice out of the dock leaf. Alternatively, a mild antihistamine cream will counteract the itching.

* nettles
* 450g potatoes
* 50g butter
* 850ml chicken stock or Marigold vegetable stock
* salt and pepper to taste
* 4 tbsps cream or sour cream

Wash and peel the potatoes and cut them in half. Wash and roughly chop the nettles. Melt the butter in a saucepan, add the leaves, cover and cook for a few minutes until the leaves are soft. Add the potatoes and the stock, and bring everything to the boil. Turn the heat down and simmer until the potatoes are cooked through and soft.

Remove from the heat and allow it to cool before putting in the blender (ask an adult to help you with this bit).

To serve, stir in the cream or sour cream and season to taste.

Festivals

SAINT VALENTINE'S DAY

Saint Valentine was a Roman priest and Christian martyr, beheaded around AD 270, on 14 February. Legend has it that he restored the sight of his jailer's daughter while he was imprisoned and awaiting execution. He is the patron saint of, among others, love, lovers, engaged couples, marriage, young people as well as bee-keepers and fainting.

* No one quite knows where the practice of sending Valentine's Day cards comes from. Some say that St Valentine sent the jailer's daughter a farewell note the night before he died, signing it 'from your Valentine'; others say it's to do with birds beginning to choose their mates on that day. Either way, tradition dictates that if you have your heart set on someone, 14 February is your chance to tell him by sending an anonymous card.

You can send a home-made card or a simple note. What's fun is to drop some clues into the envelope to keep the object of your affection guessing. Compose a romantic rhyme, and lace it with clues as to your identity; or spray a little perfume into the envelope. Disguise your handwriting by using your left hand if you're right-handed, your right if you are left-handed. Always write the letters S.W.A.L.K. in capitals over the seal on the back of the envelope. This stands for Sealed With A Loving Kiss . . .

And if you don't get one . . .

Don't worry. It's a well-known fact that most Valentine's cards are sent by girls to themselves, since boys are too embarrassed to be caught dead doing that sort of soppy nonsense. Your parents can usually be trusted to send you one, but just in case it always pays to pop a back-up one in the post. Just remember not to use your local posting box — otherwise the postmark will give you away immediately.

APRIL FOOL'S DAY

* On 1 April it's customary to play all sorts of pranks and tricks on family and friends, but traditionally the jokes must end at midday . . . otherwise the joke is on you. In France they call a prank a *Poisson d'avril* or April Fish, and pin paper fishes to the backs of unwitting victims and cry '*Poisson d'avril*' when the fish is noticed.

See Chapter 8, Dastardly Tricks, for some innocent prank inspiration.

MAY DAY

* The First of May, or May Day, is one of the oldest pagan festivals and celebrates the height of spring. Traditionally on May Day the fairest girl in the village was crowned with flowers and chosen as Queen of the May. Hawthorn, or May blossom, was gathered to decorate the doorframes of houses, and girls and boys danced round the beribboned maypole.

On May Day, the morning dew is believed to have magical properties. To make your skin beautiful, get up extra early on 1 May and wash your face in dew.

But . . . don't be tempted to get married in May, for as the saying goes:

> *Marry in May*
> *And you'll rue the day!*

Spring Flowers and Their Meanings

BLUEBELLS

Bluebells are a wonderful sight. They usually bloom in April, and like shady woodland, where they grow in clusters, often forming what's known as a 'blanket' of bluebells. It used to be the case that if you had said something horrid to a friend (or your mother), then you could say sorry with a bunch of bluebells since in the language of flowers they signify regret, humility and thankfulness. Sadly, these days you're not allowed to pick them. That's progress for you.

However, there is no law stopping you from playing In and Out the Dusty Bluebells with your friends:

All but one of you join hands in a circle. Lift up your hands to make arches. The girl not in the circle weaves in and out of the arches while the others chant:

> *In and out the dusty bluebells*
> *In and out the dusty bluebells*
> *In and out the dusty bluebells*
> *Who shall be my partner?*

When the singing stops, she stops behind someone in the circle. She taps that person's shoulder and says:

> *Tippy tippy tappy on your shoulder*
> *Tippy tippy tappy on your shoulder*
> *Tippy Tippy tappy on your shoulder*
> *You shall be my partner*

She then grabs that person by the waist and they weave through the arches together. On and on it goes, until there are far too many people in the line and everyone collapses in a fit of the giggles.

DAFFODILS

Yellow is the colour of springtime, and for many nothing says spring more than a nice bunch of daffs. In the language of flowers they signify unrequited love (like yellow roses too), sunshine and respect. In the language of William Wordsworth (1770–1850), they have come to signify pure poetic delight:

I wandered lonely as a cloud
That floats on high o'er vales and hills,
When all at once I saw a crowd,
A host of golden daffodils;
Beside the lake, beneath the trees,
Fluttering and dancing in the breeze.

Continuous as the stars that shine
And twinkle on the milky way,
They stretched in never-ending line
Along the margin of a bay:
Ten thousand saw I at a glance,
Tossing their heads in sprightly dance.

The waves beside them danced, but they
Out-did the sparkling waves in glee:-
A poet could not but be gay
In such a jocund company:
I gazed – and gazed – but little thought
What wealth the show to me had brought:

For oft when on my couch I lie
In vacant or in pensive mood,
They flash upon that inward eye
Which is the bliss of solitude,
And then my heart with pleasure fills,
And dances with the Daffodils.

PRIMROSES

* Give someone primroses and you're saying: 'I can't live without you.' Another classic yellow spring flower, it is not to be confused with the wishy-washy shade of yellow paint popular in the late 1980s.

LILY OF THE VALLEY

* This flower says 'sweetness, happiness, you've made my life complete', which is why it's often used in spring wedding bouquets. It's extremely pretty, with delicately scented bell-shaped white flowers. A common theme in the decorative art nouveau movement of the late nineteenth and early twentieth centuries, lily of the valley is a popular scent for soaps and bath salts.

BLOSSOM

* Apple and pear tree blossom only lasts a few weeks, but it is so delicate and beautiful that just looking at it makes the soul happy. In Japan, the ornamental cherry tree, or *sakura*, produces fleeting pink and white flowers, sometimes lasting only a day or two. The Japanese love and revere the tiny blooms, celebrating their appearance with numerous festivals and special blossom parties, and they are often represented in art and decoration.

Odette Churchill (1912–95)

At the outbreak of the second world war, French-born Odette Brailly was married to an Englishman named Roy Sansom, and living in London. Despite having three daughters, she was recruited into the SOE (Special Operations Executive, a secret spy organization set up by Winston Churchill) in 1942. She was sent to Nazi-occupied France as a radio operator for the British agent Peter Churchill (no relation to Winston). They were eventually betrayed by a double agent, captured and tortured but gave nothing away. They survived, despite being sent to a concentration camp, and Odette was awarded the George Cross, the greatest honour for civilian gallantry. She later married Peter Churchill (Roy having died during the war).

There is a touching end to this tale. In later life her house was burgled and her George Cross taken, but after an appeal, the medal was returned with a note from the burglar:

'You, madam, appear to be a dear old lady. I am not all that bad – it's just circumstances. Your little dog really loves me. I gave him a nice pat and left him a piece of meat. Sincerely yours, A Bad Egg.'

Rosa Parks (1913–2005)

In 1955, in the southern American state of Alabama, segregation (the separation of black people from white people in public places) was in full cry and the motiveless and open killing of black people by members of the Ku Klux Klan (a horrible organization that believes white people are superior to black people and which, sadly, still exists today) was still common. One day a black seamstress and civil-rights campaigner called Rosa Parks refused to give up her seat on the bus to a white passenger. At the time, the first four rows of seats in buses in Alabama were reserved specifically for white passengers; black people had to sit at the back of the bus. What Rosa Parks did may not seem very special today, but in 1955 it was a courageous act of protest.

Mrs Parks was arrested and fined; but her action led to a bus boycott that lasted over a year, and a law against segregation on public transport. Her protest was a milestone in the struggle for equality, and also proves that Lao Tzu (an old Chinese philosopher) was right when he said that a journey of a thousand miles starts with a single step.

EASTER

Easter is a time for feasting – mainly on chocolate – and for keeping busy during the holiday blowing and painting eggs and putting the final touches to your bonnet for the Easter Parade.

Blowing Eggs

* First, using a fairly large sharp needle, very carefully pierce a hole at the top and bottom of the egg. This needs a little caution and a delicate touch so as not to crack the egg in the process. Twist the needle round to make the holes a little bigger, otherwise blowing out the contents of the egg will be impossible and make your cheeks burst with the effort. Wiggle the needle round to help break up the white and yolk. You can also give the egg a fairly vigorous shake at this point to break up the contents further, which makes blowing easier.

  Place the pointed end of your egg to your lips, and blow as hard as you can over a bowl. Persevere – the egg whites are the hard part, but once they are all removed you will be relieved to find the egg yolk should flow out much more easily and quickly. (We wouldn't recommend saving the egg for cooking – a lot of spit tends to get mingled with it during the blowing process!) Keep blowing until the egg is completely empty.

  Rinse the egg a few times, blowing out the water to make sure it is completely clean inside, then wipe it carefully with a cloth, and allow it to dry for 30 minutes or so before painting and decorating.

Decorating Eggs

BLOWN EGGS

* Place the dry egg in a clean egg cup or an empty egg carton for painting. Use bold poster paints, glitter glue, felt-tipped pens or crayons to decorate the egg to your own design with faces, diamond patterns, spots or stripes, for example. For a more fancy Fabergé-style jewelled egg, you can add dots of glitter, gold or silver nail varnish, or glue-on sequins. Finish it off by tying a fine velvet, lace or gold metallic ribbon round the centre.

* Decorate the top half of the egg first and allow it to dry completely before turning it upside down and decorating the other half.

The blown eggs can also be dipped in natural dyes to create delicate shades of colour (see page 64), then tied round with ribbon or some lace. Before dipping the egg in the dye, seal the holes with a few drops of candle wax – this prevents the egg getting filled with dye each time you dip it.

UKRAINIAN EGGS OR 'PYSANKA' EGGS

More elaborate painted eggs can be made in traditional Ukrainian style. The technique involves painting on designs using a pinhead or a matchstick dipped in melted candle wax to make patterns and shapes on the egg. The egg is then dipped in dye, decorated with more wax, and dipped again in a darker shade of dye to build up layers of colour and pattern.

* You can either use natural plant dyes or buy special egg dyes in different colours from a craft shop. Use a clean, dry, blown egg, or an egg which has been boiled for three hours so that it will be preserved.

Use a white egg and think of a design using several colours. Any part of the shell you cover with wax will remain white. Start with a light dye colour first, perhaps a pale yellow, and dip the egg in the dye; then let it dry. Dip the matchstick or pinhead in melted candle wax and draw another layer of design. Everything covered with this new layer of wax will remain yellow when you dip the egg in the next colour dye – deep orange, for instance.

Repeat the process, gradually using darker dye colours – a deep red or black is usually used as the last layer of colour – adding more wax design after each layer of dye has dried completely.

When you have dipped the egg in the last layer of dye, carefully hold it near a candle flame or place it in a hot oven for 5 minutes to melt the wax. You may need to wipe the egg free of wax with a clean dry cloth several times and then reheat it to get rid of all the layers of wax. Experiment with designs using stars, dots, stripes and teardrop shapes.

ONION SKIN AND PETAL PATTERN EGGS

* Dampen some white uncooked eggs and press some flowers or small nicely shaped leaves on the shells of the eggs. Then wrap them tightly in several layers of brown onion skins and fasten them with a rubber band or string to secure well.

Boil the eggs for 10 to 15 minutes. When you remove the onion skins you'll find the shells will be patterned with the shapes of the leaves or flower petals and have a mottled brown effect from the onion skins.

MARBLED WAX EGGS

* Using a potato peeler, grate small amounts of different coloured wax crayons into a small bowl. Pour over some very hot water and stir a little to mix so that the wax melts. Lower your clean white hard-boiled or blown egg into the bowl with a spoon so it is completely immersed in the liquid and swirl it around for a few seconds, then take it out. The melted coloured wax will have made a marbled pattern on the egg. Leave it to dry in an upturned egg box. When the wax has hardened, the eggs can be painted with a clear varnish for a lasting glossy effect.

EASY EGG DYE WITH FOOD COLOURING

* Make sure your eggs are clean – wash them well and wipe them with some vinegar to remove any dirt. In a small bowl mix about 2-5 teaspoons of food colour with one teaspoon of vinegar and add between half to one cup of hot water. The vinegar helps the dye to take well on the eggshells. Allow the liquid to cool, then dip in your egg so it is completely covered. The longer you leave the egg in the food dye, the darker the shade. Remove the egg with a spoon, pat dry with some paper towels and leave to dry in an upturned egg box.

For a stripy effect, wind a rubber band several times around the egg, or stick on strips of thin tape or some stickers – the covered parts won't be coloured by the food dye. Remove the covering and dip them again in a slightly darker shade of food dye for a layered effect. You can also draw a design on the egg with a white crayon before dipping –faces, spots or stars, for example. As with the Ukrainian eggs, the food dye won't colour the areas decorated with crayon. Experiment with different effects and layers of crayon and different tints of food colourings.

NATURAL PLANT DYES FOR EGG DECORATING

On Easter Monday at her home in Ireland, Rosemary always went early in the morning to collect the fragrant, bright yellow gorse flowers which were in full bloom on the hills near her house. Then she'd fill a big pot with water, put in the flowers and eggs and boil them together. The gorse gave a brilliant yellow colour to the eggs, which she would then decorate with paints and crayons.

*   You can use all sorts of plants, flowers, spices, fruit and vegetables to dye the eggs different colours and shades. There are two ways to dye them: boiling the eggs with the dye material gives a more even and more intense, vibrant colour; or cool-dipping where the plant material or spices are boiled separately for between 15 minutes to an hour to create the dye. As a rule of thumb, the longer you boil the dye stuff, the more concentrated the dye becomes and the deeper the colour of the egg. After boiling, the dye is strained and then allowed to cool before the eggs are dipped for colouring. Keep them in the liquid for anything between 5 minutes to overnight depending on the depth of colour you want. The dipping method creates more subtle, delicate shades.

    Use white eggs for dyeing because they will take the colour best. The dyed eggs have a matt finish – if you want to give them a satiny shine, allow them to dry on a rack or draining board, then rub them all over with a little olive or vegetable oil to give them a gloss.

    If you want to keep the eggs for decoration, use blown eggs and dip them in cooled dyes rather than boiling them in the dye liquid.

Here are some ideas for making different natural dyes:

* **Delicate yellow:** gorse flowers, carrots and carrot tops, celery seeds, mango skins, orange or lemon peel. Experiment with ground cumin or saffron.

* **Deep yellow:** 3 to 4 tablespoons turmeric boiled with enough water to cover the eggs.

* **Orangey yellow:** curry powder, as above.

* **Orange or a rich, reddish brown:** boil the skins of 12 to 15 yellow onions. The colour will deepen from orange to a darker reddish brown the longer the eggs are boiled or immersed in the dye.

* **Pink or red:** boil the skins of 12 to 15 red onions, or some fresh chopped beetroot, frozen raspberries or pomegranate juice.

* **Brown or beige:** coffee, tea, walnut shells.

* **Brown-gold:** 4 tablespoons dill seeds.

* **Brown-orange:** 4 tablespoons chilli powder.

* **Green:** nettles, privet leaves, lady's mantle, dock leaves, spinach or carrot tops.

* **Blue:** for a delicate robin's egg blue, chop up half a red cabbage and boil for about 30 minutes. This dye doesn't work so well when very hot, so use already boiled eggs and dip them in the cooled liquid. Leave the eggs to soak to allow the colour to deepen. Try blueberries for a deeper blue.

* **Grey:** black soya beans or try red or purple grape juice.

* **Black:** blackberries.

TIP: *Adding 2 tablespoons of vinegar to the boiling water helps the eggs take on the colour.*

SURPRISE CHOCOLATE CHICKEN EGG

You can prepare these chocolate eggs in advance and give your parents a pleasant surprise at breakfast on Easter morning. You will need:

* blown eggs
* needle
* milk chocolate
* white chocolate – for marbled effect

Blow the eggs as described on page 61. Melt the milk chocolate in a bowl over a saucepan containing hot but not boiling water, then carefully pour it into the empty eggshell. Wipe the eggshells clean to remove any chocolate which has spilt over the edges and leave them in the fridge or a cool place overnight to set.

For a marbled effect, grate some white chocolate and add it to the already melted dark chocolate, stir gently to mix before pouring into the eggshell.

HOME-MADE CHOCOLATE EGGS

Moulds for making chocolate eggs can be bought from good kitchen shops or specialist companies.

The key to making chocolate eggs at home is to temper the chocolate. This involves heating the chocolate to a particular temperature, allowing it to cool, then re-heating it before pouring it into the prepared mould. The process of tempering the chocolate guarantees a glossy, polished finish to the chocolate.

The chocolate should be added to the mould in thin layers, so each layer sets completely before the next layer is added. You will need:

* 300 to 600g good-quality chocolate, depending on the size of your mould – plain chocolate should contain at least 70 per cent cocoa solids
* flavourless oil – sunflower is good
* egg moulds
* cooking thermometer

* First prepare your moulds – make sure they are perfectly clean and dust free, then wipe each mould with some paper towel dipped in a flavourless oil. This helps give the eggs a glossy finish and also makes it easier to remove them from the mould.

Chop or break the chocolate into small, even pieces and put $^2/_3$ with the thermometer into a glass bowl. Melt the chocolate using a bain-marie. To do this, put the bowl in a saucepan containing just a few centimetres of water over a very gentle heat. Make sure the bowl fits snugly in the saucepan so no water or steam comes into contact with the chocolate as it heats – otherwise this will spoil the chocolate and make it grainy.

Stir the chocolate until completely melted, making sure that the water does not come to the boil, and heat the chocolate until it reaches 40°C. Remove from the heat and add the remaining chocolate, stirring until it is all melted and the temperature has fallen to 27°C.

Put the saucepan and bowl back over a low heat and bring the temperature up to 32°C for dark chocolate, 30°C for milk chocolate and 28°C for white chocolate.

Spoon a thin layer of chocolate into each half of the mould, swirling it around or using a clean pastry brush to make an even layer. Use a knife to make a clean edge around the top of the mould to ensure a good fit when the two halves are put together. Allow to cool completely before reheating the remaining chocolate to the required temperature and adding another layer to the mould. Clean the edges each time with a knife. Add at least three or four layers of chocolate to the mould then put it in a cool place to set completely. Carefully remove the two halves of the chocolate egg from their moulds.

To fit the two halves together, heat a knife blade by putting it into a cup of boiled water, then run the blade over the edges until the chocolate melts slightly. Fit the halves together, applying slight pressure – try not to handle the egg too much as you may melt the chocolate with the heat of your hands.

You can put a surprise inside your egg – small chocolate eggs, small chocolate bunnies or a little card – before joining the two halves.

EASTER BISCUITS MAKES 14

* 110g butter
* 225g plain flour
* 110g caster sugar
* 100g currants
* ½ tsp mixed spice
* ½ tsp cinnamon
* 1 egg
* 1 tbsp brandy
* 1 tsp lemon juice

Preheat the oven to 180°C/350°F/gas mark 4. Grease two baking sheets.

In a large bowl, rub the butter into the flour with your fingers until the mixture looks like fine breadcrumbs. Add the sugar, currants, mixed spice and cinnamon.

Beat the egg in a bowl and mix with the brandy and lemon juice. Add to the dry ingredients and mix with a fork to make a firm, doughy mixture. Use your hands at the end and knead the dough lightly so it holds together well for rolling.

Turn out onto a floured board or tabletop and use a rolling pin to roll out to about one centimetre thick. Cut out in rounds with a pastry cutter, preferably one with serrated edges, and place on the greased baking tray.

Bake for about 15 to 20 minutes or until just golden brown. Allow to cool on the baking tray for 15 minutes, then place on a wire tray to cool completely.

If you'd like to offer the biscuits as an Easter gift to visitors and friends, divide them into sets of three (to represent the Holy Trinity) and wrap each set with a ribbon tied in a bow.

For Easter Bunny biscuits, you can use a bunny-shaped pastry cutter and add an extra currant to each biscuit before baking for the bunny's eye.

Easter Cards

Here are some ideas for easy cards to make for Easter.

EASTER EGG BASKET CARD

*   Fold a piece of A5 craft card in half – this will be your actual card. On a separate piece of differently coloured card, draw a pretty basket shape and cut it out. On the back of the basket shape, pipe a little glue down each of the edges, leaving the top glue free. Now stick the basket to the front of your card. Cut out some egg shapes in different coloured card, and decorate them with paints or coloured crayons, sequins, ribbons and so on. Write messages on the backs of the eggs – one for each member of the family, for example. Slot the egg shapes into the basket.

EASTER EGG CARD

*   Draw a large egg shape on some card and cut it out. Glue on coloured foil paper to cover the egg shape, or make a colourful mosaic pattern with foil sweet wrappers and coloured cellophane. Tie a bow with coloured ribbon and glue it to the middle of the egg. Glue the egg shape to the front of your card.

EASTER BONNETS

Traditionally Easter was marked by wearing fancy new clothes and an elaborate and newly trimmed bonnet for the Easter Parade.

* Dig out an old straw hat or look for interesting hats in charity shops and car-boot sales, then invite some friends over for a day of millinery activity – decorating the hats with ribbons, scarves, paper or fabric flowers made from scraps of felt or silk, buttons, sequins and feathers.

You can also make a basic hat from a paper plate. Cover the plate with crêpe or tissue paper, or paint it all over with poster paint and then decorate it with paper flowers and ribbons. Cut small holes on either side of your plate and thread some ribbon through so that the hat can be tied on securely.

For a pointed or cone-shaped hat, cut a slit from the edge of the plate to the centre, then fold and glue before decorating.

To make a hat from card, you will need:

* 2 large sheets of craft card
* scissors
* glue or a stapler

Wrap a sheet of card round your head in a cylinder shape so it fits your head size. Decide how tall you would like your hat to be, and cut the card to fit. Glue or staple the card together to form the hat shape.

For the brim, put a large dinner plate on the second piece of card then draw round it and cut out the circle. Place your hat top in the centre of the circle and trace round it, then draw another circle 4 centimetres inside this one. Cut out the smaller circle. Snip tabs to the line of the circle you drew round the hat top and glue the tabs up inside the middle of your hat to attach the brim. For the top of the hat, cut a circle about 3 centimetres wider than the diameter of the open end of your hat. Cut tabs about 3 centimetres long and fold and glue them inside the top opening.

* Allow the glue to dry properly, then cover the hat all over with coloured crêpe or tissue paper – yellow is traditionally the Easter colour. Staple or glue two lengths of ribbon to the inside of the hat, one on each side, to tie around your chin.

To decorate the hat you will need:

* yellow and other coloured crêpe paper
* tissue paper
* paper doilies
* ribbons and fabric scraps
* little Easter chicks
* mini chocolate eggs
* coloured foil and cellophane from Easter egg and sweet wrappers.
* feathers
* twigs

You can trim the hat to your own design – it can be as simple or as elaborate as you wish. Here are some examples of what you might do:

* tie coloured ribbons round the hat in a large bow at the front

* stick pieces of paper doilies to the brim for a lace effect

* cut out flower shapes from scraps of fabric and felt

* make paper daffodils by cutting the trumpets from egg boxes and the petal shapes from card, and gluing the petals to the base of the trumpets. Paint them bright yellow

* make flowers by twisting strips of coloured tissue paper into flower shapes, or pick some fresh flowers from the garden – primroses and daffodils, for example

* make a nest for holding mini eggs with twigs and straw, add feathers and some Easter chicks to the nest

MAKE-UP AND BEAUTY

The first thing to say about make-up is that it's not compulsory. If you never get interested in make-up at all, that's fine. All that will happen is that you will save yourself a lot of pocket money, as well as having one less thing to row about with your mum.

Talking of which, if there's one thing parents aren't awfully keen on, it's make-up. Some will tolerate it in small quantities, or for special occasions such as parties or school plays, but mostly they object to it on a day-to-day basis. Their excuse is that you're pretty enough anyway; but really they just don't like the thought of their little girl growing up.

The way to deal with this (and stop it becoming a source of conflict) is to be sensible about it. Avoid unnatural, garish colours and don't wear too much. This makes sense not just in terms of keeping mum and dad happy; it's also a good rule to apply to make-up in general. For instance there's no point in wearing foundation when you have lovely young skin. After all, the whole point of the stuff is to *improve* your appearance subtly, not to make you look like a cousin of Coco the Clown.

Skin

All girls want silky-soft, smooth skin. Mother Nature, on the other hand, has other ideas: SPOTS!

There's nothing more depressing than a spot. There's also not a lot you can do to stop yourself getting them. But you can cover them up.

The first thing to remember about spots is that the more you squeeze them, the worse they get. Basically a spot is just a build-up of bacteria in the skin's pores. Fiddling with it only introduces more bacteria into the skin (your fingers are never as clean as you think they are, especially under the nails), and makes the surrounding skin sore. The best thing to do is leave well alone – and try one of these two suggestions:

Tea-tree oil: You can buy this in most chemist's or health shops. Dab a little on before you go to bed. It will help disinfect the spot, and should calm the inflammation. Avoid using harsh disinfectants such as surgical spirit or TCP because they dry out the surrounding skin and just make the whole thing look worse. A good alternative to tea-tree oil is witch hazel.

Concealers: These are skin-coloured creams specifically designed to hide spots or minor blemishes. You can buy them in a chemist's or from make-up counters. You don't need to spend a lot of money, but do take care to choose the right colour. Ideally, you want a concealer that is a shade lighter than your own skin. To find out what that colour is, try a little on your face while you are in the shop (most places have testers) and then look at the colour in natural light. If you can barely see it, then it's the right one for you. If in doubt, err on the lighter side, since a concealer that is too dark will only draw more attention to a blemish.

To apply the concealer, put a small amount onto a clean cotton bud and dab it onto the spot. Then blend into your skin using a clean finger. Repeat the process if necessary. Remember that you will never be able to cover a spot completely, so don't worry if you can still see it a bit. Whatever you do, don't be tempted to keep piling on concealer. You'll just make the spot look more obvious.

Lips and Cheeks

LIPS

Once you've got your perfect base, it's time to have some fun. Lips are the most obvious place to start, as it's hard (although not impossible) to go wrong.

Just a slick of moisture will make your lips look pretty, even without the addition of colour (and anyway lipstick is not much more than coloured lip balm). Vaseline is a good cheap option, and chances are you'll find some at home, probably in the bathroom cabinet. Beeswax-based lip balms are also very moisturizing, although they don't have the same glossy effect as Vaseline.

It's very important to keep your lips soft, and you can do this by gently exfoliating them on a regular basis. A good way to do this is to put a small amount of salt (or sugar, depending on your taste) into a bowl, add a teaspoonful of olive oil and mix. Dip your finger into the mixture and gently rub over your lips using circular movements. This will get rid of any dry skin, and also improve the appearance of your lips by increasing blood circulation. Another way to exfoliate lips is to use your toothbrush – only do be careful not to get carried away by brushing too hard – and be sure to moisturize afterwards.

CHEEKS

When applying blusher or colour to the cheeks it's important to get the colour in the right place. Stand in front of the mirror. Smile. Now, the idea is to put the colour on what's known as the 'apple' of your cheeks. Those are the bits that plump up when you smile. Try it again. See?

* Never put colour under your cheekbones or on the side of your face, and never, ever, on your temples. Lots of books and magazines will tell you how to apply colour to your cheeks according to your face shape. This is silly: blusher should always go on the apple of your cheeks no matter what the shape of your face because the whole point is not to alter the way you look, just to enhance it. Only very skilled make-up artists with lots of experience and vast quantities of foundations, brushes and clever lighting can truly alter a person's face shape.

Apply cream blusher using your fingertips using clockwise circular motions. Blend. Don't panic if it goes a bit wrong first time around: wipe the colour off and start again. It's also worth remembering that most lipsticks will double very happily as cheek colour – unless they're either really dark or really frosty, in which case we wouldn't recommend them anyway on the basis that they're too tarty.

If you have a powder blusher you will need a brush. Many powder blushers are sold with their own brushes, or you can buy brushes separately (although these tend to be very expensive). A soft paintbrush or even a piece of cotton wool will make good substitutes. When applying blusher with a brush, try not to use the bottom of the bristles but the side. Apply in sweeping motions, moving upwards and outwards, and then back in towards your nose, in a circular motion.

If you accidentally apply too much blusher, you can tone it down by blending it. To do this, take a powder puff, if you have one, or a large piece of cotton wool will do, and pat off the excess colour. It's best not to use your fingers as you can sometimes make it go streaky.

Eyes

The eyes are the one area on your face where you can experiment with colours, and really let your imagination run riot. This makes them the most fun to apply make-up to and the most difficult, since once you start playing with colour, mistakes become more obvious.

Let's begin with the basics: eyeliner and mascara. If you learn to use these properly, then you won't go far wrong.

EYELINER

A good, soft eye pencil is the basis of every make-up bag. Black is the most popular colour, but brown is more foolproof. Liquid eyeliner looks stunning and is excellent for creating movie-star eyes, but it requires a lot of practice.

* Start by drawing on your hand. This will help you get an idea of the consistency and feel of your eyeliner. Now rub a finger over the top of it. How does it blend? Does it smudge evenly or not?

  Find a comfortable place to sit – in front of a mirror, obviously. Tilt your head back slightly so you're looking down at yourself. Starting on the outer edge of your top eyelid, draw a line as close as you possibly can to the line of your lashes. Stop about halfway across the eye. Repeat on the other eye. Now, gently run the pad of a finger over the eyeliner, softening the line as you go. You should end up with a very subtle smudge, which will frame your eyes and emphasize them without looking too obvious.

  Don't pull or distort the skin around your eyes. Try not to squint, as this will crease your eyelid and give you a wonky line. Looking slightly down with your head tilted back while arching your eyebrows is best, as this allows you to see what you are doing and ensures your eyelashes don't get in the way. This technique, once you've mastered it, can be the basis for putting on all eye make-up. As you get better at it you can get bolder, taking the line all the way across to the inside of the eye, and going under the eye too.

* For liquid eyeliner, it's best to start from the inside of the eyelid, as you'll want to create an outward sweeping motion. How much liquid eyeliner you get on your eye depends largely on the pressure you apply to the brush. Light pressure will produce a thin line, heavier pressure a much thicker one. Start at the socket end of the eyelid using very light pressure. The idea is to increase the thickness of the line as you move towards the outer edge, creating a natural upward 'flick'. It's very important to keep a steady hand when you do this, so if you can, rest your elbow on a stable surface such as a dressing table or a desk. Slowly and carefully, and remembering to breathe, trace a sweep of eyeliner as close to your eyelashes as you possibly can. To begin with you'll probably get in an awful muddle. Don't worry. Practice makes perfect. Just keep a cotton bud and a little light make-up remover handy to correct mistakes.

Never put liquid eyeliner under your eye. It looks very weird.

MASCARA

Mascara is the easiest and most effective way of emphasizing your eyes. If you're fair, choose a brown or a brown/black colour. Darker hair and skin tones can get away with a black or a blue/black colour.

* Using the same head position as for the eyeliner, i.e. with your chin raised slightly and looking down at yourself in the mirror, sweep the mascara wand upward from the base of the lashes. It's easiest to start on the outer lashes (which tend to be longer and thicker and therefore need more mascara), and work your way towards the inner lashes (which are smaller and need less).

If you wiggle the brush very slightly from side to side at the base of the eyelashes, this ensures that most of the mascara is deposited near the eyeline and prevents clogging further up (clogging is bad). It also helps separate the lashes evenly.

TIP: *You may have seen people pumping their mascara wand in and out of the tube to get more mascara on it. Don't do this: it just pushes air into the tube, which makes the mascara dry out more quickly. For this same reason, always replace the top tightly.*

EYELASH CURLERS

Used properly, these are a girl's best friend. You can buy heated ones but, to be honest, the old-fashioned ones with a little rubber strip and a scissor pressure action are just as effective. They're especially good if you have long, straight eyelashes, but they improve any type of lash, long or short, thick or thin. They give you that wide-awake look more effectively than any eyeshadow or eyeliner.

* Always use them before you apply your mascara. Slip them over your lashes about halfway down their length. Make sure all the lashes are inside the 'curl zone'. Gently close the curler. Hold for about five seconds, and release. Repeat on the other side.

TEA AND CUCUMBER

If you have sore, puffy or tired eyes, try one – or both – of the following

* Camomile tea bags. Camomile calms and soothes. Soak a couple of camomile tea bags in cold water and then put them on your eyes for 10 to 15 minutes.

* Cucumber patches. Slice an ice-cold cucumber straight from the fridge. Place a slice over each eye and relax for 10 to 15 minutes. This is especially good for de-puffing and brightening the whites of your eyes.

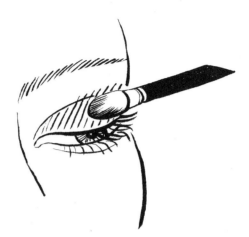

EYESHADOW

Knowing how to apply eyeshadow depends on getting to know the shape of your eyes and what looks good on you. If you have close-set or small eyes, for example, dark colours on the lid will make them look smaller and/or closer together. For wide-set eyes, it's the opposite.

* The best way to find out what suits you is to experiment. The easiest colours to begin with are soft pinks, beiges and off-whites. These are very hard to get wrong, and you can wear them on their own or with a little bit of eyeliner or mascara.

Eyeshadows can be applied either with a brush or with the pad of your finger (the ring finger is best, as it tends to be about the right size). If you are using a brush, load it with eyeshadow, then gently tap it to remove any excess. Then, starting nearest your nose, apply the shadow to your eyelid, moving gradually towards the outer edge of your eye. Repeat on the other eye.

TIP: *Whenever you're doing eyes, it's best to do each in turn in stages, rather than doing one whole eye and then the other – that way you ensure you get an even look.*

Use your finger to blend colour.

Always apply eyeshadow before eyeliner or mascara because, however skilfully you put it on, you will always get a slight dusting of colour on your lashes which will spoil the line of your eyeliner and mascara.

EYEBROWS

In the past it has been fashionable to pluck eyebrows very thin. PLEASE, PLEASE, PLEASE DO NOT DO THIS – unless you want to spend the rest of your life regretting it.

In fact, it's best not to pluck your own eyebrows at all. But since you will probably attempt to do so anyway, here are some tips. Done properly it will create an illusion of more open eyes (diagram A); done wrong and it will look as if you've had an accident with a very small lawnmower (diagram B).

* Study your eyebrows carefully in the mirror. Familiarize yourself with their natural shape. You must never try to alter this – it never works, and you just end up looking weird. If you do decide to tidy, never pluck from above the brows, only from beneath. And think in terms of pruning, not reshaping. You can take out stray hairs in between your eyes, too, but never pluck away at the inside edges of your brows. Ideally, you should be able to drop a straight line down from the inner end of your brow to the inner corner of your eye.

diagram A   *diagram B*

When plucking, always pull in the direction of growth: this will make it hurt less; it will also ensure that you pull the hair out by the root, rather than snapping it off, which is bad for the hair and makes it grow back faster. To make it even less painful, gently stretch the skin while you pluck – this helps the hairs come out faster. Holding an ice-cube on your eyebrow before you begin plucking helps numb the area. Afterwards, apply a little cooling aloe vera gel (you can get 100 per cent pure gel, which is the best) to soothe any redness and generally calm things down. If you can't get your hands on some aloe vera, then witch hazel will also help.

DO NOT under any circumstances do any of this with a razor.

TAKING IT OFF

Learning to remove your make-up is just as important as learning to put it on. You should never, under any circumstances, go to sleep in your make-up. It's very bad for your skin (and if you're wearing eye make-up it will give you sore eyes); it's slovenly as well.

* The best way to remove light make-up is with a mild facial wash. If you suffer from spots, choose a gently medicated one (soap is not ideal as it dries out the skin, which doesn't help). Massage your face in gentle, circular motions, paying particular attention to the areas around the nose and chin. Rinse well with warm water. Repeat if necessary. Pat your face dry with a towel and apply a toner, such as rose water, and a light moisturizer. To do this, first warm a little in the palms of your hands, and then spread over the cheeks, forehead and neck.

Most cleansers will not remove eye make-up, and in any case you probably don't want to risk getting them in your eyes because they'll sting. So, for eyes you'll need a specific eye-make-up remover. Soak a cotton pad in the remover, shut your eye, and gently stroke the pad over the top of the eyelid, using a downward sweeping movement. Repeat until all your eyeshadow and mascara has been transferred to the pad. Then, folding the pad in half, run the clean folded edge over your bottom lashes to take off any colour. Do the same to the other eye.

ON STAGE

Whether acting from a script or just plain acting up (as our grandmothers liked to put it), every girl, however shy, maladroit or tongue-tied will have something to gain from practising the art of performance (or at the very least becoming a half-competent stagehand). As William Shakespeare wrote: 'All the world's a stage/And all the men and women merely players.' By this he did not mean we should all become actors and actresses. He meant we all put on a show at some point in our lives, and he was, of course, right.

Embellishing for dramatic purpose (such as, to take a random example, exaggerating your ability to climb a tree) should not be confused with lying (saying you can climb a tree when in fact you cannot), which is wrong. Learning to distinguish the difference between the two, both in your heart and in others', is a key component of growing up.

On an entirely practical level, however, performance for performance's sake is both entertaining and fun. Whether it's simply learning the words to your favourite song or producing a full-blown stage play, there are lots of ways to while away the hours with yourself in the starring role.

Ballet

Myth: *Every little girl dreams of becoming a ballet dancer.*

Reality: *Not true. Being a girl does not automatically make you a fully paid up member of the pink tutu and legwarmer brigade. It does make it quite likely, though.*

* If you do like ballet, in all probability you will already be familiar with the basics. Just in case you're not, here are some useful things to know. Remember, it takes years of practice to become a real ballerina, but just a small amount of chutzpah and a vivid imagination to be a successful amateur.

First, the fun part: the kit. All ballerinas have ballet shoes. These are generally made of pink leather, although white is common too, as are satin and canvas. Insisting on wearing red ballet shoes marks you out as a rebel and a troublemaker, both of which are generally to be avoided. Boys obviously wear white ballet shoes, as well as white socks; girls wear tights, usually flesh-coloured but the colour can vary according to the rest of the costume. Some sort of floaty skirt is usually in order, as is a leotard. Legwarmers are optional, but useful, as is a tracksuit top to complete the full ballerina-at-rest look.

Proper ballerinas tend to walk in a precise, elegant way, with their feet turned slightly out and their backs very straight. This is because they are taught to hold their heads up high and never slouch and generally pay attention to their posture. In addition, they brush their hair and keep it in neat bunches or a ponytail, and present a clean and tidy appearance.

The Basics

There are five basic positions in ballet, and five basic arm movements too. Endless combinations of the arm and foot movements form the basis of all classical ballets.

first
position

FEET

* First position
* Second position
* Third position
* Fourth position
* Fifth position

All ballet movements begin and end in one of these five positions.

second
position

third
position

ARMS

* First position
* Second position
* Third position
* Fourth position
* Fifth position

Fingers should be held softly and gracefully – don't clump them or over-stretch them. Shoulders should be pulled back and down: the idea is to make your neck look as long and elegant as possible. Think lovely graceful swans.

fourth
position

fifth
position

FIVE THINGS YOU MAY NOT KNOW ABOUT BALLET

* Pointe shoes, which allow ballerinas to dance on the tips of their toes, are not made of wood as many people think. They are made of layers of fabric which have been strengthened with glue. Ballerinas can wear out several pairs of pointe shoes in a single performance.

* Tutus were first worn by female ballet dancers in the 1830s. In those days they were ankle length, but as the years went by tutus got shorter. Modern tutus are usually hip length and stand out stiffly.

* The foundations of classical ballet were laid in seventeenth-century France at the court of King Louis XIV, who was a keen dancer himself. Because of this, all ballet terminology is in French.

* The greatest ballet composer who ever lived was Pyotr Tchaikovsky, born in Russia. His three ballet scores, *Swan Lake*, *Sleeping Beauty* and *The Nutcracker*, are still the world's favourite ballets.

* Britain's national company, the Royal Ballet, was founded by Ninette de Valois in 1931.

TWO THINGS TO TRY AT HOME

* Little jumps (or *petits sautés*). Begin with your arms and feet in first position. Bend your knees halfway (*demi-plié*) and jump as high as you can. Remember to keep your head up, your neck straight, your shoulders back and your arms in position. Point your toes too. As you land, finish as you started, in first position and with your knees slightly bent.

Arabesque. This is one of the basic ballet positions, and there are many variations, depending on your age and expertise. In the *arabesque à terre* (on the ground) the supporting leg is straight, with the knee turned out; your other leg is extended behind you, toes pointed. Your arms are in first position (although you may want to use one to help keep your balance). The idea is to create the longest possible line from the tips of your fingers to the tips of your toes.

Musical Evenings

In the days before television and the Internet, entertainment at home usually consisted of accomplished young ladies performing on the piano, or, in some extremely genteel cases, the harpsichord. Old ladies might make acid comments such as, 'You do not play too ill, Miss Bennet.' Young gentlemen would be extremely polite and turn the pages of your music for you. Even in this rushing modern age, musical evenings can be fun and, in some cases, funny.

If your parents have tortured you by making you take violin or clarinet lessons, you are almost duty bound to subject them to three hours of Bach. If you want to make them laugh, belting out 'It's Raining Men' while wearing disco gear works every time. The key to a successful musical evening is to have a theme.

FOR A CLASSICAL EVENING

* Take three or four simple pieces you feel confident with. Bach, Mozart or Debussy are good choices. For the full effect, put on your best smart frock, and light the room with candles as if you were back in the eighteenth century. If you have a brother or sister, you can get them to introduce you with great ceremony. If they are very good, you might let them participate in a duet. Appropriate refreshments (macaroons, lemonade, sherry for the grown-ups) are always welcome. Make sure the seating is arranged formally, the telephone is turned off and respectful silence is observed. If you are past grade five and feeling broke, you could always make a small charge for admission. A hand-printed programme is a nice touch.

FOR AN EVENING OF SHOW TUNES

* The secret of show tunes is that you should be prepared to go all out, and ham it up with the best. You should also have a proper over-the-top costume of some kind, and possibly be prepared to do a silly dance.

It is best to do this in a group, so get some friends to help and a kind pianist or guitarist to accompany you. You need to divide the room into a stage area, lit with spotlights (anglepoise lamps work very well for this purpose), and a space for the audience, pitch dark, for the full effect. Stage make-up is preferred. You can encourage the audience to join in the choruses.

Great songs for this kind of evening are: 'Sit Down You're Rocking the Boat' from *Guys and Dolls*, 'Cabaret' from *Cabaret*, 'I Could Have Danced All Night' from *My Fair Lady*, 'The Rhythm of Life' from *Sweet Charity*, 'Tomorrow' from *Annie*, 'Mack the Knife' from *The Threepenny Opera*, 'Shall We Dance?' from *The King and I*, 'Put on Your Sunday Clothes' from *Hello, Dolly* and 'Well, Did You Ever?' from *High Society*. Of course you will have many favourites of your own. If you want to make your mother cry sentimental tears of pride and joy, just sing 'Edelweiss' from *The Sound of Music*.

FOR AN EVENING OF MODERN MUSIC

* You can do this any way you like; use a microphone or karaoke machine if you have one, go it alone, or sing to a CD. Some smokin' dance moves are always welcome. You can choose a theme – disco dolly or hot rocker – but really all you need are your favourite songs and a willing audience. Oh, and plenty of glittery eyeshadow.

Putting on a Play

First, as Mrs Beeton might have said, write your script. You can, of course, choose something already published, but most plays are rather long, and you will not get the same kind of satisfaction as you would performing something you have written your very own self.

HOW TO WRITE A PLAY

* A one-act play is a good way to start, and the easiest option. Drama, as all the sages tell us, is conflict. So, to think of a good plot, you need to invent a character who wants something very badly, and then, in the age-old tradition, put many obstacles in their way. (Remember the obstacle does not have to be external; it can be some inner failing or flaw or blind spot.) Stick to a specific place and a short time span, rather than letting the action ramble over months or years.

Imagine your heroine first. She is probably based on you, but with a little dramatic licence. You don't have to start writing any dialogue or scenes yet; just find out what she loves and hates, what she dreams of, whether she adores dogs or loathes the smell of bleach. You may not use all of this, but you must know it for the character to become three dimensional. Make notes. (A special notebook devoted only to your play is useful.)

Once you know your character inside out, give her a goal, and imagine what might stop her reaching it. You can draw inspiration from your favourite stories.

Then you need . . .

SECONDARY CHARACTERS

* You can have fun with these. You can have the comedy sidekick, the ally, the best friend, the greatest enemy, the love of your life, or just someone who comes on to pour the tea. It is important these characters provide a contrast to the heroine, otherwise it all becomes a little same old same old.

THE PLOT

You do not have to work this out in minute detail – inspiration comes as you go along – but you do need to decide on the beginning, the end and a few key points in between. Some writers like to make a chart and put it up on the wall.

* You do not need to work over your plot sweating at your desk, chewing the end of your pencil and feeling as if you are doing some particularly fiendish maths homework. The best way is to think about your main character whenever you have a moment. Let her and her possible story percolate through your brain, when you are in the bath, out walking, or on a long drive. Try and see her clearly, as if you were running a film in your head. Send her in different directions and see what happens: how does she react to different people and events? Let your imagination fly like a swallow going south for winter.

  Make sure you carry your notebook with you wherever you go. When a good idea strikes, write it down at once. If you don't, you will have forgotten it by the time you get home.

  Another good tip in this development stage is to turn yourself into a human detective. Watch how people walk, what they do with their hands, whether they fiddle with their hair. See if you can tell from purely physical clues whether they are happy or sad, nervous or bold. Listen for their funny verbal tics and how they use their favourite words.

THE PLAY ITSELF

With the spine of the plot in place, you are ready to start the actual writing. A play is written entirely in dialogue, with a few stage directions, e.g. JANE falls over; HORATIO exits stage right; STEPHANIE rips off her disguise to reveal that she is, in fact, a boy.

Unlike real life, the dialogue is not just there to enable people to chat about nothing much or swap knitting tips, it must move the action along and reveal character. You are telling a story in speech.

There are several great rules for dialogue. First, it must sound natural when spoken aloud.

Each character should have a distinct way of speaking. You know how it is in life: some people speak in short sentences, others ramble. Some people can never come to the point, some people say one thing when they clearly mean another.

Never, on any account, try to do dialect. It will sound like the Worzels. Also avoid too many you knows, sort ofs, kinds ofs, ums and ahs.

Avoid long speeches. This is not Speaker's Corner in Hyde Park or the Houses of Parliament. Only Shakespeare can do lengthy soliloquies. He is the master and may do anything.

Finally, you should understand how a play is laid out on the page. This is very simple. Have a look at one to get the idea. Stage directions are in italic with character's names in capitals. At the start of each new speech you should put the character's names in capitals and if you have stage directions for his or her entrance put them after the name in brackets and italics. So, for example:

MARIA: (*waving her handkerchief and sobbing*) Goodbye, my darling.

REHEARSALS

Once you have your script, hand out copies and be fabulously bossy about making everyone learn their lines. It is very hard to rehearse without the use of both hands.

Someone should be appointed as the director; her word is final although suggestions from the actors are permissible. If one person is not in charge, rehearsals will degenerate into squabbling.

Performance

You can stage your play as simply or elaborately as you like. Ideally you should have a good space where a proper curtain can be hung and spotlights rigged up. You can perform a play in your front room, if you rearrange the furniture and make a decent gap between you and the audience.

* You will need a prompter, in case anyone forgets their lines. The prompter should sit in a spot where all the actors can hear her, have a torch to follow the script and be invisible to the audience.

  You will need props. Some obvious stand-bys are water pistols painted silver for guns, cold tea for whisky, a length of wood covered with foil for a sword. Otherwise, gather up books, newspapers, spectacles, umbrellas, radios, etc. If you find you need a lot of props, you might consider employing a prop mistress, whose job it is to make sure each item is in its correct place at curtain-up.

  You will need costumes. If you are a genius with the sewing machine and live in a house where the cupboards are treasure troves of spare swatches of fabric, then you can put on a medieval pageant. If not, then your own clothes, cleverly chosen, will do perfectly. We do, however, strongly recommend the use of hats. These are very good for getting you into the theatrical spirit.

  You will need make-up. Even the boys must wear make-up on stage, or they will look pasty and absurd (or even more pasty and absurd than they already do, were such a thing possible). You will need a good foundation (not too orange), an eyebrow pencil, lipstick, rouge and lashings of mascara. To age someone, apply dark shadows under the eyes and by the sides of the nose, and gently trace a few wrinkles along the forehead with a grey eyeliner.

CORPSING

* The irrepressible desire to laugh, most often encountered at a tragic or crucial moment in the action is every actor's nightmare. Should this happen, you may need to turn away from the audience until the fit passes. Think of something very sad to bring you back to gravitas.

DASTARDLY TRICKS

Obviously, as responsible adults, we don't recommend that you perform any of the tricks in this chapter. But you will have noticed the word dastardly in its title and closer inspection will reveal that this is an excellent description of its nature. Basically, the bottom line is don't come crying to us if you end up in detention or get yourself grounded. One of us (who shall remain nameless) once spent several afternoons writing out 'I must not cover the blackboard in Vaseline' whilst the other got the entire school held back on account of her fondness for Penguin biscuits. If you are going to attempt any of these things, make sure you don't get caught. If you do get caught, don't blame us. And if someone else does one of these things to you, don't be sad, get mad. Then get even. Read on ...

SNEEZING POWDER

Use with caution and try not to get it into your victims' eyes!

* Sprinkle a small pinch of white pepper on a clean tissue. Offer it to a younger brother, grandfather or your teacher with an angelic smile on your face, suggesting that they might like to clean their nose (hint they've something unseemly about their left nostril).

* An alternative method is to lightly powder your victim's pillow with a pinch of pepper before bath time, when no one is looking, of course.

HONEY ON DOOR KNOBS

* This doesn't need explanation and can be fun if you live in a block of flats.

KNOCK DOWN GINGER

* Knock on someone's door and run away as quickly as your legs will carry you.

ITCHING POWDER

* 1 handful rosehips
  (or more if you want a lot!)

* Using your nails, split open the rosehips' red skin to reveal the hairy seeds inside. The tiny hairs on the seeds cause the itching. Scrape the seeds out of the hips and put them in a small bowl. Put it in a warm place, near a radiator or in the airing cupboard, and allow the seeds to dry for 10 minutes or so. This increases the efficiency of the itching powder.

Store the powder in a jar or box and use sparingly! Just a pinch or two down an unsuspecting victim's back will bring about an itching fit that will be a joy to witness! Small amounts may also be sprinkled inside pyjama bottoms or tops just before bedtime. That's actually quite cruel, and we don't really advise it.

The flesh of the rosehip can be eaten raw — it's a delicate sweet taste and is nice to nibble on while you're preparing your weapon.

TRIP WIRES

* Attach a piece of cotton between door frames — works well if your brother or sister is being really annoying and you want to trip them up or just irritate them.

WATER BOMBS

* Fill some balloons with water. Drop them from a height into the path or onto the head of your unsuspecting victim. Plastic or paper bags will work too, but move quickly if you are using a paper bag as it will go soggy and collapse in your hands if you are not careful.

JELLY BOMBS

This is a great variation on the classic water bomb, made with jelly.

* 1 block or more of jelly cubes
* balloons or freezer bags
* funnel (optional)

* Prepare the jelly following the instructions on the packet. Let it cool just enough so you can dip your finger in it without getting burnt, then pour into your jelly-bomb containers. If you are using balloons you'll need a funnel — stretch the balloon opening over the funnel nozzle to prevent spillage. Fill the bombs just three quarters full. Seal the freezer bags or knot the balloons and put them in the fridge until just set. A slightly liquid jelly will have a wonderful explosive and messy impact, while a firmer jelly bomb will have more bounce on the victim's head.

CLINGFILM ON TOILET TRICK

* Another good trick is to wait until everyone has gone to bed, then take a roll of clingfilm and stretch it over the toilet bowl as tightly as possible. Try to get it very smooth with no tell-tale wrinkles. Put the toilet seat down. When the next person goes for a wee, they'll get their pyjama bottoms and legs rather wet.

CLASSIC SACHET OF KETCHUP UNDER THE TOILET SEAT

Next time you are eating in a fast-food restaurant, take a few extra sachets of ketchup or salad cream from the counter so you can try this classic caper on a member of your family.

* Lift the toilet seat. Most toilet seats have sort of plastic knobs on the underside. Carefully put the sachet on the ceramic toilet rim, placing it exactly on the spot where the knob will touch when you put the toilet seat back down. Gently lower the toilet seat on top of the sachet. Quietly and quickly leave the bathroom.

  Loiter nearby flicking through a book until the next desperate person runs in and plonks their bottom on the toilet – and SPLAT!

CHINESE BURNS

Caution – for use in extreme emergencies only. NEVER try this on a baby or a much younger brother or sister or child younger than you in the playground. That would be bullying.

Chinese burns are horrible and hurt a lot and should only be inflicted in extreme situations. Show some pity – don't twist too hard or too long.

* Get hold of your adversary's wrist with both your hands and twist it by applying pressure in opposite directions. Continue to twist until the victim either apologizes for whatever wrong they've done, submits or shouts for mercy.

  TIP: *Parents' and, of course, a bully's wrists, are a bit more sturdy and can withstand a longer and more vigorous burn.*

APPLE-PIE BEDS

This is a good trick for sleepovers. Stealthily sneak into your intended victim's bedroom and give them an apple-pie bed.

* From the bottom of the bed, fold the bottom sheet up over itself and tuck it in underneath the mattress about three quarters of the way up the top end of the bed. When the unlucky person gets in and stretches out, looking forward to a peaceful night's sleep, their feet will jam up against the sheet, and they'll have to get up and make the bed all over again.

  You could also stuff some prickly things under the bottom sheet – a toy dinosaur, a hairbrush . . . you get the idea. Oh, and if you dip someone's finger in a glass of water while they are sleeping it makes them wet the bed (not pleasant for anyone).

LUMPY MATTRESS

* Put large, uncomfortable objects under the mattress – a brick, a saucepan or a watering can – the more bizarre and lumpy the object the better.

ODD THINGS IN THE BED

* To torment a brother or sister, try placing random, unexpected objects in their bed each night – a saucepan one night, a banana the next . . . Slip a hairbrush under the sheet for a prickly effect, put a whoopee cushion under the pillow, half-fill a balloon with ice-cold water and slip it between the sheets in winter.

SPIDERS

* If you find a nice big juicy spider, slip it into your mum's handbag.

SLUGS, WORMS OR FROGS IN THE BED

Need we say more?

Food-Related Tricks for Very Greedy Gluttons

EMPTY CHEWING GUM PACKET

* Next time you get some chewing gum, keep the wrappers and foil and carefully rewrap the foil so it looks as though there is still a whole packet left. Offer a stick to your friends and watch their faces fall as they discover the empty gum trick.

WORM IN SANDWICH

* Do you have a very greedy brother or sister, or a girl at school who always asks for a bite of your sandwich at lunchtime? If you get fed up with someone scoffing your food, why not prepare a 'special' sandwich just for them? Make the sandwich look as delicious as possible – add lettuce, tomato, cheese and mayonnaise so it is dripping out of the side, but slip in a couple of nasty surprises – experiment with a smelly sardine combined with a worm and add some chocolate buttons for a truly ghastly mix. That should stop them scoffing your food!

TRICK EGGS

This is a traditional breakfast-time trick which never fails to amuse or grow dull with repetition. In fact, part of the fun is the fact that your mum, dad, brother or granny falls for it every time!

* Next time you have a boiled egg for breakfast, eat it carefully so as not to crack the shell. When you've finished it, quietly and furtively turn the now empty shell upside down and put it in a clean egg cup. When your mum or dad or brother (or whoever is laziest and gets up last for breakfast) comes to the table, sweetly offer the lovely newly boiled egg in the new clean egg cup with a clean spoon. A nice touch is to serve it with freshly made toast soldiers. Watch as they smash the empty shell to smithereens as they eagerly try to tuck in!!!

Simple Teatime Tricks

Put salt instead of sugar in the sugar bowl and let unsuspecting guests stir it into their tea.

Use salt instead of sugar in cakes — or add sand or chilli. The cakes will look delicious but will taste quite horrid. See your guests wince when they tuck in. (Rosemary once did this completely by accident when she made a date and banana cake. But the joke was on her — she had added salt by mistake to a big jar of vanilla sugar. Unfortunately her mother-in-law was staying at the time, which is always tense-making, and the cake was truly revolting.)

CUSTARD PIES

> * shop-bought empty flan cases
> * tin ready-made custard
> * shaving cream

* Fill the flan cases with custard and top with generous squirts of shaving cream. Wait until everyone sits down for tea, and start a custard-pie fight. It might be better to have the pie fight in the garden so you can really make a mess.

BUCKET OF WATER TRICK

Another classic trick, this is very simple and effective.

* Carefully place a small plastic bucket of water on top of a door. The trick is to have the door just a tiny bit open so that the bucket can balance between the door frame and the door. When your victim opens the door, the bucket of water should fall on their head.

TIP: *Instead of water, you could fill a bucket with jelly, popcorn, autumn leaves or lots of tiny pieces of torn paper, or simply position a large cuddly toy on top of the door so that a large soft gorilla lands on your granddad rather than a bucket of cold water.*

STICKY NOTE ON THE BACK

* Stick a note on someone's back so they walk around in happy ignorance with 'I love xxx' (insert name of the nastiest boy at school or creepiest teacher) stuck to their shirt all day. Find an excuse to pat the victim on the back and while doing so subtly put the sticker on their back without them suspecting foul play. This is a skill and a fine amusement in itself!

SARTORIAL SNEAKINESS

This is a trick for last thing at night in readiness for the next morning's rush to get to school on time.

* Sew up your mother's, father's, brother's or sister's shirt or blouse cuffs. You can also sew up the pockets of school blazers or your parent's work jackets. Put them back where you found them and wait for the uproar the next morning.

Lesson Disruptors

CONFUSE TEACHERS BY SITTING AT DIFFERENT DESKS

* When your teacher turns their back to write on the blackboard, everyone very quietly gets up and swaps tables or desks. Try not to giggle or snigger while their back is turned and wait to see how long it takes them to get confused. Swap again or swap back next time they turn their back or leave the room.

BUZZING BEES

* This is great for particularly dull classes. The whole class makes a quiet but high-pitched buzzing noise and pretends that some bees have come through the window.

One pupil pretends to get hysterical and has to be calmed down with a glass of water and possibly a visit to the cloakroom or school nurse.

Jokes, Jokes, Jokes

* Why did the robber take a bath?
So he could make a clean getaway!

What's green and goes up and down?
A gooseberry in a lift!

Knock knock!
Who's there?
Cows go.
Cows go who?
Cows go moo not who.

Knock knock!
Who's there?
Howard.
Howard who?
Howard I know?

Why did the orange cross the road?
To play squash!

What lies in a cot and wobbles?
A jelly baby!

What did the mayonnaise
say to the fridge?
Close the door, please, I'm dressing.

What did the orange squash
say to the water?
I'm diluted to meet you.

What do you call a teacher
wearing earplugs?
Anything you like! She can't hear you!

What time was Adam created?
A little before Eve . . .

* Why is Cinderella never picked
for the hockey team?
Cos she runs away from the ball!

What do sea monsters have
for supper?
Fish and ships!

What do you call three ducks
in a crate?
A box of quackers!

What do you call a cannibal
who eats his mother's sister?
An aunt-eater!

Why are fish smarter
than elephants?
Because they live in schools!

What sort of coat has no
sleeves and is put on wet?
A coat of paint!

What did the big hand say
to the little hand?
I'll be round again in an hour!

Which is the strongest day
of the week?
Sunday . . . all the rest are weak days!

What is black and white
and red all over?
A newspaper!

What do you need to open
the gate to the graveyard?
A skeleton key!

* Why are some snakes like a
baby's toy?
Because they are rattlesnakes!

Which part of a fish weighs the most?
Its scales!

What did the Spanish lady
say to her Spanish hen?
Oh, LAY!

When is a piece of wood
like a head of state?
When it's a ruler!

When is a length of string
like a piece of wood?
When it's got knots in it.

What did one street say to the
other street?
Meet you at the corner?

Knock knock!
Who's there?
Luke.
Luke who?
Luke through the keyhole
and you'll find out.

Did you hear about the granny
who drowned in a bowl of muesli?
*She was pulled under by a
strong currant!*

Why was Goliath so shocked when
David slung a stone at him?
*Because such a thing had never
entered his head.*

* 'Doctor! Doctor! I feel like
a pair of curtains.'
*'Come on now, lad,
pull yourself together!'*

What do you call bears with no ears?
B!

Why was six scared of seven?
Because seven eight nine!!

Why did the sausage roll?
Because it saw the apple turnover!

When is a door not a door?
When it's ajar!

Knock knock!
Who's there?
Isabel.
Isabel who?
Isabel really necessary on a bike!

What's grey, has four legs
and a trunk?
A mouse going on holiday!

What's grey, has four legs, a trunk, a
loud Hawaiian shirt, a big sombrero
and a smug smile on its face?
A mouse coming back from holiday!

How do you start a teddy bear race?
Ready? Teddy. . . Go!!!

What do you give a pig
with a sore finger?
Oinkment!

SUMMER

Long hot days and balmy nights, lazy mornings, bare feet and ice creams, sunshine and strawberries, Wimbledon – AND NO SCHOOL! That's why summer is the best time of all.

Picnics

While the weather is fine, any meal eaten outdoors, in the park, on a walk or just in the garden, will turn into a picnic. In the summer, all you have to do is lay a table or put a cloth or blanket on the ground in the garden, and mealtimes instantly become an exciting treat.

TIPS FOR PREPARING A PICNIC BASKET

* Line your basket with a clean tablecloth, add cloth or paper napkins.

* Fill some small glass bottles with lemonade/barley water/elderflower cordial and make stoppers out of rolled up pieces of clean paper. A little piece of tin foil with an elastic band around it also makes a good stopper.

* Paper or plastic tumblers are better than glasses for picnics.

* If you have plenty of napkins, plates are not necessary for picnicking, otherwise pack small plastic plates.

* Pick a small posy of flowers and put it in a jam jar to decorate the picnic blanket.

* Pack a plastic bag for rubbish.

PICNIC FOOD

* add a little honey to cocktail sausages then cook till crisp in a slow oven

* hard-boiled eggs or quails' eggs

* cherry tomatoes

* cucumber/carrot/celery sticks

* chicken drumsticks

* olives

* hummus, taramasalata or tzatziki are always popular, with carrot sticks, baby sweetcorn or mangetout for dipping

* something sweet never goes amiss

SANDWICH TIPS FOR PICNICS

* use the freshest bread possible

* use a variety of bread – sliced loaves, baguettes, pitta bread, Turkish flat breads, Turkish sesame loaves, crusty rolls or flat corn bread for wraps

* sandwiches are smarter and more appetizing if cut into triangles and squares – with the crusts off, if you prefer (if you are going to a park or a river, bring the crusts along in a bag to feed the ducks)

* use half white bread, half brown bread to make two-tone sandwiches

* use butter or olive oil spread very sparingly

* if you don't like butter, spread the bread with mayonnaise instead

SANDWICH FILLINGS

* very finely sliced cucumber

* finely sliced tomatoes – delicious on very fresh, buttered white bread, with a pinch of sea salt and white pepper

* raspberry jam

* cream cheese and cucumber

* Marmite à la Nigella –beat 50g butter with a couple of teaspoons of Marmite

TEDDY BEAR PICNICS

Invite your favourite teddies out for a picnic in the garden or the park in fine weather. It is polite to send invitations to the bears a day or so in advance.

* Teddy bears don't tend to have huge appetites, but their favourite sandwiches include honey, jam or marmalade and a plain old glass of milk. Bring some nice napkins to wipe the jam and honey from their fur when they've had enough to eat.

HOW TO TELL IF SOMEONE LIKES BUTTER

✻ Hold a buttercup under someone's chin. If you see a gold reflection, they are
fond of butter.

DAISY CHAINS

In summer the grass on the lawn in the garden or park will be covered in
daisies. Choose daisies with good, long, preferably plump stalks. Thin stalks
are harder to split and may be too delicate and break. Using your thumb nail,
make a nail-sized slit in the stalk, thread the next daisy through the slit, then
make a slit in that daisy, thread another through that slit, and so on, until the
chain is the required length.

✻ Make bracelets, necklaces, crowns, tiaras and garlands. You can make
daisy-chain jewellery for your dolls or teddy bears, too, and for your dad or
granddad. Lace them round his neck and on his head while he's snoozing in
the sun under the newspaper.

Alternatively, a daisy-chain competition may be held. The player who makes
the longest chain in a given time – say, in the half-hour before tea is ready – is
the winner, and is crowned Queen of the Daisies for the rest of the day and
garlanded with daisy chains. And gets an extra strawberry with their ice
cream at teatime!

FAIRY HOUSES

Fairies usually live in hedges and little bushes, so you should look out for them and help make their houses more comfortable.

In Rosemary's garden at her family home in Ireland she had a hedge with wonderfully gnarled and knotted hawthorn bushes where the fairies lived, but in towns and cities they sometimes live in bushes or in the roots of trees in parks.

* Choose the tree or bush you think is most likely to be a fairy's house and carpet it with moss and flower petals. Acorn cups make good bowls for water and basins for the fairies to wash their faces and clothes. Small fluffy feathers are very soft for pillows; if you live in the country, you might find some lamb's wool which fairies love to sleep on. Empty snail shells make good sculptures for fairy banqueting rooms. Find pieces of wood to make a grand dining table and benches for the fairies to sit on. You can leave very tiny things for them to eat too – they like small garden peas, berries and rose petals. Our editor Venetia and her sisters say that fairies like blackberries for breakfast, but a whole blackberry is too big, so you will need to split it into tiny fairy-sized blackberries. You can do this with raspberries too.

Mark out a garden path with tiny pebbles in different colours and make a fairy garden with flowers and twigs. If you dig a little hole and place a small bowl or cupcake tin in it, this could be a garden pond.

Fairies usually come out at dusk, and don't like to be seen, so leave the house just before bedtime so they can find your gifts and eat their supper while you are sleeping. In the morning, when you go back to the fairy house, you might have a little clearing up to do to get the house spick and span for them again ✳

Summer Garden and Park Games

HIDE AND SEEK

This is a fun variation of the classic game to play outdoors in the garden or at the park.

* Pick straws to choose who is to be the first seeker. Get as many pieces of grass or twigs of varying lengths as there are players. The player who pulls out the shortest piece shall be the first seeker.

  The seeker stands at a chosen home base, closes her eyes tight, and counts out loud to fifty. The other players run as fast as they can and find clever hiding places. As the seeker nears fifty, she should call out loud, 'Forty-eight, forty-nine, fifty! Ready or not, here I come!'

  When the seeker spots someone in their hiding place, she calls out, for example, 'I see Florence behind the chestnut tree!' and Florence must come and stand at home base. If, however, another hider can catch Florence's attention and waves at her from their hiding place without the seeker spotting them, Florence is then freed and can attempt to escape from home base and hide again without being noticed by the seeker. If two or more players have been spotted and are at home base, and are then freed by another player waving at them, they can attempt to hide themselves again without being spotted.

  The look on the seeker's face as she turns round to find all her prisoners have escaped once more, and the expression of puzzlement as she tries to work out where the hidden person is waving from, is great fun indeed.

BABES IN THE WOOD

* This is a game of hide and seek in pairs. There is, naturally, the Wicked Witch, who is trying to find the Babes. The Wicked Witch counts to fifty with her eyes closed as the Babes run off in pairs to hide and keep hidden and silent. If she finds them they must run for their lives for home. If the Witch touches one of the Babes before they reach home, she becomes the Wicked Witch.

BLINDFOLD HIDE AND SEEK

*This is best played somewhere with lots of trees and bushes, such as the park. One player covers her eyes with a blindfold and all the other players stand in a row. One by one they step forward without speaking, and the blindfolded player tells them where to hide. When they have all gone, the seeker removes her blindfold and shouts out, 'Here I come!' and off she runs. The hidden players must try to get back home without being touched. The player who is caught or the last player home becomes 'it'.

TOUCH THINGS

*Players each find a good little stick, then stand in a line with it in their hands. Before the game starts, one player, who will be the umpire, decides on a number of things to be touched – trees, stones, garden chairs, benches, flower pots, rabbit hutches, bushes, flowers, grandmothers, aunts, etc. Players must remember the list of things to be touched and race to touch each one before they can go home. If a player fails to touch everything with their stick, she becomes the umpire and decides the next list of things to be touched. This game can also be played indoors.

Anyone for Tennis?

Another sign that summer is well and truly here, and that school will be out for summer in just a matter of days, is when Wimbledon starts.

The second week of Wimbledon always coincided with the start of the school holidays in Ireland and, in Rosemary's memory at least, with a scorching heatwave. Watching the tennis on television got her all fired up and keen to play matches herself. The grass wasn't even or well mown enough to play in the garden, so she used to have furiously competitive matches of wall tennis against the back wall of the garage.

THE TENNIS MATCH

If you have a park with tennis courts nearby, book one. At home in the garden you can mark out your own tennis court on a concrete yard or lawn with chalk or string. Place some chairs at either side of your court or knock some sturdy stakes into the ground and use some string and a sheet to make a net.

* Get into the spirit by dressing up in a white T-shirt, white ankle socks, and the shortest white skirt or shorts you can find.

  Pack your bag with a towel (for wiping the sweat from your brow). Bring some bottles of water or lemon barley water to quench your thirst during the match.

  Appoint someone as umpire. Younger siblings can be ball boys and girls.

  Psych each other out by glaring angrily across the court while waiting to receive or serve. When it is your turn to serve, don't forget to tuck the spare tennis balls into your pants.

  Get into the spirit and tension of the game: punch the air in victory when you score a dazzling point; argue with the umpire if you disagree with an out call; curtsy to the audience if you win the match and have received the silver plate!

WALL TENNIS

* Find a good expanse of wall preferably without breakable windows. If there are windows, this adds excitement and a degree of difficulty to the game. For example, you might decide that if the ball hits the window or windowsill on a serve, it qualifies as a let, and results in a second serve.

  Mark out the boundaries of the court and mark a line on the wall to represent the net.

  Points are scored as per classic tennis. If the ball goes up onto the roof, but rolls or bounces back down again, play continues as normal. If the ball goes over the roof, or gets stuck in a drainpipe and doesn't come back down, this is a lost point — you could even impose a penalty for a lost ball.

Summer Drinks and Syrups

Summer is a thirsty time. All that running about, playing tennis, bicycling, collecting, playing and swimming in the hot sun is thirsty work. It's important to drink lots of water every day, but especially when you are hot and sweaty.

Home-made drinks are easy and quick to make and really delicious. The syrup base below from Darina Allen's Ballymaloe Cookery Course *is simply sugar boiled with water, to which you can add different herbs and flowers for different flavours. This syrup is then diluted with water in a large jug or bottle and served cold with ice, or you can use it to flavour puddings, fruit salads and compotes. The syrup keeps well in the fridge for a long time or can be frozen.*

BASIC STOCK SYRUP MAKES APPROX. 800ML

* 450g sugar
* 600ml cold water

* Dissolve the sugar in the water over a gentle heat and bring to the boil. Boil for 2 minutes, then allow to cool. Store in the fridge if not using immediately.

LAVENDER SYRUP

* To the basic syrup recipe add 1 to 2 tablespoons of lavender flowers, then bring to the boil. Strain through a fine sieve when cool, and store in the fridge.

MINT SYRUP

* To the basic syrup recipe add 4 to 6 sprigs of fresh mint (spearmint is especially good) then bring to the boil. Strain through a fine sieve when cool, and store.

ROSEMARY SYRUP

* To the basic syrup recipe add 2 sprigs of fresh rosemary, then bring to the boil. Strain through a fine sieve when cool, and store.

SWEET GERANIUM SYRUP

* To the basic syrup recipe add 6 to 8 sweet geranium leaves, then bring to the boil. Strain through a fine sieve when cool, and store.

STRAWBERRY MILKSHAKE MAKES APPROX. 4 GLASSES

* 500g strawberries
* 900ml milk
* 225g best vanilla ice cream
* 50g caster sugar
* ice cubes
* 75ml double cream, whipped
* whole strawberries to garnish

* Whizz the strawberries in a blender. Add the milk, ice cream and sugar and whizz again until smooth. Put ice cubes into some nice tall glasses, pour in the milkshake and add a dollop of whipped cream. Top each glass with a whole strawberry. You can adapt this recipe using different fruits – mango or raspberry, for example.

ANNA'S ELDERFLOWER CORDIAL MAKES 1.2 LITRES

Elder comes into bloom in late May and early June and grows profusely among the hedgerows in the countryside and in the city. As soon as you see its lacy creamy-white flowers in bloom, you know summer is here and it is time to start collecting the blossoms to make the summer's supply of elderflower syrup for cordials and champagnes and for lots of delicious sweets and puddings.

* 16–20 elderflower heads
* 900g granulated sugar
* 1.2 litres boiling water
* 25g citric acid
* 3 unwaxed lemons

* Wash the flower heads thoroughly several times in clean cold water to remove any insects and dirt (elderflowers can often have green- or blackfly). Shake the flowers to remove any excess water.

Put the sugar in a large bowl and pour on the boiling water. Stir till the sugar dissolves and allow to cool. Add the flowers and push them down so they are thoroughly covered with the syrup. Add the citric acid. Cut up the lemons roughly, skins and all, and add. Cover and leave to steep at room temperature for 24 hours. Next day, strain through a clean tea towel or muslin cloth, squeezing well to extract all the elderflower and lemon juices. Pour into clean and well-rinsed bottles and store in the fridge.

To use, dilute the syrup to taste with tap water, or make a sparkling drink by using fizzy mineral water. Add a sprig of mint and some ice cubes to the jug before serving.

NOTE: *Citric and tartaric acid are used to help preserve the elderflower cordial and can be bought in grocery shops and at the chemist. Tartaric acid is not the same as cream of tartar – last year Rosemary couldn't find tartaric acid anywhere and had no idea what it was so tried to make this cordial with cream of tartar which gave it a slight taste of baking powder – not good!*

LEMON BARLEY WATER

MAKES 1.15 LITRES

* 2 unwaxed lemons
* 85g pearl barley
* 1.15 litre water
* sugar or sugar syrup (see page 110), to taste

* Use a potato peeler or zester to thinly peel the skins from the lemons. Squeeze the lemons and reserve the juice.

Put the skins in a saucepan with the pearl barley and half the water. Remove the pulp from the lemons and add to the pan. Bring to the boil and simmer for 30 to 40 minutes. Remove from the heat and mash the pulp. Let it stand for an hour or so.

Scoop out a tablespoon or so of barley, and put into a large jug. Strain the cooked pulp into the jug, add the squeezed lemon juice and the rest of the water.

Sweeten with sugar or sugar syrup to taste. Cover and put in the fridge to cool before serving. This barley water is even better on the second day.

BOTTLES

* It's nice to store your cordials and other home-made drinks in nicely shaped and coloured glass bottles. Always wash old bottles thoroughly in hot soapy water and be sure to rinse them several times before use. Adding a dash of white wine vinegar or some lemon juice helps to get the bottles squeaky clean and sterile for reuse.

HOME-MADE LABELS

* Make some home-made labels for your bottles. Cut some squares of paper – you can use a textured writing paper in cream or white, or brown wrapping paper. Write the name of your drink or cordial on the label, along with the date on which it was made, and draw some flowers to decorate it.

Growing Lavender in the Garden

Lavender thrives in sunny climates. In Provence in France, for example, you'll often see whole fields glowing with its violet-blue flowers. Plant lavender in big terracotta pots, or in flower borders in the garden, in a position where it will get lots of direct sunlight and where the soil is light and free-draining. It will flower at the beginning of summer and should continue to the end of August and into September. Cutting out the flowers and stems as they fade will help keep the lavender flowering all summer long. The dried lavender flowers can be kept in bunches and allowed to dry further by hanging them upside down away from direct sunlight, or you can start to collect the petals and keep them in a clean airtight glass jar to use later.

At the end of summer, in late August, when the lavender has finished flowering, collect all the blooms. When you harvest the flowers cut the whole stalk so it has a few leaves at the base; look out for any dead or woody stalks and remove those too by cutting them back to the ground. This will help the plant grow back into a nice shape and stop it getting straggly and unhealthy.

Once you have harvested your lavender flowers, pull the flower petals from the stalk with your fingers over a large bowl to collect them. It's best to clear the kitchen table so you have lots of space to work. Spread a clean tablecloth or a sheet over the table before you start — this will help when tidying up and gathering stray flower petals at the end. As you work, the whole house will become infused with the lavender's strong, almost medicinal and soothing smell, which will linger for weeks.

Once you have collected your lavender petals, you are ready to start making lavender water (see recipe on page 139) or lavender bags, or you can use them in cooking.

LAVENDER BAGS

Lavender bags are quick and easy to make and are a good summer present. Place them in drawers to make your clothes smell sweet and in wardrobes to keep moths away, put them under running hot water to scent your bath, or on your pillow at night to help you sleep.

* Use any small cloth bags you may already have in the house, or make your own. A clean handkerchief can be used to make an instant lavender bag. White ones with lace round the edges are perfect. Place a handful of lavender blossoms in the centre of the hanky and gather the edges together to form a little pouch. Close the bag and tie it with a ribbon. Make a good strong knot, then tie a tight bow.

  Alternatively, using a saucer or side plate as a guide (the larger the circle, the bigger the lavender bag), cut out circles from some cloth. Cotton, linen or muslin are good materials to use. Scraps or odd ends of cloth can be used up, or recycle old sheets, shirts or cotton dresses which are past their best. Wash and iron the cloth if it is recycled to make it crisp and clean before cutting.

  If you use pinking shears (scissors for cutting cloth with crimped blades) this will stop the edges of the cloth from fraying, and you will not need to hem them. Place the lavender at the centre of the circle, gather up the edges and secure with a ribbon as above.

HAIR AND HAIR CARE

One of the unassailable joys of being a girl is HAIR. Long, short, straight, curly, thick, wiry, fine, red, brown, blonde or black; hair is a universal source of fascination. And excitement.

Which Style?

For most of us hair is just there. Don't torture it. Love it and enjoy it. To begin with your hairstyle will in all probability be determined by your mother's wishes. Some mothers take an active interest in their daughter's hair, plaiting it or otherwise styling it for them and making sure it gets a proper brush at least twice a day. Others find it a chore, and favour a short or shortish hairstyle that is more practical than aesthetic. Once you're old enough to make your own hair decisions, pause to think about the following questions:

* **Do you like sport?** If so, very long hair or a style that requires lots of looking after is probably not such a good idea.

* **What sort of style suits your hair?** If you have very fine hair, for example, keeping it long may not necessarily be the best thing for it as it can make it look lank. Equally, if your hair is very curly, or has a tendency to stick up, it might benefit from extra length and weight to help keep it under control.

* **How much time do you want to spend on your hair?** If you like to get up early and are organized, then long hair is fine. Otherwise, having short hair gives you one less thing to worry about in the morning. On the whole, long hair is more high maintenance than short hair – but it's also more versatile.

BRUSHING

* Whatever your hair type, never leave the house without brushing it. Not only does brushed hair contribute to a good appearance, it also clears out old hairs and improves circulation to the scalp. Try not to tug or scrape your scalp. There's an old-fashioned rule that says you should do 100 strokes when you brush your hair. You can try this if you like, but personally we think it's a waste of time. Twenty to thirty strokes is fine – or whatever it takes to get it looking presentable.

WASHING

It is a myth that you need to wash your hair every day. (It is also, by the way, a myth that if you don't wash your hair at all it will eventually become self-washing. It won't. It will eventually become very smelly.)

* How often you need to wash your hair depends entirely on you and your hair type. If you are in and out of a swimming pool all the time, for example, you will obviously need to wash (and condition, see below) your hair a lot. The same goes for sporting types (sweaty hair is on the whole very unattractive). As a general rule, every other day is fine for normal hair. But if your hair is very thick and takes hours to dry then you might want to limit it to twice a week. If it's fine and flyaway, then wash it every day using a good volumizing shampoo to stop it looking limp and lifeless.

   Afro hair needs masses of moisture. So a shampoo that claims to be for 'curly hair' does not necessarily mean it will be right for yours.

CONDITIONING

* Again, this very much depends on your hair type. Dry, curly and very thick hair will benefit from frequent conditioning because it prevents it looking coarse and frizzy as well as making it easier to control. If you have oily hair, you don't need to condition every time you wash. The same is also true if your hair is fine and lacks volume – but you can still use a conditioner once a week.

TREATMENTS

There are squillions of things you can buy in the shops, but there are also plenty of equally effective (if somewhat messy) home alternatives.

* **Lemon juice is the most famous natural lightener, and it really works.** The only drawback is that if you use too much it can make your hair go like straw, so you need to condition as well. Lemon doesn't get on very well with chlorine, so avoid swimming pools for a few days when you've used any dye, otherwise you might end up with green hair!

* **Camomile is also wonderful for blonde hair.** Add a spoonful of honey to a cup of camomile tea, let it cool and then use it as a rinse.

* **One small cup of coffee can add depth and shine to brunette or darker-coloured hair.** Don't use instant if you can help it – use leftover cafetière coffee or espresso if you can get your hands on it. Let the coffee cool, pour it over your hair and leave it on for 10 minutes before thoroughly rinsing it off.

* To enhance russet tones, rinse your hair with a cup of cooled **rosehip tea.**

* **Henna is a good,** natural way to put red tones into your hair. It's easy to use and you just mix it to a paste and leave it on your hair for a couple of hours before washing it off. It has the added advantage of conditioning your hair and making it look more luxuriant.

DON'T ever be tempted to colour your hair using food dye. At the first hint of rain the colour will run all down your face. Not a good look.

GENERAL TIPS AND TREATMENTS

* **Coconut oil is a dreamy natural conditioner and smells of the tropics.** Warm a little in your hands and work it through the hair (you may need to do this two or three times, depending on how long your hair is), cover your head in one of those cheap disposable bath hats or cling film, then wrap your head in a towel. Leave it for an hour, and then shampoo thoroughly.

* **Eggs are also famously good for the hair.** Whisk two egg yolks into half a cup of water and massage it in. Leave it for 15 minutes and then shampoo well. If you leave the eggs in, they will act as very strong styling gel, which is excellent for spiky hair.

* **More shine.** If you can bear it, do your final rinse with COLD water. This closes the cuticles (the little shafts on the outer part of the hair), making the hair smooth and shiny. It's also very good for waking you up in the mornings.

NOTE: *Did you know that while you sleep your hair loses loads of moisture? Always braid or at the very least twist your hair into a few sections – make sure you do this all the way to the ends to avoid split ends – secure them with a hairpin or an elastic band and cover your head with a cotton scarf before going to bed.*

BIG HAIR

*   An easy way to get volume is this: pull your damp hair onto the top of your head and secure it with a covered elastic band, then blow dry the hair closest to your scalp. Let the hair down, turn your head upside down, and dry the rest. Va-va-voom. This is much better than back-combing, which also adds volume but damages the hair shaft in the process.

AFRO HAIR

Afro hair has very specific requirements. Natural hair (i.e. hair that hasn't been chemically treated) can be worn short, in plaits or in cornrows – the latter being especially useful if you are on holiday for a week or two since they stay in for a while and can be gently shampooed. Always use a wide-toothed comb because fine-toothed combs can pull the hair out. Also buy a brush: one with natural boar bristles is best.

*   Don't blow-dry your hair, always towel it dry since the heat can irritate some scalps. This will take some time so get your mum to help. If you must blow it dry, work in small sections on a low setting and preferably with a comb attachment. No matter which you decide, never allow your hair to air dry – this leads to breakage and dries it out.

After the hair is dry, divide it into small sections again and apply a light hair lotion or oil starting from the scalp outwards; use more on the ends which like to frizz. The softer your curls, the lighter the moisturizer you will need. Avoid products that are petroleum based. Plant oils (like olive or almond) and butters (such as shea) penetrate and nourish hair best.

BIZARRE HAIR FACTS

* The ancient Egyptians liked to dye their hair blue, or anoint it with gold dust.

* Women in ancient Greece lightened their hair with saffron.

* At the beginning of the eighteenth century, women liked to comb their hair into fantastic styles which could reach two feet tall.

* Crimping was invented in 1872.

FAMOUS HAIR

* **Cleopatra:** Did not in fact have straight black hair with a heavy fringe as portrayed on screen. She quite probably had red hair, which she wore in odd little bundles of curls, including one style known as the Melon. Do not try this at home.

* **Audrey Hepburn:** Audrey Hepburn made the short crop famous in the film *Roman Holiday*, when she had all her princessy long hair chopped off so she could ride around Rome on a scooter with gorgeous Gregory Peck.

* **Twiggy:** The face of 1966. Her famous urchin cut was created at Leonard's of Mayfair and took seven hours to achieve. It came to epitomize the new hopeful feeling of the swinging sixties.

* **Jennifer Aniston:** An actress who starred in the American television sitcom *Friends*, Jennifer Aniston pioneered the Rachel (named after her character in the series). All over the globe, young girls rushed to have it copied, with varying degrees of success. It was a long, chunkily layered bob and, with the addition of highlights, made its wearer look not unlike an Afghan hound.

Hair Styles

THE CLASSIC PLAIT

Very simple to do and never goes out of style. You can also do plaits in pigtails or, if your hair is very long, you can curl them round like sausages – but only if you're starring in *The Sound of Music* or playing *Star Wars* with your brothers.

* Brush your hair first. Divide the hair into three equal sections. Take two sections in your left hand, keeping them separate with a finger, and hold the third section in your right hand. Cross the section in your right hand over the middle section. Now cross the left section over the new middle section (which was originally the right-hand section). Take the right-hand section and cross it over the new middle section (which was the left-hand section) It's actually really easy to do. Practise on a small section of hair to begin with, or on a friend.

THE FRENCH PLAIT

* This is very chic, and is also a good way to keep your hair out of your eyes. You do it in exactly the same way as a normal plait, except that you start from the very top of your head, with three thin sections of hair. With each plaiting motion, you weave in a new piece of hair from the side of your head to join the plait, right to left. The trick is to add only a thin piece of hair with each new plaiting action, otherwise the thing becomes bulky. Also make sure the new sections are equal on each side, so you don't get an uneven effect. Your hair must be well conditioned for this, otherwise it may become tangled and difficult to manage. You may also find you need to keep smoothing out the different strands to keep them separate. Once you get to the hair away from your scalp, you just finish the plait as normal and secure the end with a covered elastic band.

You can embellish it all you want – a pretty ribbon, or some diamanté grips placed at the sides or down the centre of the plait. Some people like to smooth it down with a little hair wax warmed in the hand or jazz it up with some hair glitter.

A French plait takes a bit of practice, but once you have mastered it, you can do it with your eyes closed. It is very useful for a Bad Hair Day, when hair is greasy or plain wayward.

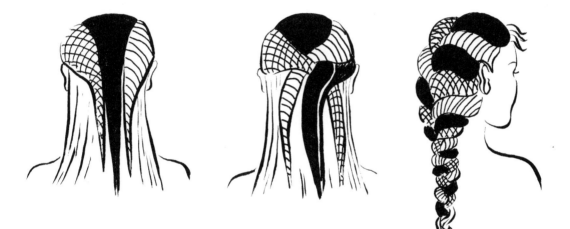

THE PONY TAIL

The low pony tail is quiet and elegant. Gather your hair at the nape of your neck and secure it any way you like. It looks especially good with a velvet ribbon (a good formal look to adopt for visiting aunts or evening trips to the theatre); in summer, tie it with a romantic chiffon scarf and waft around the garden looking mysterious.

The high pony tail is swishy and fun. Once you have put your hair up, tease out a few delicate strands around the side of the head to soften the look. If you have layered hair, you can pull up the shorter pieces of hair from the tail end of the covered elastic and anoint them with a minute amount of hair wax so you get a funky spiky effect. Do not overdo this.

THE PONY TAIL BUN

The word bun always sounds terrifying, but it is slightly better than the horrible 'up-do', so don't be put off.

* Put your hair into a high pony tail, and then pull the end through the covered elastic one more time so you get a bun effect with the ends of your hair hanging out. If your hair is very long, you will have a lovely loose flip curving out over the back. You can play around with this, adding a little wax or gel so it falls separately, or just in one section – see what suits you best.

  If you have shorter or layered hair, you will be left with some spiky ends. Using wax or gel, gently pull these out in different directions so you are left with a lovely little sunburst of hair high up at the back of your head.

CURLING

Almost everyone with straight hair goes through a stage of yearning for curls. There are many different ways to achieve this.

* When your hair is almost dry, divide it into sections of about a centimetre each, twist and twist until they curl up on themselves like a little snail, and secure them with a kirby grip. Leave them for a couple of hours. Some brave people sleep like this although it is uncomfortable. The end result is a mass of crazy curls. You will need to play around with them using your hands and some wax or gel, as the ends have a tendency to kink.

* For a truly curly look, make many tiny plaits all over your head, and leave them for a few hours before undoing them.

* For big loose curls, the soft Velcro roller is hard to beat. And, although having a head full of mad pink rollers is quite an alarming look, it gives lovely results. Wrap sections of combed, just damp hair round the rollers, making sure the ends of the hair are tucked in neatly, then blow dry. At this stage, you can add a fine mist of holding spray, but make sure you do so at arm's length. Remove the rollers gently, shake out the curls and tease them out with your fingers.

FRINGES

* There is no answer to the eternal fringe/no fringe debate. Mostly, they're like curls, in that people who have them wish they didn't, and those who haven't got them want them. It's up to you. You can experiment with how you might look with a fringe by finding a life-sized picture of someone with one in a magazine, cutting it out and placing it over your forehead. Or you can get a friend to pin your hair up in an approximation of one. But really you can't know what you're going to look like with a fringe until you get one.

NEVER EVER . . .

* **Use elastic bands on your hair.** They will cause it to break and split and it will HURT. Always use the special covered ones.

* **Don't twist your hair round your finger,** even if you are sitting in double maths and it's quadratic equation day. It will damage the hair shaft and contribute to split ends which cannot be repaired – the only solution to split ends is to cut them off!

* **Don't blow dry your hair on a really high heat very close to your head.** No prizes for guessing what will happen. Yes, that's right, FRIZZ.

* **Don't scrape your hair back into a really tight ponytail.** Apart from looking nasty, it will drag on the hair roots weakening your hair and making it more likely to fall out.

* **Don't have your parting in the same place all the time;** it weakens the hair along the parting.

* **Don't wash your hair with soap;** it will make your scalp sore and dry and you will get dandruff or, worse, psoriasis (a form of eczema) on your scalp, which will in turn damage your hair.

THE GREAT OUTDOORS

If you're lucky enough to have some wild open spaces at your disposal you will never be bored. Tired, muddy and hungry, yes. Bruised and battered, perhaps. But bored – never.

Falling

Learn to walk before you run; learn to fall before you climb. Knowing how to fall properly is an art. Done well it is exciting, it looks great, can be very funny – and besides, crutches are such a bore.

* Start by perfecting the stage faint, itself an invaluable accomplishment and a useful exit strategy for all manner of uncomfortable situations (non-completion of maths homework, getting out of PE, wanting the morning off school). Practise it on a lawn or in a room with a thick carpet.

Bend your ankles, bend your knees and let yourself go floppy, collapsing vertically at first, until you start to topple. The trick is to be very loose, very relaxed, and not to stick out a hand or try to catch yourself; you are supposed to be unconscious. The aim is to hit the ground from the ground up, so that the bits nearest the floor land first, softening the impact. A crumple is really what you're looking for – first your calf, then your thigh, then your waist, then your shoulder. For added drama, and to dissipate the impact, you may wish to add a half roll. Land with your eyes shut (or if you're feeling really confident, rolled back in your head). Resist the temptation to open one eye to check the reaction.

Once you've mastered this technique, you can use it to tumble off everyday objects, such as garden walls and top bunks. Higher challenges require a higher degree of skill: land feet first, everything bent, and topple sideways very quickly, catching the secondary impact on your shoulder. Now the roll is the most important thing; you do not want to absorb all the shock through your shoulder. Roll over once, twice, three times if you feel like it. Remember: you are not trying to avoid the ground; you are trying to befriend it at speed.

TIP: *When falling out of trees you should beware roots, knobbles and the trunk. Push yourself away from the trunk if you are close to it.*

Climbing

Climbing is not only a useful skill to master, but it also comes in handy whenever there are boys to be impressed (or taken down a peg or two).

There is always an element of risk in climbing – be it trees or walls. At first it is wise not to climb higher than you are prepared to fall. Even a few feet up, adrenaline will make your eyes sharp and your muscles quiver; you will feel a little scared, but thrilled. Breathe deeply, relax and do not let yourself panic. It is all about keeping cool under pressure. If you find you enjoy it, join a climbing club. In the meantime, here are some tips to get you started.

The secret of climbing is to be really close to whatever you are ascending, close and vertical, not bowed outwards or bunched. This gives gravity much less chance of pulling you off, and saves strength and energy.

Here are some basic pointers . . .

* **Professional climbers have a rule:** maintain three points of contact at any one time. E.g. two feet and one hand, or two hands and one foot. Shift only one grip at a time.

* **Stay calm.** A good climber never panics. Take your time.

* **Grip.** Hold on firmly, but do not cling.

* **Do not worry about how high up you are:** you are perfectly safe, otherwise you would be falling – no?

* **Plan your next move before you execute it.**

* **Enjoy your situation.** Here you are, in the world of birds and squirrels. Be happy.

* **Climb in the moment.** By all means plan ahead, but concentrate on the present. Do not worry about getting stuck higher up, or how you are going to get down.

TREES

When climbing trees, stay close to the trunk. Branches are strongest at their root. Even a small one, no bigger than a twig, can provide a decent foothold if you can jam your toes into the point where it joins the trunk. Look carefully. A thin young branch may be much stronger than a thicker, older or dead one.

* When you are ready to descend, do so slowly, concentrating only on the couple of feet below you. Think laterally. Look around you. Your best route may be sideways. Occasionally you might have to go up and round to go down. If you fall, grab as much as you can of the tree on your way down, slowing yourself as much as possible.

Throwing

It's a myth that girls can't throw. It's just that boys are generally better at it because they have been practising since they were first able to pick things up.

* Turn side-on to your target. If you want to throw far, aim up 45 degrees from the ground, draw your arm back and breathe in. When you let fly, do it with real venom. Put some anger into it and exhale violently. The perfect throw does not come from your arm, but from your back foot. If throwing right handed, bend your right leg slightly. Now, release everything like a whip: the energy travels all the way up your leg, through your back, through your shoulder, arm and wrist. Follow through: your whole body is a sling, and a sling does not stop when it releases. There. You have just thrown further than ever before, and people are looking at you with new respect. Practise.

When you get good you will find your whole arm ripples as if a wave has shot down it and your wrist makes a snapping motion. Things will really start to fly. At this point people will start being nice to you in case you decide to throw something at them.

Shooting

Shooting is not necessarily about killing things. It is a sport like any other, difficult to do well, intensely satisfying when you hit, and fun to practise. Although boys are very macho about it they have no natural superiority. It requires delicacy, a light touch and control; some of the best shots in the world are women.

There are some ground rules:

* Never, ever point a gun at anyone, loaded or not.

* Treat all guns as if they are loaded.

* Never walk with a loaded gun.

* Imagine an infinite red line stretching out either side of the muzzle, at ninety degrees.

* Handle the gun so that no one is ever in front of that red line.

* A gun can be lethal.

Building a Campfire

When you are outside in summer or winter a fun thing to do is to build a campfire to sit around with your friends while you chat, cook or play word games.

* Find a suitable clearing, either in a wood (if it is raining) or in the fields (if it is a fine day). Decide on your spot for the fire, clear away a metre square space on a piece of ground, and if there are stones around put them around in a small circle.

Collect dry leaves, hay or newspaper into a small bird's-nest-like shape and cover with dry twigs. Light the inside of the nest first and blow the flame gently from one side, until the fire catches. The key here is to have patience. Bit by bit cover your bird's-nest with more substantial wood or twigs that you collected

earlier. Don't smother the flames, let the air get through, and keep blowing from the side to help things along, if necessary. After about an hour you should have a robust fire, ready for anything.

NOTE: *You should douse your fire with water before you leave, and remember to take all your rubbish home with you.*

A Few Good Things to Cook on the Fire

MARSHMALLOWS

Find a long twig and dig one end into the soft marshmallow. You should never put any food into a flame, rather you should look for the best glowing embers in the fire and hold the marshmallow stick about 20 centimetres from the fire. Gently turn the marshmallow as it begins to go brown. When lightly brown and toasted, it's ready. Wait to cool a bit and nibble the toasted marshmallow from the outside inwards. It is sometimes possible to get two rounds of toasting from a marshmallow; once you've nibbled off the outside toasted bits you can put the fresh mallow back in the fire. Keep turning the stick so the mallow doesn't fall off.

HOT POTATOES AND BAKED BANANAS WITH CHOCOLATE

Both of these you can cook in the fire, in tin foil. Baked potatoes will only cook properly if you have had a really good fire which has been burning for at least 4 hours. Prick the potatoes, wrap them well in tin foil and poke them (using a stick) right inside the ashy embers at the bottom of the fire.

* Check them a couple of times but, as a rule, if it's the end of a good fire, they should be cooked within an hour.

Bananas will cook quickly and can be done in smaller fires that haven't been burning for so long. Peel the banana but keep its skin, make about five cuts vertically across the banana and put a square of chocolate into each of the incisions. Re-cover the banana with the banana skin and wrap the whole thing in tin foil. Place in the warm ash of the fire for 10–15 minutes. Wait for the package to cool (be careful as bananas and chocolate are full of sugar, which gets VERY hot when heated up), unwrap and eat with your fingers, straight from the foil.

A CAN OF BAKED BEANS

* If you are eating potatoes, you could accompany them with a nice can of beans. Find yourself a sturdy stick (no thinner than the width of your thumb, with no traces of rot). Now here's the tricky bit – it needs to have two prongs at one end, so that it looks like a 'Y' – a good rummage in the woods should produce quite a few. The fork on your stick has to be long enough for you to fit your tin of food in the 'Y', so that it feels like it's nestling tightly inside. Wait until your campfire has burnt down a little so you've got some really hot coals, dampen your stick so it doesn't catch fire, take the lid off the tin and use the stick to hold it over the coals, being careful not to burn yourself. Stir from time to time until it's really hot and pour over hot potatoes or eat straight from the tin.

Stargazing

Doing this on a clear night is an awesome activity, full of power and mystery. All you need is a very basic grasp of astronomy.

* The first thing you should do is find the Pole Star. There are two easy-to-spot constellations of stars that will help you find it immediately.

If you were at the North Pole the Pole Star would be directly above your head, so the first thing to do is to find out which way is north. You can do this with a compass, or from watching where the sun has set that night – it always sets in the west. So, from the west you can find all the other bearings: north, east, south, west – an easy mnemonic (memory aid) is 'never eat shredded wheat'.

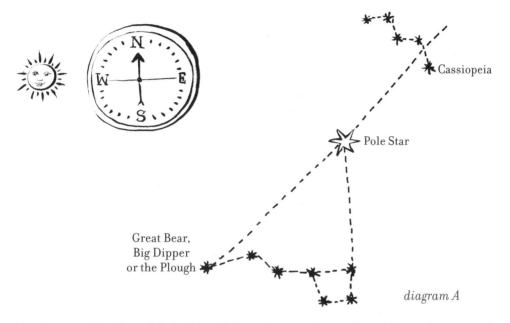

diagram A

Once you've found it look well into the northern sky and see if you can find a bright cluster of stars in the same pattern as in diagram A – well done, this constellation is called the Great Bear (also known as the Big Dipper or the Plough) and once you have spotted it, everything is simple from here on. It looks like a saucepan with a handle, and the two bright stars at either end are called 'pointers' because they point you directly to the Pole Star. If you cannot see these pointers you may be able to find the Pole Star from the other group of stars, known as Cassiopeia, which is shaped like the letter W. This group revolves around the Pole Star and is sometimes upside down. When the Pole Star is on its meridian, absolutely true north, a line can be drawn through one arm of the W across the Pole Star to a point between the two stars in the tail or handle of the Great Bear, as shown in diagram A.

Once you've found these very simple bearings you can go on to learn the whereabouts of other things in the sky such as Venus, Mercury, Jupiter, Saturn, the Milky Way and Sirius. There are an infinite number of heavenly bodies, and an infinite number of things to be learned from and about the stars.

Helen of Troy

The tale of Helen of Troy is one of history's greatest love stories — but to call it history's greatest love triangle would be more accurate. It is described by the Greek poet Homer in his epic poem The Iliad and is intertwined with the ten-year war fought between the Greeks and the Trojans of which Helen was, we are to believe, the cause.

The story is a bit confusing, and there are conflicting accounts. But, in a nutshell, here it is: Helen was the most beautiful woman in the world and almost every great hero wanted to marry her. Her father Tyndareus, king of Sparta, decided the fairest thing to do would be to have a competition and the winner could claim his beautiful daughter's hand in marriage. In the event, Menelaus, brother of King Agamemnon, triumphed, and he and Helen were duly married (history does not relate Helen's views on this arrangement, but she does not appear to have minded too much). In order to ward off trouble, Tyndareus made all the heroes promise to protect the union between Helen and Menelaus, so when Paris, son of King Priam of Troy and brother of the brave and noble Hector (universally known as Troy's greatest warrior), got it into his head that Helen should be his, all hell broke loose.

As ever in Greek legend, the gods are to blame for most of the carnage. Paris had been told by Zeus to judge who was the fairest of three goddesses, Aphrodite, Hera and Athena. Each one offered him a gift as a bribe and Aphrodite's gift was to be able to marry the most beautiful woman in the world — and only Helen met that description. Paris was keen on women so he chose Aphrodite. Off he went to claim his prize and persuaded Helen to go back to Troy with him. When Menelaus, who had been off somewhere doing important hero work, got home to discover her gone, he immediately summoned all the other Greek warriors and, led by his brother Agamemnon, they sailed to Troy and laid siege to the city, resulting in thousands of dead and much suffering on both sides.

As for Helen herself, no one is really sure who she wanted to be married to, since no one seems to have bothered to ask her opinion. In the end Troy was defeated; some say she went back to live with Menelaus, others that she perished with Paris. Still, her story does prove one thing: being the most beautiful woman in the world isn't all it's cracked up to be.

Romeo and Juliet

* Set in medieval Verona, the story of two 'star-cross'd lovers' is the subject of William Shakespeare's most famous tragedy. It is a tale of young lives cut short by hatred and prejudice. Juliet is the thirteen-year-old daughter of the noble Capulet family, Romeo the son of their sworn rivals, the Montagues. Why the two families hate each other is unclear — they just do, and have been feuding for generations.

Romeo and Juliet meet at a ball thrown by Juliet's parents, the aim of which is to get her to meet Count Paris, who hopes to marry her (in medieval Italy you were thought quite grown-up at thirteen). It being a masked ball, Romeo is free to move around in his enemy's house without being discovered. The pair instantly fall in love, initially without either realizing who the other is. Soon, however, Romeo declares his true identity, and there ensues one of the most famous theatrical set pieces: the balcony scene. Juliet stands at her bedroom window, with Romeo below. 'Romeo, Romeo, wherefore art thou Romeo?' she proclaims, meaning not 'Where are you, Romeo?' but 'Why are you Romeo?' — in other words, lamenting the fact that he is the son of her father's enemy. There and then they resolve to marry in secret, and with the help of Juliet's nurse a priest is found, and he performs the marriage ceremony.

Sadly, it doesn't end there. Juliet's fiery cousin Tybalt picks a fight with Romeo, who refuses to defend himself, since his secret marriage to Juliet now makes him a member of Tybalt's family. Instead, Romeo's friend Mercutio takes up his sword on Romeo's behalf and is killed. Furious, Romeo pursues Tybalt, kills him and is exiled from Verona for his crime.

Juliet's father brings up with her the prospect of marriage to his friend Paris — but she refuses, saying she loves Romeo. In desperation, she turns to the priest who married them and he suggests a magic potion that, when drunk, will make Juliet seem dead. The priest will then send a message to Romeo telling him she is not really dead, and instructing him to meet her at her family's crypt so they can escape together.

BUT . . . Romeo never gets the message. Distraught on hearing his beloved is dead, he procures some (real) poison of his own and rushes to the crypt to see Juliet one last time before drinking the lethal draught and dying. Soon after, Juliet awakes. Finding her poor Romeo dead beside her, she stabs herself and dies.

HEAVENLY SCENTS

There is something magical and comforting about natural aromatics such as rose, orange blossom and lavender water, and essential oils with exotic names like musk, ylang ylang, frankincense and myrrh. They conjure up images of the Orient, the spice route, Arabia, Persia, Java and Ceylon, and eastern bazaars with stalls piled high with fragrant powders in shades of golden caramel to deep red.

Spices, herbs and aromatics are used not only in cooking, but also for their medicinal and even sensual qualities. Aromatic oils are believed to help calm the nerves, help digestion and sleeping problems, be good for the heart and soul and the skin, and even help to kill bacteria.

The benefits can be practical or emotional: rose water gives a rosy outlook; dill, aniseed and parsley help digestion; garlic is both an antiseptic and good for the blood; lavender is soothing and promotes deep sleep; rosemary is uplifting and antibacterial; mandarin energizes. And ginger is said to make people more loving – why not slip some into your arch-enemy's lunchbox when she is not looking?

Rose-Petal Perfume

As very young children, Rosemary and her sisters were lucky enough to live in the house that their grandparents had built in the north of Ireland.

The gardens had been planted with roses: climbers, standards, tea roses and, most importantly, very old varieties whose fragrance in high summer was quite intoxicating. When her parents took over the house the garden went to seed, but the roses grew wild and unruly over walls and across unweeded beds.

The rose-petal perfume we made was kept in glass jars and smelt lovely for a day or two, but weeks later we'd find the jars lurking forgotten in a corner with the perfume looking slightly brown and no longer smelling so sweet.

So, before we get complicated with more sophisticated methods involving alcohol to preserve your rose water, here is the basic method.

* rose petals
* water

* Half-fill a jar with rose petals and add enough water to come three quarters of the way up the jar. Leave the petals to soak for one or two days in a warm sunny place and then strain the liquid into a clean jar through a fine sieve or clean J-cloth. Squash the petals a little to get all the rose-ness out of them.

Use the perfume liberally all over your face, hands and body, or pour some into the bath. Alternatively, pour it into a nice bottle and give it to your mother or grandmother as a pretty, surprise gift.

Scented Waters

Scented waters can be made from flower petals, herbs, leaves and seeds, or you can even experiment with tree bark and roots, bruised nuts and flower buds. They are made by soaking the petals, or whatever you are using, in distilled water (boiled water left to cool) for at least a couple of weeks in a sunny place and adding clear, scentless alcohol as a preservative — vodka is good for this. The water is then strained off the petals and can be stored in the fridge for up to two weeks. Floral waters are delicately fragranced, while essential flower oils are stronger-smelling. We've given you the recipes for lavender and rose water and you can adapt these for other ingredients.

You can add the scented waters to the bath and some can be used as refreshing and cleansing toners for the face and body. Lavender and witch hazel are astringent, in other words good for cleaning slightly oily skin and preventing spots. Rose water is good for all skin types, but is particularly good for soothing dry and sensitive skin on the face.

The vodka in the following recipes will kill any bacteria and helps to preserve the scent, otherwise your scented water will go smelly very quickly.

Roses

ROSE WATER

* 2 cups distilled water
* ¼ cup vodka
* 1 large clear bottle

* 2 cups strong-smelling rose petals (organically grown if to be used for drinking or cooking)

* Use the same method as for the lavender water. You can make a stronger-scented rose water by adding one or two drops of essential rose oil.

Lavender

Lavender in particular is known for its soothing and calming qualities. Lavender oil and lavender bags are wonderful for helping you relax and unwind at night — add a few drops of lavender essential oil to a running bath, or place a lavender bag by your pillow before going to bed. Lavender water can also be sprayed directly onto your pillow to help you get a good long night's sleep.

Lavender is also a good antiseptic and is now an ingredient in many commercial kitchen cleaners and washing products.

LAVENDER WATER

* 2 cups distilled water
* 1½ cups lavender blossoms
* ¼ cup vodka
* 1 large clear bottle

* Put the lavender flowers into your clean and well-rinsed container. Add distilled water then the vodka. Stopper the bottle and shake well. Put the bottle in the sun — a windowsill which catches direct sunlight is perfect. After two weeks the water will be ready. Strain the liquid through a coffee filter or clean muslin cloth into another very clean and rinsed glass bottle and store in the fridge.

ORANGE-FLOWER WATER

* Orange-flower water is made when the essential oil neroli is extracted from orange blossom. If you want to use orange-flower water on your face or body you can find it in aromatherapy shops. It is used a lot in Middle Eastern cookery to flavour desserts and puddings and, along with rose water, can be bought in most Middle Eastern and Turkish groceries. We wouldn't recommend using this cooking orange-flower water on your skin, as it probably has lots of sugar and chemicals in it, but it's hard to tell as on our bottle the ingredients are all in Arabic!

In France orange-flower water is mixed with hot water and honey as a bedtime drink. Poor ill-fated Marie Antoinette apparently swore by it for maintaining the purity of her delicate alabaster complexion.

You can make your own water by mixing a few drops of neroli oil with a teaspoon of clear odourless alcohol and then adding a cup of distilled or spring water.

Orange-flower water is a good pick-me-up for oily and dull skin and is used as a base for face creams and masks; it will brighten a peaky or dull complexion. Use it to scent the body and hair.

FLOWER REFRESHER

* Mix equal amounts of rose water, orange-flower water and lavender water and pour into a bottle with a spray top. Use as a toner after cleansing and to refresh the skin throughout the day.

HUNGARIAN WATER

This wonderful astringent lotion is said to be the first herbal product made and marketed. According to legend, it was originally made by gypsies, who used it as a hair rinse, headache remedy, mouthwash, foot bath and aftershave and claimed it to be a cure-all. Whether or not this is true, Hungarian Water is a very refreshing tonic for the face and is also wonderful as a hair rinse, especially for dark hair.

This recipe comes from Rosemary Gladstar's *Herbs for Natural Beauty*.

* 6 parts lemon balm
* 4 parts camomile
* 1 part rosemary
* 3 parts calendula
* 4 parts roses
* 1 part lemon peel
* 1 part sage
* 3 parts comfrey leaf
* vinegar to cover (cider vinegar or white wine vinegar)
* rose water or witch-hazel extract
* essential oil of lavender or rose

* Place all the herbs in a clean wide-mouthed jar. Add enough vinegar to cover the herbs generously. Cover tightly and put in a warm place for two or three weeks.

Strain the mixture through a clean muslin cloth or coffee filter. To each cup of Hungarian Water add between half to one cup of rose water or witch hazel and a drop or two of essential oil if desired. Put into a clean bottle. It does not need to be kept in the fridge and will keep indefinitely.

Hungarian Water makes an unusual and lovely gift. Look out for pretty old scent bottles at flea markets to fill for gifts, or reuse empty perfume or glass bubble bath bottles. Make sure you wash and rinse them really well before filling with your home-made water.

Storing Floral Waters and Infusions

Glass bottles with spray tops or atomizers can be bought from shops selling natural beauty products – Neal's Yard and the Body Shop both sell them. Or, better still, keep and reuse glass perfume bottles when they are empty.

* Wash the empty bottles well in very hot water with a few drops of detergent.

  Rinse thoroughly in clean warm water to which you've added a dash of white wine vinegar or lemon juice (this helps get them squeaky clean and sterilizes them).

  Then simply fill with your own floral water. Try using different combinations of scents. For example, you could combine rose water, lavender water and orange-flower water. Keep small amounts in the bottles but keep your main store in the fridge. They'll keep for a couple of weeks.

Basic Infusion Methods

You may want to use the herbs or flowers as a tea. Here are two ways of making an infusion.

HOT INFUSION

* This is really just like making a cup of tea: put a teaspoon of the herb/leaf/flower in a cup, pour on boiling water and infuse for about 5 minutes, strain and drink. To make a larger quantity the rule is the same as for tea making – one teaspoon per portion or cup, plus one teaspoon extra for the pot. Then leave it to brew for about 10 minutes. The strength of the infusion can be varied to taste.

COLD INFUSION

* Put one teaspoon or more of the herb or flower petals in cold water or milk and leave it to steep for several hours. Then either drink it as a tea or use it as a lotion or poultice for the skin. These infusions will keep fresh stored in the fridge for a couple of days.

Which Scent Suits Your Personality and Style?

There is a lot to be said for having your own signature scent. Every girl should think about acquiring one. Even if you don't fancy wearing perfume, the smell of your soap or regular shampoo will be YOUR signature scent. Wear it with pride.

The smell of someone's scent becomes associated with that person – it lingers on a scarf or a much worn jumper even when washed, on winter coats, even handbags. A bedroom takes on the scent of the user, and certain smells become associated with different people, houses, times and places.

Rosemary's mother's scent was called Blue Grass. She can still remember how the little glass bottle on her dressing table delighted her, how forbidden and mysterious it was.

Her Granny's scents, however, were Germolene and TCP . . . Her dad's was a subtle mix of farmyard manure and Old Spice. It takes all sorts.

Marilyn Monroe, when asked what she wore to bed, famously answered, 'Chanel No. 5.'

There *is* something very grown-up and significant about choosing which is your favourite scent. So here are some things to consider when thinking about what fragrance and perfume might suit you. And don't worry if you get sick of your signature perfume and decide it's not the one for you. Fob it off on a sister or cousin, or wait until you run out and then, in good time for your next birthday or Christmas, give some subtle hints to family members.

Different moods will clearly suggest different scents, and once you start developing a 'nose' you can experiment by mixing different scents together to match how you might feel that day.

Daytime scents tend to be lighter and more subtle than night-time scents, which are usually heavier and muskier. By combining two together or adding a dab of essential oil, experiment with changing the mood of your scent.

How to Apply Scent

There's nothing worse than overdoing your perfume. Too much, and you will give yourself and those around you a terrible headache or even make them feel sick. It's probably best to save your scent for special occasions — wasting precious perfume by wearing it to double maths on a Monday morning seems a little unnecessary.

A totally charming and very clever saleswoman in a Paris department store gave Rosemary a lesson on how to wear scent a few years back. She hardly ever remembers to follow her instructions, but it's good to know how it should be done: spray your perfume in front of you with one short but generous spray and walk into the fragrance. In this way, the Parisian lady informed her, the scent subtly envelops you and your clothes in an even and not overpowering way.

* If you have a bottle of perfume with a stopper and no atomizer, all you need is one small dab with a finger on your main pulse points — traditionally on each side of the neck just under the jawline by the ears, and on your wrists.

  If you want a more striking effect and it's a special occasion, you can use your scent a little less subtly by dabbing some on the back of the neck and the back of your knees.

Antony and Cleopatra

Cleopatra was just eighteen when she became queen of Egypt, ruling jointly with her younger brother Ptolemy, to whom she was also married (things were different in those days in Egypt!). She wasn't especially beautiful — she had a hook nose — but she was by all accounts an excellent musician, charming and spoke nine languages.

Before Cleopatra met Antony, she was the girlfriend of the greatest Roman of all, Julius Caesar, by whom she had a son. After Caesar's assassination in 44 bc, the Roman Empire was divided between three rulers, of whom Antony was one. Cleopatra wowed him with her wealth, arriving for their first meeting on a golden barge dressed as Venus, the Roman goddess of love. She laughed at his jokes and flattered his ego, and before long they had three children, including twins.

But the course of true love was not destined to run smoothly. For a start, Antony already had a wife in Rome. Secondly, and more importantly for a Roman, he was so smitten by Cleopatra that he neglected his duties as a soldier and a statesman. People said he was under her spell and had become weak and pleasure-seeking.

In 31 bc Antony fought a huge naval battle against the Roman fleet off the coast of Greece and the rumours about his declining powers were soon proved true: the Romans made mincemeat of his troops. As soon as Cleopatra saw he was losing she fled, and Antony, seeing her leave, abandoned the battle and followed her, thus confirming the gossip that he was nothing more than her slave.

Back in Alexandria, Antony and Cleopatra awaited their inevitable doom. When the Roman army arrived at the gates of the city, Antony's men deserted him and joined the invaders. Furious, Antony accused Cleopatra of betrayal. She took refuge in her mausoleum and sent word that she was dead. Upon hearing this, Antony became distraught and committed suicide by plunging his sword into his stomach. Legend has it that he was taken to Cleopatra and died shortly afterwards in her arms.

Cleopatra was captured and faced a humiliating fate. However, she was still queen of Egypt and ordered a feast, including a basket of figs. What her Roman guards failed to realize was that hidden among the figs was a deadly asp. She was found dead, poisoned by the serpent's bite.

PETS AND PONIES

There are those who argue that owning a pet is nothing but trouble and mess. They are, of course, right. Pets do make a mess, they do chew your favourite shoes, they do require walking and cleaning and, yes, you do have to deal with their poo. BUT. There is much satisfaction to be had from looking after another creature – especially if it happens to be a bouncy puppy or a cuddly guinea pig.

Cats

The first cats are thought to have lived 8,000 years ago in Cyprus. The Romans introduced them to Britain. They had a horrible time in the Middle Ages, when they were associated with witches and the devil and were often tortured and burned. Nowadays, they are very popular as pets, although there is some rivalry between cat people and dog people.

Cats are independent, elegant and inscrutable. They do not have the pack mentality of dogs, and tend to meet all their own basic needs. They are brilliant hunters, using the same tactics as leopards and tigers, and can catch and kill birds, mice and even scorpions and grasshoppers. They then like to present these trophies to their owners – which can be a bit of a shock. They are carnivores and can be fussy eaters.

They love to play with string, or a ball, especially if it has a bell in it. Although discerning, they can be incredibly affectionate. Unlike dogs, they do not need taking for a walk, which means they are ideal pets for the city.

Cats come in many different types. Most common are the tabby, which is striped, often with white nose and paws; the tortoiseshell, which has patches of many different colours on its fur; the ginger cat and the lucky black cat. Sometimes mixed breeds like this are called moggies. Famous pedigree cats include the Burmese, which has silky fur, wonderful amber eyes, and comes in every colour from deep chocolate brown to lilac; the Siamese, an aristocratic cat with what are called blue points (tail, paws and face); and of course the Persian cat, with its luxuriant long hair.

* **Favourite fact:** The term for a group of cats is a clowder.

* **Best story:** *The Cat that Walked Alone* by Rudyard Kipling.

Dogs

Ah, dogs. If you want to know the meaning of unconditional love, get a dog. They are beautiful, clever, furry and will lick the tears off your cheeks during weepy movies.

* Dogs are descended from wolves, and were domesticated about 15,000 years ago, probably in China. They are pack animals, and are believed to regard their human owners as members of the pack (they must presumably think of us as quite strange dogs, who have no body hair, wear clothes and sometimes spectacles and walk on two legs). They are known as man's best friend on account of their loyalty and devotion. Because of their intelligence, they are trained as guide dogs, for search and rescue and as sniffer dogs. They can herd sheep, pull sleds across the Arctic and track scents.

They will eat pretty much anything, but it is best to feed them on a good quality dry food, as this keeps them healthy and stops their breath smelling (important if they like to kiss you a lot). Chocolate, raisins, onions and macadamia nuts are poisonous to dogs. They need plenty of exercise, a lot of affection, play, weekly grooming and fresh water at all times. There is currently some scientific speculation that dogs can laugh.

Everyone has their favourite breed, but for gentleness and friendliness the Labrador, beagle and West Highland terrier (those sweet white fluffy ones known as Westies) are hard to beat. A poodle can be charming, and a well-fed whippet is kind and elegant. There is a theory that cross-breeds are less neurotic than their pedigree cousins. The Lab – collie cross is one of the nicest: sleek, black and shiny, it has all the cleverness of the collie combined with the good nature of the Lab; they are excellent retrievers, easy to train (you can teach them to shake hands in return for a biscuit) and brilliant jumpers.

Dogs to avoid (although of course there are always lovely exceptions):

* **Rottweilers, pit bull terriers and German shepherds** – too aggressive.

* **Pugs and Pekes** – all that snoring and snuffling.

* **Chihuahuas and any other dog that has very little hair and can fit in a handbag** – just unnatural.

* **Yorkshire terriers** – too hairy and yappy.

Favourite facts:

* A cross between a cocker spaniel and a poodle is called a cockapoo (we are not making this up).

* During the second world war, a collie called Rob was parachuted behind enemy lines with an SAS unit; he had been trained to watch over the exhausted men as they slept between undercover operations.

SERIOUS DOG POINTS

* Never put your face right up to a dog's face, or maintain direct eye contact for too long. Even gentle dogs can take this as a sign of aggression.

* Never pull tails, hair, paws, etc.

* If a dog should act aggressively towards you, put your hands in your pockets, stay still and turn a little to the side, looking away. Do not run, wave your arms or shout.

* NEVER hit a dog, or shout at it. To tell a dog NO, just make two short firm sounds – 'Uh-uh'. This mimics the sounds that canine pack leaders make in the wild when they want to put a more lowly dog in its place.

* Do not overfeed your dog. This is not kindness, it is cruelty. Dogs are greedy and do not know when to stop, so it is up to you to keep their diet balanced.

Goldfish

* Despite their popularity as fairground prizes, we cannot really recommend goldfish. They don't do much, apart from open and shut their mouth. The best thing that can be said about a goldfish is that it is very easy to replace with another identical-looking one in the event of its untimely demise.

Guinea Pigs

* Guinea pigs are sweet little stocky creatures and spend most of their time eating. They come from South America, can live for up to eight years and, adorably, mate for life. They are happiest kept in pairs in a nice hutch with wood shavings on the floor, and like to eat grass, hay and some raw vegetables. They famously squeak a lot, and can become very attached to their human, pining when separated.

Favourite fact: When guinea pigs become excited, they do little jumps in the air, known as pop-corning.

Hamsters

* The hamster is smaller and quieter than the guinea pig, and likes mostly to sleep. The Syrian hamster is most commonly kept as a pet. Although incredibly soft and cute, the Syrian will fight to the death with others of its kind, so the golden rule is: one hamster, one cage. The dwarf hamster, on the other hand, is most content as a pair.

They all need a roomy cage, with some tissue or newspaper they can shred to make nests (they love making nests almost more than sleeping). They also enjoy a sand bath and a wheel to run around in. They eat fruit, vegetables and even some insects.

Parrots

*   Parrots come in many types – macaws, cockatoos, parakeets, Amazons and African greys. They are famous for imitating human speech and letting out extraordinarily loud shrieks, often lasting five minutes at a time. They live for a very long time, enjoy chewing furniture, clothes and jewellery, and tend to fling their food around when they eat. Possibly not the best pet for a quiet life.

    Best story: A British newspaper reported the story of a female macaw called Charlie, which was said to have been born in 1899 and died, aged 105, in 2004. During the Second World War she apparently belonged to Winston Churchill, and specialized in making rude remarks about Adolf Hitler and the Nazis.

Stick Insects

*   The stick insect is a surprisingly popular pet. You need a tall mesh cage so they have air, room to grow and something to climb up (they love climbing). Most types eat blackberry and eucalyptus leaves, although the Peruvian stick insect eats only ferns (and presumably speaks Spanish). All stick insects are mistresses of camouflage.

Horses and Ponies

These are not strictly pets (pets, we believe, being small enough to pick up or at least have on the sofa with you), but are the most fun to keep or dream about keeping.

It is not known when the horse was domesticated, but horses have been used over the ages for chariot racing, war, farm work, going down mines to haul coal, ranching, herding, ploughing fields, police work, dressage, three-day-eventing, showjumping, polo, hunting and racing, and just for pure pleasure.

Ponies are under 14.2 hands (four inches to a hand). They are used for showing, general riding, jumping, hunting, pulling small carriages and, of course, gymkhanas. Oddly, although they are smaller, cuter and usually furrier than horses, ponies are often considered more difficult to handle. They can be fiendishly cunning and stubborn. Many ponies find taking a quick nip out of you when you are not looking a splendid joke. But once they have accepted you as an equal, they are devoted and loyal and will carry you faithfully through all weathers.

Parents often dread the moment their child becomes obsessed with ponies since the whole thing requires vast amounts of expensive kit, a great deal of time and very hard work. Ponies must be mucked out every day, groomed, fed, exercised and occasionally taken to the vet. Once you get into showing, dressage or eventing, the work becomes even harder, since there must be daily schooling and training, very early starts to reach distant showgrounds, and the care and maintenance of all kinds of kit. So if you are very lucky and your parents do consent to a pony, be extremely grateful at all times and don't be rude to your mother when she wakes you at 5.30 a.m. on show day.

Competing

Competing teaches valuable life lessons: how to meet disappointment with fortitude, and how to accept victory with grace and modesty. The most common forms of competition are:

SHOWING

* Shows include classes for riding ponies, where you perform displays of walking, trotting and cantering for the judges. Sometimes you also need to strip down your pony (less shocking than it sounds, usually just taking off the saddle) and lead it out in a walk and trot, so the judges can see how it moves without a rider and check its action. There are also classes for working hunter ponies, where, as well as doing everything described above, you jump a short course of rustic fences. Working hunters tend to be less delicate and tougher than pure show ponies, who are judged primarily on their elegant looks.

SHOWJUMPING

* Looks do not matter here; indeed some showjumping ponies are quite peculiar in appearance. Speed, accuracy and performance are all, as ponies must complete a course of jumps in the first round, and those who go clear then compete against the clock. This can be very exciting and quite scary.

EVENTING

* This is a competition where you ride over a cross-country course of tough fences. Unlike showjumping, where the fences are made of poles and can be knocked down, cross-country jumps are fixed and solid, and often include brush, logs or water. Negotiating these obstacles requires agility, courage and cleverness in both pony and rider. Often a simple dressage test must be completed first, and a short course of show jumps afterwards, so a very versatile pony is needed.

DRESSAGE

* This is where a pony and rider complete a series of prescribed moves, known as the dressage test. It is slow, painstaking and requires hours of patience and practice, but can be incredibly rewarding when you get it right. The feeling of horse and rider moving as one is exhilarating. Dressage has been described as ballet for horses.

GYMKHANAS

* A gymkhana is an event in a field which involves ponies and silly games. Some of these include:

  * **Bending**: in which the pony has to weave its way in and out of a row of poles.

  * **Sack race**: the rider must lead her pony the length of the arena while hopping inside a sack (the rider, not the pony).

  Gymkhanas also involve anxious mothers with competitive picnic baskets, being sick with nerves and crying when your pony refuses three times to jump and is eliminated. They also involve rosettes. Red or blue are best, but any colour will do. You will be awarded your rosette by one of the fierce judges, then you must tie your rosette to your pony's bridle and do a victory lap around the arena while your mother cries (again).

PONY CLUB

* The Pony Club was founded in England in 1929 to teach young people all about ponies and riding. The Pony Club organizes shows, endurance riding competitions, quizzes, working rallies (where riders go to learn about all aspects of horsemanship) and, of course, Pony Club camp.

  Pony Club camp, which takes place in the summer, is where riders take their ponies for a week away, and indulge in all things horsey. There will be training – such things as riding over small jumps without stirrups or reins, long rides, various competitions, and often a cross-country course.

Great Horses in History

BUCEPHALUS

* Bucephalus, born around 355 BC, was the most famous horse of antiquity. He was described as having a black coat with a white star between his eyes, and being of the 'best Thessalonian strain'. He was famous for being a wild horse that no one could tame except the twelve-year-old Alexander the Great, who was allowed to keep the horse. He named him Bucephalus because the horse's head seemed 'as broad as a bull's'. He carried Alexander faithfully through many wars, and finally died in battle in 326 BC. Alexander loved him so much that he founded a city in Bucephalus' honour.

RED RUM

* The only horse in history to win the Grand National three times (he also finished second twice). He was trained by Ginger McCain on the Southport sands, galloping up and down the beach to reach peak fitness. He also liked to go swimming in the sea. He became so famous that he got fan mail from all over the world and was invited to open supermarkets. He lived to the grand old age of thirty, and a bronze statue of Red Rum now stands at the Aintree racecourse, the scene of his historic triumphs.

MARENGO

* Napoleon's famous grey Arabian horse. He carried the emperor through four battles, including Waterloo, and was wounded eight times. Like all Napoleon's horses, he had trumpets blown close to him, cannons fired beside him and dogs sent running through his legs, all to train him to remain calm and steadfast in battle. It was said that he could gallop eighty miles in five hours. He was captured by the British at Waterloo, and spent the rest of his life in England. He died aged thirty-eight, and his skeleton was displayed at the Army Museum in London. All except for one hoof, that is, which was presented to the officers of the Brigade of Guards to serve as a snuff box.

PARTIES

The point of a party is for everyone – including the hostess – to have fun. This is impossible if you're rushing around trying to sort out the food or organize party games. What you really want is for everything to look effortless and relaxed – and to do that you'll need to plan ahead.

The Invitations

Try to send out invitations at least three weeks in advance. Make sure you include the following vital information:

* where and when

* reason for party (e.g. birthday)

* start and end time

* dress code and/or theme of party

* how to RSVP (this stands for *répondez s'il vous plaît* which is French for 'reply if you please') – generally an invitation will ask guests to reply yes or no, to a given address or telephone number, by a certain date

* directions: if your party is at an outside venue, photocopy a map of the local area and highlight the address for your guests

Making your own handwritten invitations adds to the fun and excitement of it all – and gives you a chance to show off your creative side. Here are some ideas . . .

SURPRISE WITH SIZE

* If you're having, say, a fairy-themed party, send out teeny fairy-sized invitations in the smallest envelopes you can find; or if you're having a dinosaur party, a gigantic poster-sized invitation will get the message across loud and clear (and will make sure no one forgets to come!).

DIFFERENT SHAPES

* Invitations don't have to be square – literally. Make a template of the shape for your card – star shape, ballet-shoe shape, insect shape, football shape, etc. – and cut out.

PHOTOGRAPHS

* Arrange fridge-magnet letters and numbers on the fridge detailing the date, place and time of the party, photograph the fridge door and print.

  Alternatively, use alphabet and letter building-block cubes on the floor and ask someone to take your photograph surrounded by them, or arrange Scrabble letters and numbers on a nice background and photograph.

LETTERS

* Cut out individual letters and numbers from the newspaper or magazine (like blackmailers do in films!) to form the wording for your invitations.

Party Food

Dancing, clowns and balloons may spring to mind at the mention of a party, but the food is always the best bit as far as we're concerned. Here are some of our favourite treats.

MARMITE SANDWICHES

* Soft granary bread is best suited to Marmite sandwiches. Make them using soft butter (not margarine, please), and spread the Marmite very thin. Cut off the crusts and cut them into soldiers (for some reason, they taste much better this way). If there are Marmite haters among your guests, provide them with strawberry or raspberry jam sandwiches, made using the same method.

COCKTAIL SAUSAGES IN HONEY

* Preheat the oven to 180°C/gas mark 4. Put your uncooked cocktail sausages (roughly four per person) on a baking tray. Drizzle some runny honey over the top and shake them up a bit. If you like, you can sprinkle them with sesame seeds. Cook in the oven for about 20 minutes, turning halfway through to make sure the melted honey covers them properly. Very sticky and very yummy.

POTATO WEDGES

* Preheat the oven to 180°C/gas mark 4. Wash as many potatoes as you need (one per person should be enough, although if there are boys coming you may need more). Leave the skins on. Slice them in half lengthways; then slice those pieces in half again, also lengthways. Arrange the wedges on a baking tray (you can cook them at the same time as the sausages, but keep them on separate trays). Drizzle over some olive oil and sprinkle with a little salt (shuffle them around a bit to make sure they're properly coated). Pop them in the oven for 20 to 25 minutes, turning halfway through. Serve on a large plate with a small pot of tomato ketchup and/or mayonnaise for dipping.

TRAFFIC LIGHTS

* The essence of simplicity. Cut some red Leicester (or any other orangey cheese) into cubes, roughly the size of a die. Do the same with a cucumber, keeping the skins on (obviously you won't be able to manage precise cubes, but do your best). Thread a cube of cucumber, a cube of cheese and, finally, a small cherry tomato onto a toothpick and *voilà* – traffic lights. If you prefer, you can use green peppers instead of cucumbers, or even a bit of crisp green Granny Smith apple.

YOUR PARTY TABLE

* Always have the table set and ready before your guests arrive. If you're having a theme (see overleaf), carry it through to your table decorations. For example, if you're a big fan of Paddington Bear, use brown paper labels as place-setting cards; if you're having a Halloween party, splatter your tablecloth with blood (red paint) and hide fake spiders under your guests' napkins. It's always a nice touch to sprinkle the tablecloth with little sweets – Smarties or Jelly Tots always go down well – and you can give your guests something to smile about by leaving a joke written on a little rolled-up piece of paper on each plate.

Themed Parties

A theme is always fun for a party, and it gives your guests a good starting point for dress (and, of course, present) ideas. It also makes life easier for you, as it gives you a creative focus. There are endless themes from monsters and mummies to craft and picnic parties. It all depends what sort of things you enjoy most. Here are a few of our favourites.

FOOTBALL PARTY

This is a great theme to choose if you want to invite boys, who, on the whole, tend to turn up their noses at flower-fairy themes.

* **Invitations:** football-boot shaped, Top Trumps cards with your star player, or an invitation designed to look like a ticket for a football match.

* **Dress code:** football kit.

* **Food and drink:** hamburgers, oranges cut into quarters, hot dogs, mini pizzas.

* **Birthday cake:** football-shaped with black and white icing, or football-pitch shaped with green icing and miniature football players.

ORANGE BIRTHDAY PARTY

* **Invitations:** orange, of course, and orange-shaped.

* **Dress code:** anything as long as it's orange.

* **Food and drink:** oranges, orange cheese, orange peppers and carrot sticks to dip in hummous, bowls of orange Smarties, orange juice, orange jelly and anything else you can think of that's orange.

* **Birthday cake:** orange-shaped and flavoured, with orange icing.

HOLLYWOOD PARTY

The Academy Awards (or Oscars) take place every year in February or March. It is Hollywood's most glamorous event.

* **Invitations:** Oscar-shaped, red-carpet-shaped, premiere ticket — glitter, gold, silver and lots of STARS!

* **Dress code:** glamour!

* **Food and drink:** blinis with cream cheese and smoked salmon, dips with crudités, fizzy water and elderflower 'champagne', fondant fancies.

* **Birthday cake:** white icing or whipped cream with gold candles, sparklers and strawberries.

    A fun variation on this theme is a Bollywood party, where everyone wears beautiful bright colours, ankle bracelets and does sinuous Indian dancing.

FLOWER-FAIRY PARTY

Always a favourite.

* **Invitations:** tiny cards wrapped in delicate tissue paper inside tiny envelopes; add a shake of fairy-dust glitter before sealing each envelope.

* **Dress code:** fairy dresses, fairy wings, silver wands, flowers in hair.

* **Food and drink:** miniature sandwiches, quail's eggs and cherry tomatoes, cocktail sausages, little fairy cakes with pale pink icing, fruit-juice elixirs and cordials.

* **Birthday cake:** Victoria sponge with cream filling and topping, decorated with flower petals.

Party Games

HUNT THE ORANGE

* Here is one of several orange-themed games to play. Oranges are hidden all over the house or garden. Numbers are placed randomly on the oranges. The players keep the oranges they have found and, at the end of the game, the scores are counted by adding each player's numbers. A prize is awarded to the highest score – a bar of nicely scented orange soap, some orange balloons or orange-flavoured sweets or chocolate.

PASSING THE ORANGE

* And here's another – players sit on chairs in two rows facing one another. The aim is to pass an orange from person to person all along the row using only the feet. This is not quite as easy as it sounds – the trick is to put the orange on top of your feet which you hold tightly together, to keep the legs stiff, and then tilt the feet slowly so the orange rolls gently onto the next person's. The side whose orange makes it to the end first wins.

SLEEPING LIONS

* A good game to play at the end of a party when everyone might be a little overheated and overwrought...

All the players (except one or two hunters, who may be adults) lie down on the floor in sleeping positions and must not move a whisker. The hunters walk around the room and try to get the sleeping lions to move by making them laugh, whispering jokes to them, calling them silly names and so on. The hunters are not allowed to touch or tickle the lions. If a sleeping lion moves, they get up and join the hunters. The last lion left sleeping wins a prize.

MUSICAL CLOTHES

* In a large bag, place as many items of clothing as you can gather from the dressing-up box and around the house. These might include fairy and princess dresses, cowboy outfits, pyjamas and nightdresses, feather boas, gloves, old glasses, wigs, hats, false moustaches and beards, scarves, overcoats and shoes, men's shirts and evening dresses.

Players stand in a circle, and when the music starts, the bag is passed round. When the music stops, the player holding the bag has to take something out and put it on. The game continues until the bag is empty. The winner is the person wearing the most clothes.

FASHION DESIGNERS

* Players divide into pairs or small groups. Each team is given some newspapers, sticky tape and scissors. One child in each pair/group is the model to be dressed by the other(s). You might specify a theme in advance (punk rock or Oscars) and have winners of different categories – say, most original, highest degree of technical dressmaking skill, with pleating or frills, for example.

THE NAME GAME

* Players sit in a circle on the floor. The first player starts the game by asking, 'What vegetable do you like best?' for example. The next player replies as quickly as she can with the names of two or three vegetables starting with the letters of their name. So, if the player is called Constance Anne Swift, she could reply, 'Cucumbers, aubergine and swede.' The same vegetable cannot be named twice. If it gets too difficult with vegetables, the game can be played for another round with fruit, animals, foods, flowers, etc. It's also great for embarrassing people about their middle names!

MUSICAL STATUES

* Put on some funky music. While it is playing, everyone has to move about, dancing and grooving vigorously. When the music stops, everyone stands as still as a statue. The referee (usually an adult) must judge if anyone is moving even just the slightest bit once the music stops. If someone keeps on dancing or wobbles at all, then that player is out and retires to the sofa. Keep playing until the last statue is left standing quite still.

THE BUMPS

* Not a game so much as a ritual. The birthday girl is held by her arms and legs by four of her 'friends'. She gets her bottom bumped on the ground once for every year of her age. When or where this will happen during the course of a party no one knows; the guests must ambush her when she is least expecting it. Vigorous squeals of protest are allowed, and even encouraged. It is acceptable to refuse to speak to the bumpers for at least 5 minutes after the event. Retaliate if you wish, but remember: revenge is a dish best served cold. In other words, wait until they least expect it, then strike. A worm in their party bag, for example.

MUSICAL BUMPS

* Similar to musical statues, but when the music stops each player must sit down on the floor. The last player to sit down is out. If a player makes a false move and sits down before the music stops in an attempt to cheat, that player is also disqualified and must step out of the game.

SPIN THE BOTTLE

* Spin the bottle can be played as a daring kissing game if there are boys at a party. What you do is sit in a circle on the floor or at the table, and lay an empty bottle on its side. The first person spins it, and must kiss the person at whom the bottle neck points when it stops. That person takes the next turn to spin the bottle. If the bottle lands pointing at another girl, then the person who spun the bottle should kiss the boy next to that girl.

KIM'S GAME

* In advance, prepare a tray with a number of items on it (matchbox, needle, thread, cup, saucer, spoon, apple, banana, pen, etc.). Players are shown the tray for a short time, and must try to remember all the items. Cover the tray up with a cloth, and the players must write down a list of everything they remember. The player who remembers all or most of the items is the winner.

TEASPOON RACE

* Players sit in two rows on opposite side of the table. Each puts a teaspoon in her mouth. The player at the end of the row places a sugar lump or a grape in her spoon and gently tips it into the next player's teaspoon, and so on to the last player in the row. The team which passes their sugar lump to the end first, and without dropping it, wins.

PARTY BAGS

* By no means essential, but an excellent way of thanking your guests for coming and giving them something to remember your party by. Don't go over the top: a paper bag containing a few sweets and a little memento – a toy or a slice of birthday cake – will do fine.

THANK YOU LETTERS

It's very important that you thank everyone for your presents. So you don't get in a muddle, keep a note of who's given you what as you go along. That way, when it comes to writing your letters you can be specific. Here's an example:

Dearest Aunt Flo

Thank you so much for the wonderful flower press you gave me. [A few specifics go down well.] *I have already filled it with daisies from the garden, and Mum says that when her pansies come out I can have a few of those too.* [A little polite enquiry never goes amiss.] *I hope your ankle is better – I feel awful about you slipping on that spilt jelly.* [And, finally, a cheery sign-off.] *Do send my love to Uncle Thomas, and hope to see you both really soon.*

Sleepovers and Pyjama Parties

Everyone knows that the point of sleepover parties is to make sure not much sleeping gets done. Have a secret stash of goodies for your midnight feast, put a big PRIVATE sign on your bedroom door and devise a secret password to keep intruders out. Any adult who wishes to enter without knowing the correct password must pay a forfeit – something like a tray of hot chocolate is always a good one, or extra supplies of popcorn.

Once you've hunkered down, here's what you can do . . .

TRUTH OR DARE

This is a variation on spin the bottle. Draw straws to see who goes first. The person at whom the bottle points is asked, 'Truth or dare?' If they choose 'Truth' they must answer completely honestly ANY question asked. If they choose 'Dare' they must perform the group's chosen dare.

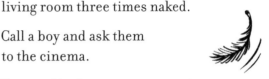

Possible truth questions:

* Who is the last person you held hands with?

* Who would you like to kiss, if you could kiss anyone in the world?

* What is the worst lie you have ever told?

* What is the worst thing about your best friend?

* Who do you hate most at school?

Possible dares:

* Have a cold shower.

* Run round the garden or living room three times naked.

* Call a boy and ask them to the cinema.

* Eat a garlic clove.

* Lick the carpet five times.

PILLOW FIGHTS

Sleepovers usually involve a pillow fight at some point during the night. There are no rules for pillow fighting – everyone just grabs a pillow and whacks each other until either a pillow bursts or one of you collapses in a sweaty heap.

NO MIRROR MAKEOVER

Everyone has to make themselves up as glamorously as they can – without looking in a mirror. Or one of you is blindfolded and has to attempt to make up a partner without looking.

GHOST STORIES

A great way to round off the night. Extinguish the lights, light a candle or two, gather around the flame and tell the spookiest ghost stories you can think of. For inspiration, read out loud a story by one of the great masters: *The Legend of Sleepy Hollow* by Washington Irving, about a headless horseman who haunts a wood; chapter two of Bram Stoker's *Dracula*, when the young Mr Harkness arrives at the vampire's castle; *The Canterville Ghost* by Oscar Wilde (not really that scary, but a great story).

AUTUMN

Autumn is a great time to be outside for walks in the park or along country lanes, or for long rambles in the forest when the trees will be ablaze in golds and reds. This is the best time for collecting leaves, acorns, conkers, apples, nuts and seeds, and autumn hedgerows are a great hunting ground for all sorts of berries and autumn fruits. In the woods or forest this is the best time to go looking for mushrooms and toadstools.

The weather might be wet and windy, but it's not yet too cold — so as long as you've got a big jumper, a rain jacket and some sturdy boots, you can jump in the mud, splash in puddles and rummage in the undergrowth to your heart's content without your toes falling off from the cold.

MOVE THE CLOCK BACK AN HOUR

* British Summer Time ends in October and the clocks go back an hour, so you get an extra hour in bed. A good way to remember whether the clocks go back or forward in spring or autumn is the following mnemonic: spring forward, fall back.

CATCHING LEAVES AND SEED HELICOPTERS

This seemingly idle pursuit can provide long hours of dreamy, hypnotic entertainment in the forest or countryside, in your garden or in the street on the way home from the shops or school, or when you are out for a walk in the park.

* It's not as easy as it looks – especially if it's a gusty day when the wind can send the leaves whirling past your nose and out of your fingertips. Good trees to stand under are beech, oak and plane, though any tree with lots of leaves left and a windy day will do.

  The seeds of some trees – sycamore, maple and lime – have wings on them like helicopters which send them spiralling on the wind providing a challenge for even the most skilled and dedicated leaf-catcher.

  Some people believe that catching a leaf brings you good luck in the same way that finding a penny and picking it up, or seeing a falling star, or having bird poo land on your head brings good luck.

BUILDING A BONFIRE

* Autumn is a time for tidying and clearing the garden of any dead plants, tree branches, grass cuttings and any other debris that has accumulated over the summer. The challenge is to start the fire using only one match and not having to resort to throwing the contents of a can of petrol over it or using firelighters. For bonfire-making tips see Building a Campfire on page 130.

RAKING LEAVES

Raking leaves in autumn can be seen either as a chore that has to be done or as a fun and healthy outdoor pursuit that will bring colour to your cheeks. If there are a few of you raking, you can have a competition to see who can make the biggest pile of leaves into which you can hurl yourself, then rake them up all over again.

* Store dead leaves in a shed or somewhere dry, or pile them up and cover them with a plastic sheet or tarpaulin – they will come in handy for lighting your autumn and Guy Fawkes Night bonfires. If you have a surplus, make a leaf bin and let the leaves rot down for a year or so, then use them as compost or, if you have one, add them to the wormery.

Chestnuts and Conkers

October is the month to collect chestnuts – shiny brown horse chestnuts for playing conkers, and the sweet chestnut in its spiky green shell for roasting in the embers of the bonfire or indoors on the hearth. Horse chestnuts are inedible for humans, though they are eaten by cows and were once used as horse feed.

CONKERS

To play conkers it's essential to collect only the best and hardest ones with no cracks or damage. The more dense the conker, the more unlikely it is to crack in a contest. Put some conkers in a bowl of water – the dense and hopefully worthy ones will sink to the bottom while those that are damaged or cracked or not as dense will float to the top and can be thrown away.

* Many techniques have been tried for hardening conkers for use in playground contests. Some people swear by slow cooking them at a very low temperature for a few hours to toughen them up, others think soaking them in vinegar overnight and then allowing the conker to dry at room temperature is a foolproof method. If you are determined to have a champion conker you can collect some perfect specimens and save them in your sock drawer for a whole year so they will dry and harden slowly and will hopefully be invincible.

Drill a hole through the middle of the conker starting at the centre of the lighter brown bit on the bottom – get your parents or another grown-up to do this for you using a fine electric drill (Rosemary used thin, pointed knitting needles to bore the holes so as not to crack the conker). Thread a strong piece of string about 25 centimetres or so long through the hole and tie a large knot underneath so that it is secure and the conker won't fly off when hit.

The game starts with one player holding their conker in front of them at a height chosen by the other player, with the string wrapped several times round the fingers so it can't be dropped. The second player holds their conker in one hand at an angle with the conker near their body and the string held taut in the other hand, and then fires it in an attempt to get a forceful direct hit on the other conker. If there is a hit, they get another go; if it misses, it is the other player's turn. If the conker flies out of the opponent's hand when hit, the other player should shout 'Stamps!' as quickly as possible and can then stomp on the conker and smash it, unless the opponent shouts out 'No stamps!' first, thus protecting their conker.

A winning conker takes on the score of the other player's conker in a rating system. So in a first match with two fresh conkers, the victorious conker would become a 'one-er'. If that conker then went on to beat a conker with two victories already under its belt, it would become a 'four-er' and so on, so that a really champion conker might become a 'fifty-er' or more, and potentially even live to fight another year.

If you get really good, you might even like to take part in the World Conker Championships, which are held on the village green in Ashton in Northamptonshire on the second Sunday of October–you are not allowed to bring your own conkers, but must use new conkers which are supplied.

HOW TO ROAST SWEET CHESTNUTS

The sweet chestnut is not native to Britain so it is quite rare to find them in the countryside or woodland, but look out for them in parks and gardens. It's thought the tree was brought to Britain by the Romans, who used the nuts to make flour.

* In our climate, the sweet chestnut tree doesn't bear nuts until it is at least twenty-five years old, which is perhaps why most of the nuts we smell roasting in the streets of London in winter are imported from hotter climes.

   If you are lucky enough to come across a sweet chestnut on your rambles, look out for the prickly green cup containing the sweet brown chestnuts. You will usually find between one and three nuts in each spiky case.

   Sweet chestnuts are best roasted in their shells over the embers of a log fire. But whether roasting them over an open fire or in the oven, make a cut in the brown outer shell with a sharp knife first to stop them exploding. When the shell has blackened slightly they're cooked; let them cool a bit before peeling.

Autumn Berries and Seeds

Collecting autumn berries is fun for the nature table, art and craft work, or for making jellies, wines and syrups.

The fruits of the hedgerow can be used like flowers to make an autumn bouquet — and unlike flowers, the berry and seed arrangement will last for much longer without withering and dying.

* Most seeds and berries will keep for a long time if simply dried in the air — collect ripe bunches of sycamore, ash and hornbeam keys or seeds, and all sorts of pine cones for autumn arrangements in a large pot or vase.

   If you would like to make a more permanent display or collection of nuts, acorns and beech mast, allow them to dry naturally in the air, then paint them with clear varnish to stop them shrivelling.

AUTUMN LEAF, SEED AND BERRY COLLAGE

When out on an autumn walk collect some stalks of different dry grasses, wheat or corn, some brightly coloured berries such as scarlet hawthorn, rowan, some rosehips and some different seed cases – beech, lime, poppy and honesty, for instance. As well as these, you will need:

* a chocolate box or shoe box lid, or a piece of stiff card about 25 x 20cm
* a piece of felt cut to the same size
* glue
* some braid, narrow ribbon or dried red kidney beans

* Glue the felt to the lid or cardboard. Arrange your seeds, grasses and berries on it to form a picture or scene and then glue them into place.

Below is a suggested composition – the beech nuts form the ground, the grasses a tall plant, the berries a scarlet bush, the honesty a shimmering bush, and the sycamore seed cases are arranged in the form of a bird, or perhaps a dragonfly. You could also make butterflies and moths using the honesty and sycamore seed cases.

Once you have glued down your picture and allowed your collage to dry, trim the edges of the card with the narrow braid or ribbon, or arrange some red kidney beans as a frame.

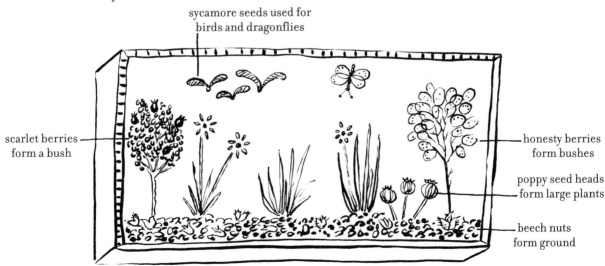

sycamore seeds used for
birds and dragonflies

scarlet berries
form a bush

honesty berries
form bushes

poppy seed heads
form large plants

beech nuts
form ground

Rosehips

You need to collect a lot of rosehips for this syrup but it's delicious and very good for you. Rosehip syrup is full of vitamins A, C and E – weight for weight rosehips have twenty times more vitamin C than oranges – so it's a good thing to make and store for the winter to help keep colds and flu away and it's good for tickly coughs. The best syrup is made from wild dog-rose hips collected from the hedgerows or you can use the hips of Rosa rugosa. *It keeps for months as long as you have sterilized your bottles properly before storing.*

ROSEHIP SYRUP MAKES APPROX. 850ML

* 900g rosehips
* 2.5 litres water
* 450g sugar

Bring 1.8 litres of the water to the boil in a large saucepan. Chop or mince the rosehips (this can be done quickly in a blender) and add them to the boiling water. Bring back to the boil, remove from the heat and leave to soak for 15 minutes then strain through a fine nylon sieve or some muslin. Return the pulp to the saucepan, add the rest of the water and bring to the boil, turn off the heat and allow to soak for 5 minutes and strain again. Pour the juice into a clean saucepan and bring to the boil once more. Leave uncovered and simmer to reduce the liquid to about 850 millilitres. Then add the sugar, stir to dissolve, and boil for a further 5 minutes.

Pour the syrup into sterilized bottles with tightly fitting screw lids.

ELDERBERRY CORDIAL

Like rosehip syrup, elberberry cordial is an excellent tonic recommended in winter to fight off colds and flu.

* elderberries (still on stalks)
* sugar
* cloves
* water

Rinse the elderberries to remove any dirt or insects and stew them, with the stalks, in a large pot, with just enough water to cover. When reduced to a mush, strain the pulp through muslin or a fine sieve, mashing it with a wooden spoon and squeezing well to get all the thick juice. Measure the juice, and for each 600 millilitres add 450 grams of white granulated sugar and 10 cloves. Boil for 10 minutes to reduce to a syrup consistency.

Allow to cool and use a funnel to transfer to sterile bottles with tight-fitting tops or corks. The cloves are a preservative, so make sure you distribute them evenly among the bottles. The cordial can be drunk immediately, but will keep well for a year or two in tightly closed bottles.

Mushrooms and Toadstools

Most fungi appear in the autumn and winter when the weather is damp. Fungi make an interesting addition to the nature table, or you might like to start your own collection. Woody kinds of fungi found on tree trunks or at the roots of trees will keep for years if simply left to dry in the air. Other, smaller or feathery mushrooms such as tiny chanterelles can be pressed using the same method as flower pressing.

SOME EDIBLE MUSHROOMS

* In France foraging for mushrooms is virtually a national sport and passionate mushroomers spend their weekends in autumn searching for the elusive and prized chanterelles and tasty morels. Wild mushroom connoisseurs recommend that freshly picked specimens are best enjoyed simply fried in butter with perhaps some garlic, chopped parsley and a squeeze of lemon and eaten with fresh bread. Cooked in this way you can add them to an omelette or to scrambled eggs.

Here in the United Kingdom there is an unaccountable wariness of fungi which dates from centuries ago, but in fact there are only a few truly poisonous mushrooms among almost 3,000 different kinds which grow here in Britain and Ireland. Most toadstools are non-poisonous and some are excellent in flavour, but some are too small or leathery to eat and some are just tasteless.

Two common misconceptions or old wives' tales about identifying a poisonous mushroom are that only edible fungi can be peeled and do not turn a silver spoon or sixpence black. This is not at all reliable, the proof being that field mushrooms can be proved edible or non-poisonous by these tests, but so can *Amanita phalloides*, the most deadly species of all, responsible for the majority of fatal poisonings!

Forests, pine woods and parks are great places for mushroom hunting, or you might be lucky enough to have some mushrooms in your garden – check under trees and in the undergrowth in shrubby areas.

Buy a good, illustrated mushroom book, which will clearly explain how to identify the different mushrooms and which are the most delicious to eat, or find out about organized mushroom foraging walks in your area with an expert guide or mycologist.

PUFFBALLS AND GIANT PUFFBALLS

* Giant puffballs can grow to over 30 centimetres in diameter and just under 30 centimetres in height and are most commonly found in pasture land. Look out for them from late August onward. They often resemble human skulls – one story tells of workmen coming across a number of them growing under the floor of a house and reporting the incident to the police, thinking they had found a mass grave. Puffballs are normally a slightly flattened oval in shape and are attached to the ground by a thick stem. The outer skin is downy at first, becoming smooth and creamy, then yellowing and turning brownish-yellow as it ages. When older, the fragile outer skin cracks and becomes spongy. When touched, the brown powdery spores are released in puffs. The flesh of the puffball is edible when young and still soft, white and cheesy.

  To cook puffballs, slice the flesh into rounds, dip in beaten egg and then cover with seasoned breadcrumbs and fry in butter until golden brown on both sides. Serve with a sprinkling of chopped parsley.

Autumn Moths

Although summer is the main season for moth and butterfly spotting, you can attract moths to the garden on mild, dry autumn nights not only by leaving a light on outside but by the smell of alcohol.

* To do this put some rotten fruit such as apples, bananas or plums outside on a balcony or windowsill. You can also try 'sugaring' some tree trunks or branches in the garden. Make a sweet alcoholic mixture with apple syrup and wine and allow it to ferment for about 24 hours. In the evening, just before dusk, paint some tree trunks with the mixture, then check outside a few hours later. Moths will have gathered to feed on the sugary solution. You can also use the sugary liquid to soak some rope, cotton rags or socks, then string the material through low branches to attract the moths.

THE FARMER WANTS A WIFE

We think of this as an autumn game – perhaps because we always celebrated harvest festival and that made us think about farmers and their wives bringing in the crops from the fields.

The farmer's in his den
The farmer's in his den
  Hey ho ma deario
The farmer's in his den.

The farmer wants a wife
The farmer wants a wife
  Hey ho ma deario
The farmer wants a wife.

The wife wants a child . . .

The child wants a dog . . .

The dog wants a bone . . .

The bone was left alone . . .

First decide who is to be the farmer and form a circle around her; hold hands and dance round singing the song. At the end of the wife verse the farmer must choose a wife from the circle, and the wife then joins the farmer in the middle, and the song continues with the last person chosen choosing next, so the wife chooses a child, the child chooses a dog and so on.

When we played it, the poor bone, who was left alone at the end of the song, always got a bit of a pounding on the head and back from all the other children, but then as consolation the bone is always the farmer in the next round of the song.

The choices can be different, depending on the number of children playing. For example a nurse can be chosen after the child, then the nurse chooses the dog.

Emmeline Pankhurst (1858–1928)

Mrs Pankhurst was the passionate and indomitable leader of the movement for the right of women to vote. It may seem unbelievable in this day and age, but it was only in 1928 that women were granted the same voting rights as men. Until 1918 they had not been allowed to vote at all, and then only women over thirty were allowed to do so. Emmeline Pankhurst, as well as her two daughters Christabel and Sylvia, and many other suffragettes protested and petitioned vigorously to have equal voting rights with men. Rebecca West (a contemporary journalist, writer and critic) said of her: 'Trembling like a reed, she lifted up her hoarse, sweet voice on the platform, but the reed was of steel and it was tremendous.'

During the course of her crusade, Emmeline was arrested, went on hunger strike, and was force-fed. By the age of fifty-four, she had been imprisoned twelve times. Just along from the Palace of Westminster there is a statue of her, looking more like a gracious rock of ages rather than the firebrand she was in life – a reminder that it wasn't so long ago that women were second-class citizens.

Boudicca (died c. AD 60)

The queen of the Iceni tribe in first-century Britain, she got in her chariot and took on the might of the Roman Empire. She won Colchester and sacked London before finding her way blocked by Paulinus, the Roman governor of Britain, and an army of 10,000 men. The night before the final battle, she drove around her tribe, exhorting her warriors to be brave: 'Win the battle or perish: that is what I, a woman will do; you men can live on in slavery if that's what you want.'

Sadly, they lost, and she did perish, but not before she'd made life extremely difficult for the invaders. She famously had long red hair and piercing eyes, and was described as 'terrifying'. Like Emmeline Pankhurst, she too has a lovely statue near the Houses of Parliament.

BEWITCHED

The secret of every successful magician is that practice makes perfect — perseverance and dedicated rehearsal will turn even the most shambolic trickster into a slick wizard of the mystical arts. Never attempt any conjuring trick in front of an audience without having rehearsed it until you have mastered, refined and perfected it.

If you are performing for an invited crowd keep the routine short so you don't lose your audience. If they start fidgeting you know you're in danger of losing them. It is therefore imperative that you prepare everything you need for each trick in advance, and have it all to hand. In this respect, it is enormously useful to enlist the help of one or more assistants.

Assistants are great, because you can get them to do all the boring stuff — and they can be bossed about for the benefit of your audience, reinforcing the impression of you as a great and feared magician. Small siblings, or even a docile pet, are perfect for this purpose.

You will need a costume and your assistant will too. This should be in keeping with yours, only suitably less spectacular. You will also need a magician's name. Mesmeralda, for example; or Violet Voilà; or Princess Presto.

Begin your magic routine with a very quick and simple trick, which is sure to grab the audience's attention. Follow with slightly more complicated or longer tricks, and always finish the show with your very best and most astounding trick — that will leave the audience begging for an encore. And remember the magical mantra: practice makes perfect. If a trick goes wrong, you can cover up by giving the impression that it was a deliberate mistake — part of the act, naturally. Or you can always blame your assistant and threaten to turn her into a frog. Either way keep calm and keep going.

Your Equipment and Stage Outfit

You might want to invest in a real magic wand and magician's hat, but as an amateur and for practising at home you can easily make a few props.

THE MAGIC WAND

* A very realistic magic wand can be made by tightly wrapping a sheet of white paper round a knitting needle or pencil, then gluing it down the side. Paint it black, leaving a white tip at the end.

MAGICIAN'S HAT

* Look in secondhand shops or markets for old top hats, or make your own magician's hat using some drawing or wrapping paper. Cut out a rectangle about 60 centimetres long and 30 centimetres wide, fold it in half, then mark a curved line. Open out the paper and cut along the line to form a semicircle, then fold the paper to a point and stick down the edge with glue or tape to make a pointed conical-shaped hat. Paint and decorate the hat with stars and glitter.

MAGICIAN'S CAPE

* A vampire cape from Halloween can double nicely as a magician's cape;
  alternatively you could use a length of black cloth to make a cloak to drape
  over your shoulders.

YOUR MAGICIAN'S PATTER

* A large part of the magician's art is the patter, or talk, as the trick is performed.
  Even the most brilliant trick performed in complete silence will not amuse
  an audience much, and in the absence of a drum-roll (although if any of
  your assistants is musically inclined, you could always take advantage to
  introduce music into your show), the conjurer should entertain as she
  performs by keeping up a steady stream of bamboozling and witty banter. The
  patter also serves to distract the audience and diverts their attention from the
  mechanics behind the trick. Practise your hand movements and stage banter
  in front of the mirror – 'Abracadabra. Hey presto!' combined with a smattering
  of basic French phrases, for example *'Et voilà!'* or *'C'est comme ça!'* or *'Hopla!*
  C'est magique!'

Card Tricks

Never reveal the secret of any card trick – no matter how much the audience
begs you to.

READING THE PACK

This is a very easy card trick, but it never fails to mystify an audience.

* Take your pack of cards and, while no one is looking, turn the first card over
  with its back to the rest of the pack. Remember which card this is. With the
  cards held behind your back, tell the audience you have magical powers and
  can predict correctly every card in the pack as it appears. Hold the pack up to
  the audience so they can see the card which you turned over first, and tell
  them what it is without looking at it. At the same time you must note the card

now facing you. Put the cards behind your back again, and slip the last card from the pack (the one that was facing you) and place it, face outwards, on top of the card you have announced. Hold the cards up again and call out the card. Repeat this until you have named enough cards to arouse suspicion as to how it is done, stop the trick, and start your next trick, quietly rearranging the pack before you do so while unobserved.

FINDING A CARD

Shuffle a pack of cards. Holding the pack in one hand with the cards face down, cut the pack. With one half in one hand, one half in the other, ask a member of your audience to take the top card from the half in your left hand and remember that card. Tell them not to let you see it. Meanwhile, take a sneakily casual glance at the bottom card in your right hand and note it. You must not be spotted doing so. Ask the member of the audience to return her card to the top of the pile in your left hand. Put the two halves together and shuffle just a few times. One at a time, throw the cards on the table, announcing the card which was picked out when it appears with a flourish. You will be able to identify the correct card, because it will very likely follow the one you have just looked at on the bottom of the pack in your right hand (as you shuffle, take care not to disturb these cards from their order).

TUMBLERS OF WATER TRICK

Ask your audience if they think it is possible to fill two tumblers to the brim with water, turn one upside down, and stand the other on top of it without spilling a drop. They will look bemused until you demonstrate how.

Fill two glasses to the brim with water and place a piece of thick cartridge paper on top of one of them. Place the palm of your left hand on top of the paper, pick up the tumbler with your right hand, and then quickly turn it upside down. Remove your hand from the paper and place the tumbler on top of the other. Now carefully pull out the paper.

With a little practice, not a drop of water will be spilled.

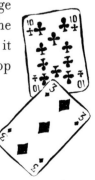

hidden cards

THE FOUR BURGLARS

This is a very simple trick once you have practised a little.

First take out all four jacks from the pack of cards. As you do this, remove any other three cards and discreetly hide these behind the four jacks in your hand. The trick is to do this without arousing suspicion or anyone noticing. Spread the jacks out in a fan in your hand, as shown in the diagram, with the three cards concealed behind the last jack. Show the jacks to the audience. Put the rest of the pack on the table face down.

Explain to the audience that the four jacks are four burglars, and the rest of the pack represents a house which they are about to burgle. Turn the cards in your hand over (the three cards you discreetly removed will now be on top of the four jacks) and explain that the first burglar (or jack) will break into the basement. Take this first card and put it back into the pack low down. The next burglar breaks in through a window, so the next card you hold is slipped in higher up the pack. The third burglar gets in through the front door; the third card therefore is placed near the top, while the fourth burglar stays outside the house keeping watch, and will give three warning knocks as a sign that they should come out quickly if he sees anyone. The last card (which is, in fact, the four jacks you have kept in your hand) is now placed quickly on top of the pack.

Give the burglars the warning by tapping the pack smartly three times with your magic wand, then lift off each of the four jacks one by one, announcing, 'Here come all four burglars running out of the house!'

A KNOTTY PUZZLE

✱ Place a scarf on the table, and ask a member of the audience to come forward and take a chair. Ask her if she can tie a knot in the middle of the scarf while holding both ends and without letting go of either of them. Unless they know the trick in advance, they will be quite at a loss as to how this can possibly be done. When they give up, ask them to stand up and give you the scarf. Fold it lengthwise. Fold your arms and pick up an end with each hand. Unfold your arms without letting go of the ends – as you do so, you will have perfectly easily tied a knot in the middle.

A TRICK WITH DOMINOES

Build a house out of dominoes by placing two upright on the table and two more resting horizontally on top of them, then two more upright and one more on top as shown in the diagram. Now, the trick is to remove the domino marked A in the picture without disturbing the others. It is quite easy.

✱ Lay another domino lengthwise (domino B). Put your forefinger through the opening in the house and rest it on the end of domino B, press down hard to flip the domino upright. It will strike against the horizontal domino A and shoot it out from the house, leaving the others undisturbed. Practise a few times to perfect the trick before performing it in public.

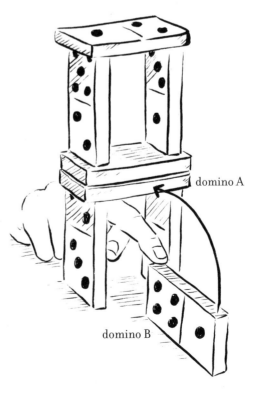

domino A

domino B

Tricks with Pennies and Coins

PALMING A COIN

With a little practice you will develop the skill of apparently being able to make an ordinary penny appear and disappear in your hand, only to reappear again from behind the ear of a member of the audience, or from their hair.

It's good to have a special, extra shiny penny, which you keep in your pocket at all times and which you consider your 'magic' penny. Then you can practise your coin tricks whenever you fancy, to help relieve the boredom of long bus or train journeys for example.

* With the back of the hand held towards your audience, hold your penny by the edges, between the first finger and thumb of your left hand, level with your shoulder (diagram A). With your forefinger and thumb outstretched, bring your right hand towards the left, as if you are going to take the coin in your right hand. With your right hand obscuring the left, allow the coin to drop into the left hand, and 'palm' or conceal it, either by holding it clenched in the flesh of the palm, or by covering it with your thumb. Keep your left hand quite open and relaxed, and as the coin falls, close the right hand tight (as if clasping the coin) and move your hands apart (diagram B).

After a few bits of banter, pretend to draw the coin from behind the ear, armpit or some other part of a person in your audience with your left hand in which the coin is palmed. They will be concentrating on the closed, but empty, right hand, believing it is holding the coin.

diagram A

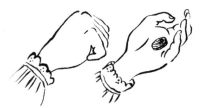

diagram B

MAKE A PENNY VANISH BY SLEIGHT OF HAND

*   Borrow a penny from a member of your audience, and show it lying on the fingers of your right hand. Now, throw it from one hand to the other a few times allowing the spectators to see it go from hand to hand. After a few tosses, catch the coin between the first and second fingers of the right hand and hold it there (diagram A). This time you only pretend to toss it to the left hand, which you clasp shut immediately as if you have just caught the coin (diagram B). Rub the fingers of the left hand a little, and then open this hand to show that the penny has magically disappeared. With the coin hidden in your right hand, make great show of making it reappear from the ear or the pocket of one of your spectators.

diagram A   diagram B

HOW TO PASS A TWO-PENCE PIECE THROUGH A 1.5 CENTIMETRE SQUARE

This trick may well seem impossible because the coin is much bigger than 1.5 centimetres in diameter, but in fact it can be done quite easily without tearing the paper. This is how.

*   Take a piece of paper and cut out a 1.5 centimetre square. Fold the paper in half, and place the coin in the fold. Carefully bend the paper upwards and outwards. You will see the coin drops through the hole quite easily. Give your friends the piece of paper and the coin and ask them to try. They will look befuddled and claim it is impossible (unless they know the trick!). Then demonstrate how it is done.

A DISAPPEARING COIN

Take a clean handkerchief and rub one corner with some uncoloured soap. Lay the hankerchief flat on a table with the soaped corner pointing towards you and place a penny in the centre (diagram A). Now fold over the (soaped) corner to cover the coin, then fold in the other corners as shown (diagram B).

Demonstrate that the coin is still in the hanky by inviting the audience to feel it. Place your fingers inside one of the folds with your thumbs underneath (diagram C) and quickly draw your hands sideways and apart, while catching two corners in your fingers and shaking out the hanky. The coin, which to all appearances will have disappeared, will be caught in your fingers.

The secret of this trick is that the soaped corner is covering the coin, and the coin will stick slightly to this corner, enabling you to catch it with ease between your fingers.

Of course, as with all good magic tricks, this needs a little practice, but with dedication you will soon be an expert. The more flamboyantly and quickly the hanky is lifted the more convincingly the coin will disappear.

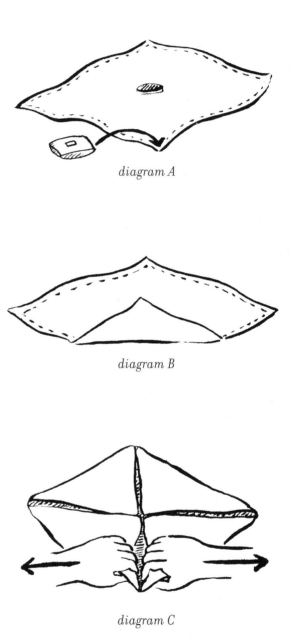

diagram A

diagram B

diagram C

A CARD AND COIN TRICK

* Balance a playing card on the tip of the index finger of your left hand. Balance a penny on the centre of the card, making sure it is exactly over the pad of your finger. Flick the corner of the card sharply with the nail of your right index finger, with a good straight flick. With a little practice, the card should spin away leaving the penny balancing on your finger.

A MATCHBOX TRICK

This is a very simple trick but well worth doing and very amusing to watch.

* Tell your friends you can make a matchbox carry out your every command. All you need is a small empty matchbox. Open the box a little and put it open side down over your knuckles with your hand held flat. Close the box so it catches the flesh on the knuckles and squeezes it into the box. Now, just close your hand into a fist and the matchbox should stand up straight on end.

  Distract the audience with your banter and by waving your other hand over the matchbox as it is raised and lowered as if by the magic force of your fingers.

MORE MATCHBOX MAGIC

You can have a good little joke with just a plain matchbox and a few matches.

* Get two ordinary identical matchboxes, cut the label side from one of them and stick it to the reverse side of the other so you have a double-sided matchbox with identical labels on each side. Take the tray out, and on its bottom glue a row of unused matches. Slide the tray back into its double-sided cover.

  When you open the box it will be empty, but when flipped over accompanied by the words 'Hey presto!', it will open to reveal a seemingly full box of matches. Alternatively, show the full side to an audience member so they can see the matches, then, without them noticing, turn the box over, hand it to them and ask them to open it. When they do, the matches will have vanished.

HALLOWEEN AND
GUY FAWKES

When we were children Halloween was quite an occasion. Great planning would go into deciding on our costumes and choosing a mask from the newsagent's shop for a Halloween party held in the kitchen or in someone's barn. Afterwards we'd go out with a gang of friends and knock on doors to collect whatever we were offered, usually sweets and nuts, but sometimes money. We didn't trick or treat as they do in America – the sight of our ghoulish outfits and the fact that we had ventured out in the dark with our turnip lanterns tied to sticks when it was freezing cold and often raining was enough to merit our rewards.

Pumpkin Lanterns

Pumpkins didn't exist when we were children, so we had to make do with smelly old hard turnips for our Halloween lanterns to decorate the tables and windows. They were devilishly hard to carve, so, if you can lay your hands on a nice jolly orange pumpkin, leave the turnips for the soup.

Pumpkin lanterns can quickly shrivel up or go a bit soggy at the cut edges, so it's best not to start too early. Wait until a day or two before Halloween night, if you can, and, once carved, sit your pumpkins on a windowsill or in a cool place. Try rubbing some Vaseline round the cut edges to help stop the wrinkling.

* Choose a nicely shaped, evenly coloured pumpkin and avoid any bruised or cracked specimens. Huge carved pumpkins look spectacular, but smaller ones tend to have firmer flesh, so they will last longer.

  Make sure the pumpkin will stand without wobbling; if it is unsteady cut a little off the bottom to even it out. Slice the lid off the top, carving out a square 'tooth' shape so it's easier to replace the lid later. Use your hands to pull out as much of the flesh and seeds as you can, then use a pointed spoon or an ice-cream scoop to scrape out the rest. Carve out the pumpkin flesh to about a centimetre in thickness so the light will shine more brightly.

  Now you are ready to carve a ghoulish face – smaller girls should rope in their parents for the tricky carving bits. Use a pencil to draw your face directly onto the pumpkin or first sketch a scary face on some paper. Keep it simple – square eyes, a triangle nose, and a nice big mouth with spooky crooked teeth. Tape your drawing on the pumpkin, then mark out the outline by making small puncture marks through the lines with a pencil. Remove the paper and carve along the outline – use a sharp pointed knife to make the first incision, then with a small serrated kitchen knife use a sawing motion to carve out the shapes.

  Put a lit tea light or candle in a holder inside the pumpkin, put on the lid and place it in the window and let the ghostly goings-on commence.

Halloween Outfits

Dressing up for Halloween in our households has always been a case of improvisation with some rapid last-minute cutting and sewing thrown in for good measure. You can buy a few accessories — a witch's hat or some devil's horns, then scout around the wardrobes and dressing-up box and create a ghastly and ghostly outfit from what you have to hand. Look out for suitable pieces in charity shops which can then be customized to fit your look — for a witch's outfit, hunt for black lace dresses and blouses, black net underskirts and chiffon scarves. For Dracula, use a man's white dress shirt with ruffles and a long black dinner jacket. For a zombie, you could buy a man's black suit jacket which you can then rip and shred.

*   Use face paints or buy a hideous mask to add the finishing touch to the outfit. After all, the aim of Halloween is not to look gorgeous, but to scare the living daylights out of everyone!

Ask permission before you start to cut up any of your mum or dad's 'old' clothes. And bear in mind that if you are planning a night of trick or treating it will be chilly, so lots of layers are advisable or you'll spend a miserable night with your teeth chattering.

WITCH'S OUTFIT

Make a cape by cutting a half circle of black silky lining material or net fabric and stitch some black ribbon to the top to tie round the shoulders. Dress all in black — wear a long-sleeved black top and skirt or borrow an old black dress from your mum. Layering different types of all-black fabric is very effective — a big lacy long-sleeved top worn under a short T-shirt, for example, will give a spider-webby look.

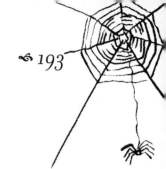
* To customize a skirt, cut out some patches from odds and ends of fabric and tack them on; use silver or gold fabric for moon and star shapes.

Wear black fishnet tights over plain bright green or red tights for a really good witchy look; make some holes in the fishnets.

Paint your nails with black, blood-red or green nail varnish. For make-up, paint your face white, then use a sponge and green face paint to add a spooky tinge. Add some black spots for warts and draw in some wrinkles round the eyes and mouth and on the forehead. Paint your lips a dark red or black – and black out a tooth or two.

Make a pointed witch's hat – you will need two large sheets of thick black art card. Cut a large semicircle from one sheet and roll it to form a pointy cone shape – staple or tape it down the edge. To make the brim, cut a large circle, roughly 30 centimetres in diameter, from the other sheet of black card and use a small plate to draw another circle inside. Cut out the inner circle and cut tabs so that the brim fits neatly into the cone – fix with glue or tape. Add some green hair – use lengths of green wool, or cut strips of green crêpe paper and glue them to the inside of the hat.

Make a witch's broom – find a good strong stick or tree branch, or use an old broom handle. Gather thin twigs from the garden and attach them to the end of the broom with thick black tape or tie them on with a black shoelace.

GHOST

The classic ghost outfit is simply a white sheet, or a pillowcase for smaller girls, with two holes cut for the eyes, and some slashes cut into the bottom.

* Or you could cut a hole in the centre of a sheet big enough for your head to fit through. Add several layers of shimmery white fabric or some white netting or lacy material, also with a hole cut for the head, over the sheet for a floaty effect.

Wear a ghost mask, or paint your face all in white – you could use flour or talcum powder – then brush black face paint round the eyes and mouth. Whiten your hair with talcum powder or spray it with silver and white hair colouring.

Ghoulish Tricks

DRACULA TEETH

Next time you fancy an orange, cut it in quarters rather than peeling and eating it in segments. That way you can make yourself a nice set of alarming and scary-looking gnashers. These are very good as an emergency fallback accessory at Halloween.

* Cut an orange into quarters. Eat the quarters. Take one section of orange peel and lay it flat on a chopping board and, using a knife, cut out some pointed teeth shapes. Open your mouth quite wide and pop the false Dracula teeth into your mouth, pith side out, in front of your own teeth and over your gums. With your Dracula fangs in place, tap someone gently on the shoulder to get their attention, open your mouth wide and flash your smile.

FAKE BLOOD RECIPE

* red food colouring
* green food colouring
* egg cup
* spoon
* corn syrup
* cup

* Pour about 2 drops of red food dye and 1 drop of green food dye (depending on how light or how dark you want your blood to be) into the egg cup and mix them together with a spoon. When you are satisfied with your blood colour, pour some corn syrup into a cup, add the food colouring and mix well.

  The fake blood can be poured down your face or used with fangs for a great Dracula effect at Halloween.

FAKE GLASS

This is a method for making very authentic-looking fake glass. Why, you might ask, would you want or need to make fake glass? Well, it can be used in combination with the fake blood at Halloween to scare the living daylights out of your granny or your parents. You can smash little sharp bits and arrange them so they are sticking out of your arm or chin, for example. If you are a little more ambitious, you could experiment with moulds to make fake glasses or props for home horror videos. Imagine the look of horror and disbelief on friends' faces if, at a party, you drain your fake glass, and suddenly start munching and swallowing it?

* Use a shallow baking tray to make sheets of glass, or a mould for plates and bowls. Be creative with the effect you'd like to achieve.

    * greaseproof paper or clingfilm
    * 2 teacups water
    * 3½ teacups sugar
    * 1 teacup corn syrup
    * clean saucepan

Line a baking tray or a mould with greaseproof paper or clingfilm – this will help stop the glass from sticking and allow easy removal.

Put the water, sugar and corn syrup in the saucepan and, over a medium heat, bring the mixture to the boil. Simmer gently until it has thickened and the water has boiled away. DO NOT be tempted to stick your finger in to see how it tastes – boiling syrup will cause a serious burn. Pour a thin layer of syrup onto the baking tray to make a sheet of glass or thinly cover the mould to make a bowl or plate shape. Allow it to cool until hardened (you can place in fridge or freezer to speed up the process).

TIP: *Don't leave your glass in direct sunlight – it will go soft and sticky. The fake glass will not keep for long, so use it quickly.*

Halloween Party Games

DUCKING FOR APPLES

Fill a large bowl or tub with cold water and float some apples in it. In pairs, or one by one, players kneel by the bowl with their hands behind their backs and must duck for the apples, attempting to get hold of one between the teeth and lift it from the basin without using the hands. (To make it even more tricky, players may also be blindfolded.) If a player is successful, they get to eat the apple.

TIPS:

* *If the apples are small, you may be able to suck one up from the bowl without getting your head wet!*

* *If you don't mind getting your hair wet, try the dive-bombing technique. Take aim, and plunge your head down into the water and pin an apple to the bottom of the bowl, then seize it with your teeth and emerge triumphant.*

* *Use your chin to nudge a bobbing apple to the side of the bowl — then grab it with your teeth.*

CHOCOLATE ON THE MOUND

We used to play this game straight after bobbing for apples while our faces were still wet. The combination of a damp face and flour was part of the messy appeal.

* On a plate, make a large mound of flour and place a chocolate on top. Put a knife by the plate. The players walk round the table and when they reach the knife they have to scoop away a slice from the edge of the flour mountain trying not to dislodge the chocolate. If the mountain collapses on your turn, you are unlucky and have to use your mouth to retrieve the chocolate from the plate of flour.

NUTCRACK NIGHT

* A way to tell your romantic fortune on Halloween night is to place two nuts side by side on the grate – one nut for the girl and one for a boy. If the nut which is the boy starts to blaze and burn, he holds you in high regard. If the nut jumps or cracks, the boy will prove unfaithful. And if the two nuts burn together, you love each other and will be married.

SCOFF THE SCONE

* This is an old Halloween game from Scotland. Spread some scones or pieces of bread thickly with black treacle, then hang them on strings attached to a broom handle. The broom is held up so the scones swing from their strings. With their hands behind their backs, the players must attempt to eat the scones. The broom may be raised just out of reach so players have to jump up to get a bite, the result being that faces are usually covered in treacle by the end of the game.

MUMMY RACE

* Divide your guests into teams of two to four players. Each team is given two rolls of toilet paper, and one person in the team is chosen as the mummy. The teams are given 5 minutes in which to 'bandage' the mummy as best as they can by passing the toilet rolls to each other to wrap the victim from head to foot. The team with the most convincing mummy at the end is the winner – and is exempt from rolling back all the toilet paper and clearing up the mess.

Bonfire Night

Guy Fawkes Night commemorates the Gunpowder Plot of 5 November 1605, when a group of conspirators including Guy Fawkes attempted unsuccessfully to blow up the Houses of Parliament in London. To celebrate this thwarted plot we traditionally have firework displays and burn an effigy of Guy Fawkes on a bonfire. In the days leading up to the fifth, children often use guys to beg for money, traditionally to buy fireworks, with the call, 'Penny for the guy.'

PENNY FOR THE GUY

Making your guy is a bit like making a scarecrow. You'll need an old pair of trousers, a shirt or an old jumper and an old white tea towel or pillowcase for the head. A pair of socks will make the feet and some gloves will make the hands.

* Tie the ends of the trousers and the shirt or jumper sleeves together and stuff them full of scrunched-up newspaper, rags or straw. Tuck the shirt or jumper into the trousers and attach it firmly. Stuff the socks and gloves and tie the openings with string, then stitch these feet and hands to the trouser bottoms and the ends of the sleeves.

   Put some newspaper or an old ball in the middle of the tea towel and tie it together round the neck. Sew buttons on for the eyes, or use felt-tipped pens to draw a face on the guy. Stick the loose ends of the tea towel well down into the shirt or jumper and use safety pins to attach the head to the collar. Dress the guy by adding a hat, a scarf and a jacket.

   In the past, children used to blacken their faces with soot before going out to collect money for the guy, which would be placed in a pram or a wheelbarrow. They'd pick a good spot, such as outside a cinema, and implore cinema-goers and passers-by to empty their pockets!

   On Bonfire Night the poor guy is put on the top of the bonfire and burnt as punishment for his dastardly plan to blow up the king.

TOFFEE APPLES MAKES 4–6

Toffee apples are deliciously crunchy and sweet – eat them while watching the firework display and while standing round the bonfire.

- ❋ 125g soft brown sugar
- ❋ 1 tsp cream of tartar
- ❋ ¼ cup water
- ❋ several eating apples

Put all the ingredients, except the apples, into a heavy pan. Stir on a low heat until the sugar has dissolved and then bring to the boil. Turn down the heat and simmer until the toffee thickens, stirring occasionally with a wooden spoon.

Test the consistency by dropping a small amount of toffee into a glass of cold water – if it's done it will immediately form a hard crunchy ball on contact with the water.

Insert strong lolly sticks or clean twigs from the garden firmly into each apple. Roll the apples carefully in the toffee and coat them generously. Put them upside down on a board covered with greaseproof paper to cool.

BOOKS, QUOTES AND FILMS

This is by no means a definitive list (that would take up this entire book, and some!). But here are a choice few books and films that we think every girl should get to know. Some are fun, some educational, some hopelessly romantic, some tragic, some just plain escapism. All, in any case, are better than watching rubbish telly.

Books

It would be impossible to list all the good books in the world; the following is a selection of classics which we loved when we were young, and still never tire of. These stories can all be read from the age of eight onwards.

The Flambards Trilogy by K. M. Peyton

* K. M. Peyton started writing when she was just nine years old. *The Flambards Trilogy* takes you into the lost era before the first world war of great, crumbling houses, gentlemen who had stables full of gleaming hunters, and rolling fields still ploughed by working horses. We follow the orphaned Christina, who leaves London and is plunged into this alien world, watch her grow from a nervous little girl into a strong and determined young woman, see her first love, follow her through the war itself, and finally come to her battle to salvage something from the wreckage of it all.

  Peyton provides a brilliant snapshot of life in the early twentieth century – prejudice against women, the poverty of the working people and the careless cruelty of the rich. She shows that kindness and determination are worth more than buckets of money. And in Christina she gives us a lovable heroine.

The Lion, the Witch and the Wardrobe by C. S. Lewis

* This is a story of four children, Peter, Susan, Edmund and Lucy, who discover a magical world called Narnia at the back of their wardrobe. There they meet many amazing and fantastical creatures, including Aslan, a brave and noble lion who is fighting to stop the evil White Witch from plunging Narnia into perpetual night. Although this is fantasy, it feels entirely real. *The Lion, the Witch and the Wardrobe* is the second in a series of seven books, known collectively as *The Chronicles of Narnia*. All the books in the series are dazzling, but this is the one that will get you hooked.

The Sadler's Wells Series by Lorna Hill

* These include *A Dream of Sadler's Wells*, *Veronica at the Wells*, *Jane Leaves the Wells* and *A Masquerade at Sadler's Wells*.

Most great books take you behind the scenes into a place you have never visited. These novels literally lift the curtain, leading you backstage into the world of the ballet. You can almost feel the lights and smell the greasepaint. The stories range from the wilds of Northumberland to the glamour of London and back to the mountains of Scotland. And of course the joy of a long series of books is that once you discover the first, you have so many more to look forward to.

The Chalet School Series by Elinor Brent-Dyer

* Madge Bettany sets up a school in the Austrian Tyrol for her sister Joey, whose health is too fragile for the treacherous London fogs. The school starts with just a handful of pupils, but grows into a grand success as children arrive from all over the world.

Part of the delight of the series is watching Joey and the other pupils grow up, marry and have children who go to the school in their turn. There are all the adventures, alarms and excursions, occasional danger and excellent school pranks that you'd expect and, in the ones set in Austria and Switzerland, a wonderful sense of the mountains and the wide outdoors. Although the first one was published in 1925, the novels are timeless. Forget *Mallory Towers*; these are the definitive boarding school books.

The Black Stallion Series by Walter Farley

* In *The Black Stallion*, young Alec Ramsey is taking a ship from Arabia to America. On the docks he sees a magnificent black stallion being loaded into the hold. The horse is kicking and screaming, as if fighting this horrible insult. The ship goes down, and boy and horse find themselves on a desert island. The heart of the story is the touching relationship that develops between them. It is a meeting of opposites – gentle boy and wild horse – and a moving story of the love and trust that can grow between humans and animals.

Luckily, there are fifteen books following on from this one and these are by far the best of all the horse stories.

The Hobbit by J. R. R. Tolkien

* This is the prequel to Tolkien's three-volume fantasy saga, *The Lord of the Rings*, but it's not as complicated and there aren't nearly as many nerdy battle scenes. It tells the story of a hobbit called Bilbo Baggins, who along with Gandalf, a great wizard, and a group of dwarves, sets out to retrieve a treasure being guarded by a huge dragon called Smaug. Along the way they meet a variety of terrifying and mysterious characters, including trolls, elves and giant spiders, and Bilbo steals a magical ring (the Ring, as it later turns out) from a weird creature called Gollum who lives deep inside a mountain. Honestly, you don't have to become one of those nutty *Lord of the Rings* fanatics to love this book.

Just So Stories by Rudyard Kipling

* Charming accounts of such things as 'How the Camel Got His Hump'. These are all short and easy to read; they are funny and wise and make you think a little. If you love these, you can go on to the *Jungle Book* stories by the same author.

The Blue Fairy Book by Andrew Lang

* Every girl should have a definitive book of fairy tales, not only because they are exciting, but because these myths and legends are where many of the great stories of literature come from. This collection contains beautifully written versions of all the classic fairy stories, from *Sleeping Beauty* to *Aladdin*.

Little Women by Louisa May Alcott

* *Little Women* (see film on page 211) is about four sisters growing up during the American Civil War. Each sister is different: the eldest, Meg, is very pretty; the second eldest, Jo (also the narrator), is clever and ambitious. Then there is Beth, shy and sweet, and the littlest, spoilt Amy. Together they learn to deal with the realities of life, overcoming many obstacles.

Tintin by Hergé

* Although these look like comic books, they are very sophisticated. Tintin, the intrepid boy reporter, the always grumpy Captain Haddock and Snowy the dog chase villains all over the world. There are many books in the series, and you will grow to love the rather strange characters – the deaf Professor Calculus, the upright butler Nestor, the bumbling Thompson and Thomson and, of course, Tintin and Snowy, always at the centre of every adventure. There are exotic locations from jungles and mountains to the moon and under the sea. Thundering typhoons!

The Incredible Journey by Sheila Burnford

* Two dogs and a cat trek two hundred miles across the Canadian wilderness to get home. They encounter many treacherous obstacles on the way, but through their touching devotion to each other and their determination they get back to their beloved owners.

The Happy Prince and Other Tales by Oscar Wilde

* These are some of the most poetic and moving stories ever written for children. They are gentle moral tales; some of them will make you cry, so it's probably best to read them alone with a box of tissues by your side – and possibly a biscuit.

The Silver Sword by Ian Serraillier

* If we were forced to choose one absolutely favourite book from our youth, this would be it. The Balicki family are Polish and are torn apart when the Nazis capture Warsaw. When their parents are taken away to labour camps, the three children are left as orphans in a chaotic city. The novel tells how they adapt and survive in a world devastated by war, and follows their long and treacherous journey to the safety of Switzerland. Although sometimes very sad, this is ultimately an inspiring story of courage and hope. And it reminds us all how lucky we are.

My Family and Other Animals by Gerald Durrell

* A book of enchanting bugs, bats, geckos and owls and an eccentric family in the sleepy heat of Corfu. This is the slightly embellished but true story of when the young Gerald Durrell, already obsessed by all forms of wildlife, spent five years on a Greek island. One brother is artistic, the other down-to-earth, and his sister would like to be glamorous and is rather vain. They accumulate lots of animal friends, hangers-on and dogs with peculiar names.

  After reading this book, you may be overcome with a pressing desire to spend all your time lying on your belly in long grass tracking the progress of the red ant. Well, we were.

The Pursuit of Love by Nancy Mitford

* Glamorous, dotty and packed with very posh people falling in love and making excellent jokes. This is the story of another eccentric family, the Alconleighs, also based on real-life characters, although they are more interested in Labradors than ants. It is very funny and filled with deliciously bizarre characters – Lord Merlin dyes his pigeons pink – but at its core it is a book about the human heart; it examines the deep, enduring bonds of friendship and the wild romantic love all girls yearn for.

Sprig Muslin by Georgette Heyer

* This is just one of many novels by Georgette Heyer. They are full of headstrong heroines, dashing men in breeches and plenty of people saying things like 'Lud, sir.' Don't be put off by the fact that these novels are quite dense, and may include some nineteenth-century words you don't recognize – once you get into the swing of them, you will feel as if you have been whisked off by a time-traveller to a world of shiny carriages, muslin dresses, aristocratic town houses and eight-course dinners. There is love, usually misunderstanding, quite often someone planning to flee to the border, brave and forthright young ladies and extremely handsome and well-dressed gentlemen. Once you have found yourself in this world, you may never want to leave.

OTHER GREAT CLASSICS
YOU MIGHT ALSO LIKE . . .

* *Aesop's Fables* by Aesop
* *Alice in Wonderland* by Lewis Carroll
* *Ballet Shoes* by Noel Streatfeild
* *Better To Arrive* by Glenda Gordon
* *The Borrowers* by Mary Norton
* *Fantastic Mr Fox* by Roald Dahl
* *Five Children and It* by E. Nesbit
* *Little House on the Prairie* by Laura Ingalls Wilder
* *The Little Prince* by Antoine de Saint-Exupéry
* *The Little Princess* by Frances Hodgson Burnett
* *Mary Poppins* by P. L. Travers
* *Mrs Frisby and the Rats of Nimh* by Robert C. O'Brien
* *Treasure Island* by Robert Louis Stevenson
* *Swallows and Amazons* by Arthur Ransome
* *The Water Babies* by Charles Kingsley
* *Watership Down* by Richard Adams
* *What Katy Did* by Susan Coolidge
* *The Wind in the Willows* by Kenneth Grahame
* *The Secret Garden* by Frances Hodgson Burnett
* *Pollyanna* by Eleanor H. Porter
* *Anne of Green Gables* by L.M. Montgomery

You may find that some of these, being of a venerable age, are out of print.
The best place to find them is www.amazon.co.uk or www.abebooks.com
on the Internet, often at very reasonable prices.

Virginia Woolf (1882–1941)

* Virginia Woolf was an author whose fascinating diaries and groundbreaking novels marked a turning point in female writing. One of eight brothers and sisters, she grew up in London and St Ives (in Cornwall). Her mother's sudden death when Virginia was thirteen left her devastated and led to the first of many nervous breakdowns. Although she never went to school or university, she began writing down her thoughts from a young age and through her brother's friends from Cambridge became an important member of the Bloomsbury Set, an influential group of intellectuals, writers and thinkers. She married Leonard Woolf in 1912.

In a too short life, she wrote a clarion call to women's independence in A Room of One's Own and published ten works of fiction, including Mrs Dalloway, which we think is one of the most admirable novels in the English language. She battled against mental illness with great courage all through her life, but, tragically, it defeated her in the end and she committed suicide.

The Nine Daughters of Zeus

* The nine daughters of Zeus were not strictly women, on account of being the mythical daughters of the mythical Zeus, king of the gods. They were the result of the union between Zeus and Mnemosyne, daughter of Uranus and Gaia, and were known as the Muses, inspiring history, tragedy, poetry and dance. They each specialized in a specific art form and were, in no particular order, Calliope (epic poetry), Clio (history), Erato (love poetry), Euterpe (lyric song), Terpsichore (dance), Melpomene (tragedy), Polyhymnia (sacred song), Thalia (comedy) and Urania (astronomy). They were essentially benign creatures, but could get very huffy if challenged and once turned some rivals into birds.

Temples were built to them, statues carved of them, cults formed around them. Much of the great culture of the ancient world was produced in their name. They are mostly represented wafting around in chiffon, dedicated to their art. Thousands of years later, muses still hold sway, although they tend to be nice girls called Arabella rather than actual goddesses.

Quotes

'Think of all the beauty still around you and be happy'
Anne Frank

'A girl should be two things: classy and fabulous'
Coco Chanel

'Grown-ups never understand anything for themselves, and it is tiresome for
children to be always and forever explaining things to them'
Antoine de Saint-Exupéry

'If a girl seems as shy as a mouse, you still have to look out for the tiger within her'
Chinese proverb

'No act of kindness, no matter how small, is ever wasted'
Aesop

'He deserves Paradise who makes his companions laugh'
Koran

'Age is foolish and forgetful when it underestimates youth'
J. K. Rowling – Harry Potter and the Half-Blood Prince

'Who, being loved, is poor?'
Oscar Wilde

'The most important thing in life is not the triumph but the struggle.
The essential thing is not to have conquered but to have fought well'
Pierre de Coubertin

'What the world really needs is more love and less paperwork'
Pearl Bailey

*
*'I'm tired of all this nonsense about beauty only being skin deep.
That's deep enough. What do you want — an adorable pancreas?'*
Jean Kerr

'Remember, no one can make you feel inferior without your consent'
Eleanor Roosevelt

'Beauty is not in the face, beauty is a light in the heart'
Khalil Gibran

'All who would win joy, must share it; happiness was born a twin'
Lord Byron

*'I mean, what am I supposed to call you? My girlfriend? My companion?
My roommate? Nothing seems quite right.'
'How about your "Reason for Living"?'*
Garry Trudeau

'Noble deeds and hot baths are the best cures for depression'
Dodie Smith

'As a woman I have no country. As a woman my country is the entire world'
Virginia Woolf

'You don't have to brush your teeth — just the ones you want to keep'
Unknown

'Dream as if you'll live forever. Live as if you'll die today'
James Dean

Fab Films

Gone with the Wind (1939)

*   Nearly four and a half hours of Hollywood histrionics, and the tightest bodice ever laced. Vivien Leigh is the feisty Scarlett O'Hara and Clark Gable the masterful Rhett Butler. Their stormy romance is played out against the smoke and guns of the American Civil War. One big glorious hissy fit of a film. You'll laugh, you'll cry, you'll get cramp if you don't remember to get up and walk around during it.

National Velvet (1945)

*   This tale of a schoolgirl who wins a horse and rides it to victory in the Grand National is so much more than the sum of its parts. It has Elizabeth Taylor in it! It has horses! What more could a girl want?

The Red Shoes (1948)

*   If you love dance, you'll love this film. It's all about a young ballerina (the divine and lovely Moira Shearer) who is torn between art (ballet) and life (well, love, actually). It has everything: drama, passion, great costumes and lashings of tragedy – all in gloriously garish Technicolor.

Roman Holiday (1953)

*   Audrey Hepburn, Gregory Peck and the Eternal City (Rome), all combine to make this one of the most romantic films ever. Hepburn is a European princess, bored and in search of adventure; Peck is a hardened reporter. Slowly and surely they fall in love. Hepburn is the epitome of chic beauty; Peck is the perfect gentleman, even when riding a scooter. It's also proof, if proof were needed, that Rome, not Paris, is the true romantic capital of the world.

Lady and the Tramp (1955)

*   As fresh as if it were made yesterday, and still the most charming of all the Disney films: two dogs from opposite sides of the tracks fall in love. Will make you laugh and make you cry, and you'll never get too old for it.

Grease (1978)

*   John Travolta and Olivia Newton-John dance and sing their way through the cheesiest, crassest musical in the history of the world ever. Zero artistic merit; excellent hairstyles. The tunes aren't bad either: 'Totally Devoted To You'; 'You're the One That I Want'; 'Summer Nights'. Perfect for sleepover singalongs.

The Secret Garden (1993)

*   This is a near-faithful retelling of the wonderful book by Frances Hodgson Burnett. Three children from very different worlds discover a universe all of their own behind a long-forgotten locked door. Ravishingly filmed, brilliant acting and gorgeous scenery. A five-Kleenex movie.

Little Women (1995)

*   In this adaptation of Louisa May Alcott's classic coming-of-age tale, Susan Sarandon plays the perfect mother and Winona Rider is determined yet winsome as the heroine Jo. There's hardship, war, illness and suitors, as well as lots of lovely snow, pretty frocks and a few universal truths. Guaranteed to make you cry, but in a good way.

Lassie (2005)

*   A rare example of a remake beating the original. Sweeping shots of glorious Scotland, Peter O'Toole as the ultimate eccentric toff, an affecting central character and, of course, the cleverest and most heavenly dog. Give the mutt an Oscar. Woof, woof.

Pride and Prejudice (2005)

*   The beginner's guide to Jane Austen. Lovely frocks, brooding men on wilful horses and more smouldering glances than you can shake a stick at. Definitive proof that feistiness can get you a happy ending AND a large mansion to go with it. Try not to be distracted by Mr Bennet's odd Canadian accent and a bewildering number of shots featuring geese and other wildfowl.

KEY: girliness · love · tearjerker · diva · hunk factor

HOME SPA

When you're grown-up and earning your own money you'll be able to waste as much of it as you like on professional spa treatments. Until that day, however, there's nothing to stop you from creating your own spa in the comfort of your family bathroom.

Skin Care

Look after your skin and it'll look after you. Skin is the biggest organ in the human body, and the one that gets the most exposure to the elements. It's also a lot more complex than it appears, and can often be an indicator of a person's general health. Good skin will make you look fab; bad skin can make you feel drab.

There are many factors that affect your skin — diet, genes, hormones — but establishing and maintaining a good skin-care routine is never a waste of time. The sooner you get the hang of it the better, and before you know it looking after your skin won't seem like a chore but will be as second-nature as brushing your teeth.

Most beauty routines recommend three steps: cleansing, toning and moisturizing. Clean skin is very important, as the cleaner the skin the fewer the impurities and the brighter and better it looks. Toning is not essential, but it is very nice, since toners generally contain things like lavender or rose which are uplifting. As for moisturizing, don't think that just because you have oily skin or a tendency to spots, you shouldn't moisturize. Moisture is good for the skin; it's oil and bacteria that cause spots.

Ideally, you should cleanse, tone and moisturize morning and night, but if you can only manage once a day, make it in the evenings so you don't take the grime of the day to bed with you.

THE MOST IMPORTANT INGREDIENTS FOR THE PERFECT HOME SPA ARE:

* **A vast fluffy towelling robe and a decent pile of towels** – ideally, white. Don't ask why, that's just what works best. If you haven't got a towelling robe at all, a dressing gown will do.

* **A clean and tidy bathroom.** This may seem obvious, but if you're trying to create a sanctuary you can't have hairy plugholes or your brother's smelly trainers spoiling the effect. You'll also need some clean, flat surfaces for arranging products and potions on.

* **Ingredients.** The following pages describe home-made remedies, all of which require different ingredients. You should decide which ones you are going to attempt and get everything together first.

* **A plan.** Broadly speaking, a good all-round spa experience should include the following: face scrub and face mask; body scrub; manicure; pedicure. You can embellish, of course. An eye mask is always a good thing to do, although it can be quite antisocial if you're spa-ing with friends. A hair pack or scalp-conditioning treatment can work wonders, although it's best not to combine spa-ing with hair colouring as the latter is messy and not at all conducive to relaxation.

* **A friend.** Or even two. Share the gloop. Compare softness of skin. Gossip, giggle, swap tips.

* **Accessories:** one large bowl and several smaller ones; a wooden spoon and a spatula (for applying gloop); hot flannels (for opening pores and generally wiping things up); tissues; toe separators (although you can use rolled-up tissue for this); nail scissors/clippers; nail brush (optional); cotton buds; cotton wool (pads if possible, otherwise balls are fine); hair bands (for keeping it away from your face); a measuring jug and/or some old bottles or cartons for mixing liquids in.

* **Refreshments.** No spa is complete without a health-giving smoothie and some divine little biscuits to keep the wolf from the door while you wait for your nail polish to dry. Fruit smoothies are best, since they're packed with vitamins and minerals which are also good for your skin. You should also have a large jug of tap water on hand, into which you've sliced a little lemon or lime – or both.

Now that you've got everything ready, you'll be raring to get down to some actual treatments.

Beauty Cupboard Basics

Here are some useful things which can be used either on their own or as part of more complicated concoctions.

* **Vaseline:** a good, cheap general all-round emollient. If you're out and about in cold windy weather it will keep your lips from getting chapped and soothe your runny nose. It's also brilliant for getting out of tight spots (if you ever get a ring stuck on a finger, for example, a bit of Vaseline will help slide it off). Use also on dry knees and elbows.

* **Sweet almond oil:** a wonderful basic oil that smoothes and soothes the skin, hair and nails without being greasy. Great as a base oil, but just as effective on its own.

* **Witch hazel:** a good all-round mild antiseptic.

* **Rose water and lavender water:** simple, effective toners.

* **Aloe vera gel:** handy for sunburn, eczema, or just to soften and nourish the skin.

Face

HOME-MADE FACIAL SCRUB

Always avoid the eye area, obviously. Grit in the eye is not conducive to a relaxing spa experience. Here are recipes for two scrubs – use whichever suits you best or alternate!

* Mash up two strawberries with a teaspoon of soft brown sugar (e.g. muscovado). Gently rub the mixture over the face, concentrating on the area around the nose and chin. Rinse off with cold water.

  Mix one tablespoon of honey, half a teaspoon of lemon juice and two teaspoons of fine oatmeal (porridge oats). Gently rub it over your face as before and wash off with warm water.

HOME-MADE FACE MASKS

Some people swear by a mashed-up banana, others by a mashed avocado mixed with a little honey. Both are moisturizing and full of goodness. Leave them on for ten minutes while lying down and think calm and beautiful thoughts.

* For the full spa effect, place a slice of cucumber (taken straight from the fridge) over each eye. Alternatively, you can soak cotton pads in water or a little cooled weak tea (camomile is best, unless you're allergic to it; otherwise green tea will work just as well; don't use PG Tips – you'll end up looking like a panda). Leave them in the fridge for an hour, and then put them over the eyes for a wonderful cooling treatment.

STEAMING

Steam can have quite miraculous effects on skin. It opens the pores, improves the circulation of the blood and helps cleanse the skin of impurities. It's especially great for gently coaxing out stubborn blackheads and lingering spots. It's also good for your lungs to breathe in the hot steam.

* All you need for a good facial steam is a large bowl, some boiling water (obviously ask an adult to help here), a towel big enough to cover your head and shoulders and something comfortable to sit on.

Wash your face and tie your hair back. Pour boiling water into the bowl or sink. Position yourself with your head over the bowl. Your face needs to be close enough to get a decent amount of steam on it, but not so close that you scald yourself. Put the towel over your head so it also covers the rim of the bowl. The aim is to trap all the lovely steam inside the towel so it can go to work on your face. Breathe slowly and deeply. Stay there for about 5 minutes.

When you're done, splash your face with cold water (to close the pores) and finish with a toner – either rose water or some soothing aloe vera gel.

If you like, you can add flowers or herbs. Lavender is excellent, as it has soothing and disinfectant properties. Lemon and mint make a wonderful combination – just a couple of slices of lemon and a few fresh leaves of mint.

Body

Given that we spend most of our lives wearing clothes, it's easy to forget that the skin on our bodies needs looking after too.

YUMMY SCRUMMY ON MY TUMMY CHOCOLATE BODY SCRUB

* Take five tablespoons of sunflower oil and four tablespoons of soft brown sugar, and add one heaped teaspoon of cocoa (NOT drinking chocolate, it must be the Real Thing). Mix thoroughly. You will have a wonderful gloopy chocolatey scrub – quite runny, so best to use it all over your skin while in the shower and be careful when applying. Wash it off thoroughly with your favourite soap or body wash, and your skin will feel like velvet.

SUGAR AND LIME BODY SCRUB

* Mix five tablespoons of olive oil with four tablespoons of caster sugar, and add five drops of lime essential oil. Please be careful when using essential oils; they are very concentrated, so you should never use more than recommended, and never use them directly on your skin. This will give you a fabulously invigorating scrub – breathe in deeply as you apply it and you can imagine you are in a Caribbean lime grove. Or a lime grove in any location you fancy, really.

BATH SACHETS

These are like little tea bags for the bath, giving you a heavenly infusion.

* Take a handful of dried or fresh lavender, wrap it up in a square of muslin, and secure the ends with string or a rubber band. Put it in your bath and let the delicious herbs steep for five minutes. You can also use dried camomile heads, which are good for calming and soothing, dried or fresh rosemary, which clears the mind, and dried rose petals, which lift the spirits.

  They are also perfect as presents.

Hair

To nourish and encourage hair growth, gently heat a small amount of almond oil. You can do this by putting the oil in a small bottle or bowl, and then putting the bottle in another bowl of hot water. After about five minutes the oil will be nicely warm (but not too hot). Apply it to the hair (no need to use gloves, as the oil is good for your hands and nails too). Pop on a disposable bath hat (or if you don't have one, wrap your hair first in cling film, then in a towel) and sit for fifteen minutes thinking happy, long-haired thoughts.

THE MOVIE-STAR WRAP

How to put your hair in a towel like a movie star. Take one medium-sized towel and bend forward so your head is upside down. If you have long hair, let it all fall down over the front of your head. Holding the towel horizontally, place its halfway point on the nape of your neck. Draw the sides of the towel in towards the crown of your head, covering your ears. Now twist it (clockwise or anti, it's up to you) and, standing up, flip the remaining bit of the towel over the back of your head. Tuck the end in underneath the nape of your head. Adjust your ears. (Some people like to keep them half in, others fully hidden. Best not have them completely out, as you can look a bit silly.) Prepare for your close-up.

Refreshments

SMOOTHIES

* The key to a perfect smoothie is FROZEN fruit. You can buy frozen summer fruits in the supermarket, or just select your own and put them in the freezer overnight. Take two handfuls of frozen mixed berries, a glass of good orange juice, blitz in the blender, and that's it. Could not be more simple or delicious. If you are feeling very naughty, you can put a little whirl of whipped cream on the top. A sprig of mint goes very well too.

  You can adapt this recipe with other fruit to your own taste – small chunks of frozen mango, banana and pineapple all work well. You can also adjust the consistency – the thicker you want the smoothie, the more fruit you use.

STRAWBERRIES DIPPED IN CHOCOLATE

These are so easy to make it's not true, plus they are supremely good both for mind and body, since chocolate, it's well known, makes you feel happy, and strawberries are very good for you. If you don't like strawberries, cherries are just as good. In winter, try using dates.

* Take a large bar of good-quality chocolate (dark is best). Break it up into pieces and put them in a bowl. This goes in a bain-marie (see page 67). While the chocolate is slowly melting (give it a stir every now and again to make sure it doesn't burn), lay out some greaseproof paper on a tray. Wash your fruit. When the chocolate has all melted, remove it from the heat. Now grasp a strawberry firmly by the stalk and dip it into the chocolate. Pop it on the greaseproof paper. Continue until all the fruit has been dipped and/or you run out of chocolate.

  Place the tray in the fridge for at least an hour. Serve with decorative sprigs of mint.

Hands

Nails should always be kept short to medium length – never long, as this is very vulgar, not to say impractical. It's also imperative to keep them clean, as dirt underneath nails harbours lots of nasty bacteria.

FILING

Filing your nails is one of the easiest ways of maintaining length and shape.

* You should always file from the outer edge of the nail inwards, using gentle, even strokes. In terms of shape, the most natural one will echo the shape of your cuticle.

  Aim to get all the nails the same length. This means filing them to match the shortest one. Remember, the rounder and shorter you keep your nails, the stronger and better they will grow. Long, sharp nails snap more easily.

CLIPPING

If you have very strong, hard nails, then clipping is a good way of paring them down before you file them.

* Clip off the outer edges first then clip off the top bit. If you just clip the nail across the top, you may very well end up damaging it.

CUTTING

* Nail scissors are best reserved for toes, as only the truly ambidextrous are able to achieve good results on both hands.

BASIC MANICURE

* a small bowl of warm, soapy (use a mild cleanser or a drop of shower gel) water
* some cotton wool and cotton buds
* a nail file, nail clippers and a nail buffer (this is like a nail file but much less rough; it makes the surface of the nails shine)
* a clean towel
* a little olive oil and some salt flakes
* almond oil
* nail polish (optional)

Start by exfoliating your hands. Pour a few salt flakes (Malden Sea Salt works best) into the palm of your hand. Add a good glug of olive oil. Gently work the mixture together with the palms of your hands. Then, for a few minutes, rub it all over your hands and wrists, using a hand-washing motion. Rinse the hands under warm water and pat them dry with a towel. Rub in some almond oil.

If your nails are very long, do a preliminary cut using clippers. If you don't have any clippers, don't worry. You can file them all to the same length. When all your nails are done, put the fingers of one hand in the warm water and leave them to soak for a few minutes (about five). This will help soften the cuticles.

Remove your hand from the water and pat dry. Take a cotton bud; dip it in some almond oil and gently start pushing back the cuticles. It helps to slowly twirl the bud as you go so you gently lift the cuticles off the surface of the nail. When you've finished each nail, run your cotton bud underneath the nail tip to remove any bits of residual dirt or dust from the filing. Do the same to the other hand. When you've finished, wash and dry the hands.

Now buff your nails – only use very gentle pressure. The aim is to shine up your nails, not buff them to oblivion. Buff from side to side starting at the base of the nail. About ten strokes per nail should do the trick.

Finally, wipe the surface of each nail with a little nail-polish remover. If you're going to apply polish, now is the time. Begin with a clear polish, either a base coat or a strengthener. As to colour, that's a matter for you and your parents. Applying polish well takes a lot of practice.

Finally, massage a few drops of almond oil into your cuticles.

Feet

PEDICURE

The technique is much the same as for the manicure.

*   Always file the toenails as short as you comfortably can (long toenails and shoes don't mix), and always cut or file them straight across. Never be tempted to file down into the sides; you'll get ingrown toenails when you're older. This probably doesn't worry you now, but you'll thank us later. Remove any hard skin with a pumice stone. Do not cut it off, ever.

     If you're just off to bed, slather your feet in almond oil and pop on a pair of socks. Your feet will be extra-super especially soft in the morning.

AND FINALLY . . .

Banana skin applied to a wart will work wonders. Here's how:

   * Wash and dry the wart and surrounding skin.

   * Cut a suitable-sized piece of unripe banana skin and put it on the wart.

   * Fix it in place with a sticking plaster and leave it on for up to eight hours.

   * Remove, wash and repeat.

   * After a couple of weeks the wart should fall off.

Verrucas can be dealt with in a similar way, only using a piece of baked onion.

Alternatively, for both warts and verrucas you can try a homeopathic remedy called *thuja*. You can buy it in most health-food shops, and it really works. Follow the manufacturer's instructions, but usually one to three pillules a day will cause them to wither and disappear within a month to six weeks.

WINTER

In winter, the days get shorter and colder as the North Pole moves away from the sun. The trees lose their leaves and most plants die down and stop flowering. As it gets harder to find food and keep warm, some birds migrate to warmer countries and many animals go into hibernation. But the good news is that after the winter solstice, the shortest day of the year on either 21 or 22 December, the days start to get longer and brighter, there's Christmas and New Year to look forward to and, before you know it, it's spring again.

How to Keep Warm in Winter

Forcing yourself out from under a warm, snug duvet on a dark cold winter's morning and getting dressed is one of life's most trying tasks. A solution is to keep your pyjamas on, and put your clothes on top of them. After all, dressing for winter is all about layering!

* If you must take your pyjamas off due to school uniform restrictions, another tip is to create a tube of heat by wearing a long-sleeved vest to bed. In the morning pull your tights on while you're still in bed and tuck the vest into your tights, then layer over your other clothes. Keeping the vest tucked in at all times stops nasty cold gusts of air blowing up your jumper during the day.

Lots of thin layers will keep you warmer than one bulky jumper, and you can take off a layer or two if you get too hot on a walk or when inside. Most body heat is lost through the head, so always wear a warm hat in very cold weather.

HOW TO KEEP YOUR HANDS AND FEET WARM

* To keep your hands warm, mittens are much better than gloves, especially if they are extra cosy sheepskin ones. To stop them getting lost, pin or sew a long ribbon to each mitten and pass the ribbon and gloves through your coat sleeves.

Before you go out on a walk on a really cold day, microwave or bake two potatoes. Wrap them in a couple of layers of tin foil, and put them in your pockets to warm your hands and snack on later if you get hungry.

To keep your feet warm in wellington boots, wear two pairs of socks – one pair made of fine wool, with a thicker woollen or even thermal pair on top. Once outside, jumping on the spot, stamping and running get the circulation going and help keep the feet warm.

When you come inside, never get straight into a very hot bath or put your feet or hands directly on a radiator or very close to the fire when they are freezing cold or you could get nasty things called chilblains. Chilblains are very painful and make your toes feel hot and itchy – to be avoided at all costs!

Snowflakes

On the 28 January 1887, the world's largest snowflake fell at Fort Keogh, in Montana, America – it was a truly mammoth 38 centimetres wide and 20 centimetres thick.

* In order for snow to fall, the air temperature has to be below freezing. Water droplets in clouds freeze to form ice crystals, and as they fall through the clouds, they bump into and join with other crystals to form a snowflake.

One of the wonders of snowflakes is that although they are always six-sided, it is believed no two snowflakes are identical – each is a unique, complex and beautiful miracle of natural design. Snowflakes can come in the form of hexagonal prisms, crystals, plates (flat), columns, needles, stars, dendrites (branching and fern-like) – the shape depends on the temperature and moisture content of the cloud in which they form.

Next time it snows, allow some snowflakes to fall on your fingers, then look closely to see if you can make out their form. Put your head back, open your mouth and catch snowflakes on your tongue as they fall.

SUCKING SNOW AND CRUNCHING ON ICICLES

* OK, this is probably a bit obvious, but if you are going to have a go at tasting snow, only ever eat extremely clean fresh snow, preferably first thing in the morning before any animals or other creatures have passed over it. If you live in the city, go out into the garden first thing after it has snowed, and take a handful from a hedge or the ground and pop it in your mouth. If there has been a really heavy snowfall, you could even take a whole bowlful of very clean snow, then squirt a dash of Ribena over it to create an instant snow-slush drink. If it is cold enough, you might find some icicles hanging from trees outside – these are good for crunching while out on a walk.

SNOWBALLS

As you will probably know from bitter experience, making the perfect snowball so that it lands with a satisfying and splattering whoomph on your unwitting target is not always as easy as it sounds.

* Firstly, the ideal snow for a snowball should be just above freezing. Too cold, and the snow will be dry and powdery and attempts to form a neat snowball will result in a crumbling mass. If it is this cold, find some snow in an area where it has warmed up a bit as it will be wetter and easier to make into a ball. Snow lying near the house, for example, will be warmer than snow lying in the middle of a field.

    While mittens are generally warmer, gloves are better for snowballing as they give more flexibility in the fingers – so put on some waterproof gloves if possible.

    Now to make the snowballs. Cup your hands together and gather enough snow to fill them. Close your hands, gently squeezing and twisting so the snow forms a ball. Don't squeeze too hard or too quickly or the snowball will fall to pieces under the pressure. When the snowball feels firm enough, gradually add a little more pressure so it grows firm and nicely rounded in your hand.

    If you are building up a stash of snowballs, all the better. Put them in a safe place as you make them. They will firm up nicely in the cold air. If you are having a battle, you might like to build a low-lying snow wall or fort from which to launch your assault, and stash a snowball arsenal there, safe from marauders.

    A few final words of advice:

    * Don't throw snowballs at complete strangers, the postman or old ladies at bus stops.

    * Don't aim directly at the face or head of an opponent at close range.

    * Don't throw snowballs at really tiny siblings – it will only make them cry.

SNOWMEN

If the weather conditions and snow are right for making a good snowball and there is enough snow on the ground, then that's all you need to get going on the more ambitious project of snowman-making.

* Start by making a snowball as above, then make it bigger and bigger until it is too large to fit into your hands. Roll the snowball along the ground to gather the snow changing direction from time to time so it remains nice and round and grows in size. It takes time, but it's good exercise and will keep you warm.

A traditional snowman is made of three balls – a small one for the head, middle-sized for the middle section, and large for the bottom of the body – but if the snow supply is limited, you can make it with one large ball for the body and a smaller one for the head.

When you are ready to assemble the snowman, lift the middle-sized snowball onto the largest ball and pat it down gently to make sure it is steady and secure. Add a little more snow round the join, packing it in tightly. Finally, position the head on the body, and again use extra snow round the join. Add a carrot for the nose, two pieces of coal for the eyes and long thin twigs for arms and hands. Hat, scarf, mittens, glasses, pipe and shoes are all optional accessories.

TOBOGGANING

If there is lots of snow, and you live near a good, steep hill, you could try tobogganing. You don't need a fancy shop-bought sledge – an old tin tray or even a heavy-duty plastic bin bag will do just as well. You might want to wear a cycle helmet and some gloves to protect your extremities both from the cold and bumps.

* Stand at the top of the hill, and lay your tin tray or bin liner out flat in front of you. Position yourself in a comfortable seated position on the 'toboggan', and ask someone to get you started by giving you a shove on the back to send you gracefully and swiftly down the hill.

SNOW ANGELS

* The best snow for making snow angels is powdery and deep. Let yourself fall gently on your back onto the snow, your arms outstretched. (If the snow is very shallow, lie down in it rather than falling to avoid head and other injuries!) Move your arms down to your waist then up to your head a few times, making sweeping movements in the snow. This makes your angel wings. At the same time, move your legs apart as wide as you can, then together again in a scissor movement. This will make the shape of the angel's skirt. Ask someone to give you a hand to pull you up without disturbing the imprint your body has made in the snow.

PAPER SNOWFLAKES

* Draw circles round a mug on some paper. Cut the circles out. Fold each circle in half, then in half again, and in half again if you can. Use the scissors to snip out little shapes along the paper folds at the bottom and the tip of your wedge shape. Repeat with other paper circles to produce different snowflake patterns by making different cuts each time. Unfold and *voilà* – paper snowflakes to decorate a window or hang by white thread from the ceiling.

MAKING A BIRD FEEDER

It's good to feed birds by putting out scraps of bacon rind, bread soaked in water and fruit all year round, but especially in winter. To survive, birds must eat at least half their own weight in food each day, and in winter when the ground is hard and frosty and there is little food around, this can be quite a struggle. According to the RSPB, putting food out in winter probably saves the lives of up to a million garden birds each year.

You can buy seed mixtures specially made for garden birds – look out for ones with black sunflower seeds, flaked maize and peanut granules. Birds, especially blackbirds and thrushes, like to eat fruit, so put out some grapes or old apples. Robins like cheese and millet, and tits love sunflower seeds and nuts.

TO MAKE A HANGING FAT-CAKE FEEDER

* small empty yoghurt cartons
* string
* scissors
* 250g lard or suet (not margarine) at room temperature
* peanuts/black sunflower seeds/wild garden bird seed mix
* raisins
* grated cheese

Make a hole at the top of the cartons and thread some string through the hole. Tie a large knot on the inside to hold the string securely in place.

In a large mixing bowl chop the lard into cubes or crumble the suet, and gradually add roughly chopped peanuts, bird seed, raisins and grated cheese. Keep adding the dry ingredients, squeezing with your fingers until the mixture holds together in a firm, thick paste. Spoon it into the individual cartons and put in the fridge for 2 to 3 hours to harden, then hang them outside in the garden in a place safe from cats.

ANIMAL TRACKS

Winter is the best time for doing a little detective work. Next time you are outdoors, look closely at the ground and learn to identify the different prints. The clearest tracks are made in clean, hard snow, but with a little practice you'll be able to pick them out in the mud near water, along lanes and in woodland.

* Follow the tracks and look out for fur and feathers, berries, nuts and seeds near the tracks to get clues about what the animal or bird has eaten and when.

  You can also make casts of the animal prints you find and display them on your nature table. You will need:

  * strip of cardboard and paperclip
  * Vaseline
  * plaster of Paris
  * water
  * bowl and spoon

  Choose a really clear and well-defined print to make your cast. Clear away any leaves or twigs. Make a circular collar from the cardboard and secure it with a paperclip and place this around the print, making sure there is no space between it and the ground. This forms the mould into which you pour the plaster of Paris. To make the cast easier to remove when it's set, lightly smear the inside of the cardboard or plastic with some Vaseline.

  Mix the plaster and water in a bowl with a spoon following the instructions on the packet, and pour the plaster into the circle over the print. Leave it to set for about 10 to 15 minutes or according to the packet instructions. When it is dry, carefully remove the cast from the circle and turn it over to see the animal or bird print in relief on the plaster. When you get home, use an old toothbrush and a little warm water to gently clean away any soil. Write the date on the back in pencil so you can keep a record.

fox

rabbit

deer

sparrow

COLD REMEDIES

If you find yourself coming down with a horrible cold, a sore throat, a running or blocked-up nose, there are some simple home remedies that really do help.

For a blocked-nose, eat something hot and spicy, like a curry, to unblock your sinuses and help you breathe. Or put a whole garlic clove in one side of your mouth and gently bite down on it every now and again to release the juice.

If you have a sore throat and cough, prepare a soothing hot drink.

* juice of a lemon and/or a 5cm piece of fresh ginger, chopped roughly
* 1 cup boiling water
* 1 tsp honey

Squeeze the lemon and/or chopped ginger into the cup of boiling water, stir in honey to taste. Drink while warm.

SPICED HOT APPLE JUICE

* 1 litre apple juice
* 1 cup water
* 1 cinnamon stick
* ½ tsp ground ginger
* 5 to 8 cloves, to taste
* 1 small orange, sliced, with peel

Put everything into a saucepan and bring to the boil. Lower the heat, cover and simmer gently for 15 minutes. Ladle into mugs and serve piping hot.

CHAPPED LIPS AND NOSES

Chapped lips and noses are an unsightly and painful hazard of cold weather, especially if you have a cold. Try not to lick your lips if they are feeling dry and cracked as this will make it worse. Slather on lots of Vaseline each morning, before you go out and again at night before you go to bed to keep your lips chap-free.

Elizabeth Bennet and Mr Darcy

✤ *Theirs is a tale of love born out of loathing, and an important lesson in why first impressions don't always count. Elizabeth and Fitzwilliam (although no one ever calls him that; he's always referred to as Mr Darcy or just Darcy) are the heroine and hero of Jane Austen's most famous novel,* Pride and Prejudice.

Elizabeth is the cleverest (but not the prettiest) of Mr and Mrs Bennet's five daughters. Mrs Bennet is a rather silly woman and Mr Bennet, as men often do when surrounded by women, spends much of his time hidden behind his newspaper. He loves all his daughters, but he only actually likes Elizabeth because she is so witty. In those days having five daughters was a difficult business because each one had to be married off to a suitable man and given a good dowry. Mr Bennet's closest male heir is Mr Collins, a smarmy vicar set on marrying Elizabeth. Needless to say, Elizabeth is not keen.

So Mrs Bennet is delighted when Mr Bingley, a wealthy young bachelor, rents a nearby estate, bringing with him his friend Mr Darcy. Bingley is charming and fun-loving; Darcy is rich and handsome – but comes across as arrogant and cruel.

To begin with Elizabeth despises Darcy, and not entirely without justification, since he seems to go out of his way to be disagreeable. For her part, Elizabeth is quick to believe bad rumours about him. But despite Darcy's apparent coldness, he gradually falls in love with Elizabeth – who is shocked to receive an unexpected and rather clumsy proposal of marriage from him. She rejects him, confronting him about his supposed mistreatment of a Mr Wickham and his attempts to drive a wedge between her sister Jane and Mr Bingley.

There follow a series of misunderstandings and dramas. Throughout, Darcy maintains his strong silent approach – but gradually his true character begins to emerge and Elizabeth sees a different side to him. It is revealed that Mr Wickham is in fact a scoundrel (having tried to seduce Mr Darcy's sister) but not before he has also seduced Elizabeth's younger siste, Lydia, and persuaded her to run away with him. Mr Darcy ensures Mr Wickham marries Lydia to prevent shame falling on the Bennet's family name and Elizabeth's prejudice towards Darcy melts away. She finds herself falling in love with him and the story ends happily ever after when Darcy proposes a second time and is accepted.

CRAFTY CREATIONS
AND GORGEOUS GIFTS

These days, everything is so cheap and mass-made it hardly seems worth making anything yourself. But you'll be amazed how much fun there is to be had from making your own creations – not to mention satisfaction.

HOME-MADE BROOCHES

Perfect for presents, clubs or just to stick on your schoolbag. You will need . . .

* coloured felt
* scissors
* a medium-sized safety pin
* needle and thread
* fabric glue (optional)
* penny piece (optional)
* buttons, beads, sequins, ribbon, fabric

Decide on the size of your brooch (5 centimetres is about right), and then draw a circle of this diameter onto a piece of felt. Draw another circle next to it. You can make two circles the same colour or two different colours, it's up to you.

Using some sharp sewing scissors cut out the circles. On whichever one is going to form the back of your brooch, sew a safety pin, using the smallest, neatest stitches you can manage. Put the top circle on your backing circle with the safety pin on the outside. Stitch round the edges to join them together. You can use a bit of fabric glue to help hold them in place while you do this. For good luck, sew a penny inside. If you do this, however, make sure you sew the safety pin on extra tight, and attach it towards the top of the circle so the weight of the penny doesn't make it flip over. This forms the base of your brooch.

Now for the fun part – decorating your brooch. You can sew buttons, beads, sequins or bits of ribbon onto it. To make a flower brooch, cut out two basic flower shapes in different fabric scraps (chiffon or other light fabrics look lovely). Make one of the flower shapes slightly smaller than the other to give a layered, petal-like effect. Arrange the fabric flowers on the brooch base, then position a bead at the centre and sew the flower and bead to your brooch.

POMPOMS

There is nothing quite as satisfying as a nice fat pompom. They're easy to make – and you'd be surprised at the number of things you can do with them. You will need . . .

* some strong card – strong enough not to bend but not so thick you can't cut it
* mug
* two-pence piece
* small, pointed scissors
* wool

Draw two circles round the bottom of a mug onto the card. In the middle of each circle, draw a smaller circle. The bigger your inner circle, the thicker your pompom will be. The bigger your overall disc, the bigger the pompom as a whole will be. The trick is to get the balance between thickness and circumference right. Get the inner hole too small and the outer ring too big and you'll get a weedy, floppy sort of pompom. The other way round and it'll be unmanageably thick. Practice makes perfect.

Cut out the two large circles, then cut out the holes in the centre. Place one disc on top of the other. It should look like a cardboard doughnut. Wind the wool round the two discs, passing it through the hole in the centre. Try to wind the wool as evenly as possible, and carry on until the hole in the middle is completely full.

Now comes the tricky bit. You need to cut the wool at the edge of the circles, guiding the point of your scissors so that it goes between the two pieces of card. You might like to ask an adult to help you first time round. The trick is to pull the wool slightly away from the centre circle with the scissors; the tension will make it easier to cut.

* When all the wool is cut, pull the circles apart very slightly and, using a long piece of wool, firmly tie all the strands together with a firm knot. Leave the ends of this length of yarn long – you might need them later to attach the pompom to something. Then completely remove the cardboard circles.

So, what next for your lovely, fluffy ball of wool? Well, you can make several and sew them onto a scarf. You could make very small ones and sew them onto the hem of a skirt. You could make one big one and attach it to a piece of elastic as a toy for a kitten or a baby brother or sister. At Christmas, a small white pompom attached to a large white pompom makes – why, a snowman, of course! Add a couple of black beads for the eyes and a large orange or red bead for the nose, wind a tiny felt scarf around its neck, and you have a gorgeous home-made present – or even an unusual Christmas tree bauble. If you're feeling inspired you could even make a little top hat out of card.

At Easter, you can make yellow Easter chicks. For the beak, cut a diamond-shaped piece of orange felt, tie a knot in a piece of cotton, thread it through the centre of the 'beak' and attach it to your 'chick' by securing it in the core of the pompom. For the feet, cut a flipper-shape from the felt and glue it to the bottom. *Voilà*: a chick. If you want your chicks to be cute and fat, make them out of one very plump pompom. Or, you can give them a separate head and body like the snowman.

Once you get good at producing pompoms, you can show off by making multicoloured ones. A robin redbreast, for example, can be achieved by winding brown wool around three quarters of your disc, then winding the rest in red. Make a beak and some eyes as before.

SHELL TRINKET BOX OR PICTURE FRAME

Each time you are at the seaside, look out for as many differently shaped and coloured seashells as you can find. When your collection is big enough, try some shell decoration. You will need:

* a shoebox or any other small, sturdy box or a picture frame
* scrap paper
* pencil
* paint
* lots of shells
* 2 paintbrushes
* craft glue
* glitter (optional)
* clear varnish

A very ordinary box can be transformed into a trinket box when decorated with seashells. The type of box you use is up to you . . . if you have a large shell collection, then a shoebox is perfect; for tiny shells, a matchbox will do. Alternatively, you could personalize an old wooden picture frame. They make fantastic presents, all the more special because of the time and effort that has gone into them.

Before you start, trace the outline of the box or picture frame onto a piece of scrap paper then paint the outside of the box and leave it to dry overnight. On the piece of scrap paper, and using your box outline as a guide, practise setting out your shells. You can use small shells to make swirly patterns; larger shells look good in the centre or at the four corners. Get a good idea of the pattern you plan to create, and mark it on the paper so you don't get it wrong when it comes to the real thing. Practising first is very important as it ensures you don't suddenly run out of shells halfway through (it has been known to happen!). Don't forget to wash the shells first in warm, soapy water, and dry them thoroughly – this will ensure they stick properly (and also that they don't get smelly).

* Now you can start gluing. You will need a strong craft glue, preferably one in a tube with a nozzle. Otherwise you can apply the glue with an old paintbrush. Using your paper pattern as a guide, start sticking the shells onto the box, applying the glue to the surface bit by bit as you go along. It is best to work symmetrically if you can – if you stick a large shell in one corner, stick a correspondingly large one in the opposite corner. That way you will avoid making the shell decoration uneven. Big shells can form the main pattern of your box; use littler ones to fill in the gaps.

  If you like, you can sprinkle some silver glitter all over the decorated box while the glue is still wet. Allow the glue to dry completely. For a lasting finish, apply a thin, even layer of clear varnish with a clean, soft paintbrush.

PRESSED FLOWERS

Pressed, dried flowers and leaves can be made into beautiful, unique cards, pictures, bookmarks – and memories. You will need:

  * several sheets of white blotting paper
  * large heavy books
  * heavy weights such as bricks

* Gather some flowers on a dry day, after the morning dew has evaporated. Good flowers for pressing include buttercups and daisies. Generally the smaller and more delicate the flower, the more successful the pressing process will be. In springtime, tree blossom makes particularly pretty flower-pressing material. If you are planning a picture, don't forget to press a few grasses and leaves too; they will add to the natural feel of your composition.

* Soon after picking, arrange the flowers with their stems and leaves on a sheet of blotting paper, smoothing out the petals gently. Don't overcrowd the paper with too many flowers. Cover with another sheet of blotting paper and place both sheets carefully inside a heavy book. Put more heavy books, bricks or other heavy objects on top and leave them in a dry place for at least six weeks.

You can buy special flower-pressing kits. These usually consist of two pieces of wood full of sheets of blotting paper interspersed with cardboard or thin wood which you then tighten using nuts and bolts.

You can use the finished dried flowers to decorate cards or make bookmarks. You will need:

* card
* glue
* paintbrush
* a sheet of clear sticky-backed plastic
* scissors

Cut the card to the size you require and then arrange your flowers, petals and leaves until you are happy with the design. Dab a tiny amount of glue on the end of your paintbrush to stick the flowers down. Allow the glue to dry.

Cut the sticky-backed plastic to the same size and carefully cover the card by peeling off the backing of the plastic a little at a time, smoothing and guiding it over the flowers and card with your hands so no bubbles are trapped. Trim off any uneven edges.

For bookmarks, use a hole-punch to make a hole in the card, thread some ribbon through and tie.

FRIENDSHIP BRACELETS

The thing to remember about friendship bracelets is this: you have to tie them onto your friend's wrist for her and they must never be taken off, otherwise your friendship is in jeopardy.

Friendship bracelets can be made from embroidery thread, wool or leather cord. Embroidery thread is ideal, since it doesn't mind getting wet, unlike wool. Very narrow ribbon also works well.

The simplest bracelet is made by plaiting three threads together, but you can experiment with different numbers of threads in different colours. To make a five-thread bracelet, you will need:

* 5 lengths of different coloured thread/wool/ribbon
* scissors
* sticky tape
* beads (optional)

Cut five equal lengths of thread (remember to take account of the fact that the plaiting process will take up some of the length, so err on the generous side; a good measure is the circumference of your own wrist, plus the same again), and tie the five lengths together at one end with a simple knot, leaving a few centimetres of untied threads above it. Tape the knotted end of your bracelet to a table, and spread the loose threads out flat in front of you. Take one of the outside threads and cross it over the two threads next to it. Repeat with the outside thread from the other side. Continue to plait your threads in this way. Try to keep the plait as smooth and even as you can. If you like, you can add a few small beads to your bracelet by threading them on as you go along. When your bracelet is long enough to fit around your wrist, tie a knot at the end of all five threads.

Untape the plait. To fit your bracelet, simply tie it round your friend's wrist with a secure knot. In summer you can wear them round your ankles – although elderly relatives may not always approve.

PAPIER MÂCHÉ PIGGY BANK

Papier mâché means 'chewed paper' in French. It is the name for a modelling technique using paper pulp and glue, but it's not actually a French invention. Like paper itself, papier mâché was invented in China in the second century AD. The Chinese had many uses for papier mâché: they made boxes, masks and even helmets, all toughened with resin and beautifully painted.

In Europe it was widely used in the decorative arts and for making toys: many dolls' heads were made out of papier mâché, and puppets are still made using it today. A more practical use for it was crafting panels for the inside of horse-drawn carriages, where it was used instead of wood.

* a round balloon
* large pile of old newspapers
* paste
* craft knife (please ask an adult to help when using this)
* a cardboard egg carton
* glue
* roll of masking tape
* a pipe cleaner
* card
* white emulsion paint
* poster paints
* clear varnish

For the paste

you can just go to your local DIY shop and buy some wallpaper paste or, if you want to make it yourself:

* ½ cup white flour
* water
* 3tbsps sugar

*

Blow up the balloon to the size you'd like your piggy bank to be and tie it. Tear the newspaper into strips of about 3 by 10 centimetres.

Now make up your paste. You might want to enlist the help of an adult the first time you try this. Mix the flour with two cups of cold water. Meanwhile, in a saucepan, bring two cups of water to the boil. Add the paste to the saucepan, stir and bring it to the boil again. Take the saucepan off the heat and stir in the sugar. As the paste cools it will thicken slightly. When this happens, it's ready

* to use. Pour it into a wide, shallow container, such as an old washing-up bowl. Now you can get to work on your pig.

Put the strips of newspaper in the paste, then lift out and allow the excess to drip off. One at a time, put them carefully over the surface of the balloon, smoothing them down with your fingers to remove any air bubbles as you go. Do two layers, then allow them to dry, then add a further two layers. If you do too many layers at once it will take FOREVER to dry.

Roughly six layers should give you the right thickness. Leave the covered balloon in a warm place (an airing cupboard, if you have one, is ideal) for a few days until it is completely dry. Then make a tiny cut in the papier mâché with a craft knife, burst the balloon inside, and remove it.

To make the rest of your pig cut the cups away from the egg box. Stick four on the underside of the pig for the legs and one on the end for the snout, using the masking tape. Twist the pipe cleaner around your finger and attach it to the opposite end of the pig for a tail. Cut out two ear-shaped pieces of card and stick them to your pig's head.

If you don't want to have to break the pig to get your savings out, cut a coin-sized hole in your pig's tummy. Make a papier mâché stopper to fit the hole (or use an old champagne cork, or even just stuff it with newspaper), and you can use your pig over and over again.

Cover the entire pig with two more layers of paste and paper, and allow it to dry completely.

Paint the pig all over with white paint. This will seal the papier mâché and disguise the newspaper print. Then decorate it how you like using bright colours. When you've finished and it is completely dry, varnish.

Don't forget, if you're giving away your piggy bank as a present, pop a coin inside for good luck. Oink.

CUSTOMIZING CLOTHES

Customizing clothes is a quick and fun way for budding fashion designers to create their own style – and a lot easier than making clothes from scratch. However, it is unwise to begin on your best pair of jeans, since you can't be sure to start with how things are going to turn out. Instead, use your imagination to revamp worn-out clothes that are already on their last legs, or pick up cheap T-shirts and tops from charity shops.

A good place to start is to decorate your clothes with fabric pens or paints. You can get all kinds (some shops even sell glittery fabric pens!). Keep your designs simple and straightforward. Try writing your name on a T-shirt, for example, or even the chorus from a favourite song. As you gain confidence, you can experiment with more detailed designs. Why not draw a picture on a piece of paper and trace it onto your T-shirt, or cut out a template and draw round the edges? Stylized animals and flowers work especially well, but you could also draw symbols, like the symbol for your star sign.

If you get tired of fabric paint, try tie-dying. It's simple and very effective. You will need:

* cold-water fabric dye
* salt
* a big old basin or saucepan
* an old wooden spoon
* rubber gloves
* old newspapers
* a pale T-shirt or top
  (100 per cent cotton is best)
* string

First, make up the dye according to the instructions on the packet (this is where the salt goes in – the instructions will tell you how much to add). Always use an old basin or saucepan for this, and an old wooden spoon, because the dye will stain. It's best to wear rubber gloves too, unless you want dyed fingers, and cover the floor of the area you're working in with old newspapers. If you can work outside, do. And don't wear your best outfit, in case you get the odd rogue splash of dye.

Next, soak your top in cold water until it's wet through – this will stop the dye from seeping all through the cloth and turning it one uniform colour. Then, take hold of the front of your T-shirt in the middle and twist it into a rope. Using the string, bind up sections of the twisted T-shirt – tie it as tightly as you can for the best results. Do the same with the back of the T-shirt. Then, immerse it in the pot of dye, stir it around with the wooden spoon, and wait. The instructions will tell you how long it'll take (it varies from dye to dye) but if you want a paler colour than the one on the packet, remove the T-shirt a bit sooner.

Once you've taken the T-shirt out, rinse it thoroughly and untie the string. You should have a wonderful pattern from where the string kept the dye off the fabric: it can sometimes look like a spider's web or the sun's rays, but the best thing is it's different every time.

WRAPPING PAPER

* medium-sized potatoes
* sharp knife (and a helpful adult to operate it) or cookie cutters — stars, hearts, or whatever's in the kitchen drawer
* newspaper
* a large sheet of white paper or brown packing paper
* several colours of paint

To make your stamp, cut a potato in half through the middle. Mark out your design on the exposed flesh of the potato. Start with easy, bold shapes, such as stars or hearts. Get a grown-up to cut out the shape you have designed using the knife. Alternatively, you can just cut out the desired shape using a cookie cutter. Press the cutter down hard onto the potato and voilà: a perfect potato stamp.

Cover the work surface in newspaper. Then lay out the paper. Work in lines from one end to the other, dipping your potato stamp in the paint. You can turn the potato to create different patterns as you print.

To make a matching gift tag, make a single print on a separate piece of paper, cut it out, punch a hole in it and thread a piece of ribbon through the hole.

MARBLED WRAPPING PAPER

* water
* large paint tray (clean!), litter tray or shallow baking tray
* oil paints in different colours
* pencil or paintbrush
* sheets of plain white paper or roll of lining paper

Pour some water into the shallow tray and add a few drops of two or three different coloured oil paints to the surface. Use a pencil or the end of a paintbrush to make gently swirling patterns on the surface of the water. Very carefully lay the paper on the surface, and then lift it off, again very gently. The paper will have picked up a delicate whirly marbled pattern. Lay the paper flat and allow it to dry thoroughly before using to wrap presents.

Nellie Bly (1864–1922)

* In the nineteenth century, when most women were sitting at home sewing, Nellie Bly (whose real name was Elizabeth Jane Cochrane) was working as a journalist in New York City. Unlike most female writers at the time she was not content with reviewing plays and writing articles about cookery – she wanted to tackle serious subjects. She faked madness so she could expose the cruel conditions in a mental asylum. Her exposé of the harsh treatment and appalling conditions in the New York Sun prompted an investigation by the authorities and ultimately led to an improvement in facilities for the mentally ill. She also spent six months in Mexico as a foreign correspondent before being threatened with arrest by the Mexican dictator Porfirio Diaz.

Soon after, she took off around the world, the first woman to do so without a chaperone. She made it in seventy-two days, six hours, eleven minutes and fourteen seconds.

Aung San Suu Kyi (1945–)

* Burma is a beautiful country in South-East Asia. Once a part of the British Empire, since 1962 it has been run by a group of corrupt generals infamous for their human rights abuses, including the use of child labour. Election results have been ignored and they have murdered or persecuted anyone who dares to disagree with them.

Aung San Suu Kyi founded the pro-democracy movement in Burma in 1988 and has been its leader ever since. All her life she has put the welfare of the people before her own in actions that have won her worldwide respect. In 1990 her party won 82 per cent of seats in the Burmese parliament – a result that the military junta ignored. The generals remain in power, and Suu Kyi has been under house arrest for many years and remains so to this day.

Known as the Lady, she always wears a flower in her hair. She was awarded the Nobel Peace Prize in 1991, and donated her prize money to education and health care.

From 1988 she was separated from her husband, Michael Aris, and their two children. Sadly Aris died of cancer in Britain in 1999; he had tried to gain entry to Burma to see his wife one last time, but the regime refused to allow him to visit.

CHRISTMAS

Christmas is such an exciting time, it's hard to know where to start. The main thing to remember is that it should not be a horrible cheap commercial spend-fest. Christmas is about family and friends. A nice home-made card, however higgledy-piggledy, is worth a hundred shop-bought ones.

Christmas Cards

If you decide to make your own Christmas cards, remember you will need lots of them — so the easier they are to make, the better. A simple potato print of a Christmas tree or star, spruced up with a dash of glitter glue, is a good option (see page 246). Or you could make a linocut to print your cards, in which case you will need:

* lino blocks
* lino cutter handle and blades (also known as gouges)
* water-based printing inks in a few different colours
* ink roller
* old plate or ceramic tile to put the ink on
* additional roller for pressing the printing paper onto the block

With a linocut, the basic principle of printing is the same as for potato printing, but with the bonus that you can keep and reuse the lino block again and again each year. To begin with, it's simplest to use one block and print in just one colour on white paper. With a little practice, you can experiment with several blocks printed one over the other to produce more complex designs in many colours.

All the equipment you need for lino printing can be bought in good art and craft shops. A gouge, which is the instrument you use to cut away the surface of the lino block and create the pattern, is similar to an apple corer or potato peeler. You buy the blades (or gouges) separately from the handle, and sometimes you can buy a set of several blades. Lino blocks themselves are usually sold in A5 size. To make smaller blocks ask a grown-up to cut them in half or quarters — use a sharp craft knife and a metal ruler when doing this.

* Gouging the lino may seem quite hard at first, so it is a good idea to start on a practice block, experimenting with a few different widths of blade to see the different effects produced and to get comfortable with your tools. It also helps to warm the block before starting by sitting on it, or placing it on top of a warm radiator for 5 minutes or so. The widest cutter is used for gouging out large background areas. Smaller V-shaped cutters are used for adding finer lines and detail to the print. As you work, always cut outwards and away from your body in case the cutter slips.

The main thing to remember when starting to cut is that everything you cut away will be blank or white on the print, while the uncut areas will be the coloured ones. Choose a simple design for your first print and draw the picture on the lino in pencil before you start. Remember that the final print will appear in reverse, so if you want to add words or lettering, 'Happy Christmas' for example, draw the letters back to front.

To make a Christmas-tree print, draw the pointed shape of the tree on the lino. Use the broadest cutter to cut away everything around the tree, then use a finer V-shaped cutter to add details such as tinsel and decorations to the tree.

When your block is ready to print, pour some ink onto an old plate or tile and roll the ink roller in it until it is lightly covered. Next, run the roller lightly and evenly over the top of your lino block. The idea is to get only the uncut lino covered in ink. Very carefully, place the paper over the block. Holding one corner, gently rub all over the paper with the clean roller so the ink is distributed evenly over the paper. Peel it off, and you have created your first print.

The first two or three prints may not be perfect, but don't despair. Repeated inking produces better and better prints as you work.

How to Decorate Your Christmas Tree

* Before you start to decorate the tree, plug in the fairy lights to check they are working – there's nothing more annoying than spending ages arranging them only to find they're broken.

Start by winding the lights round the tree, from the bottom up. It helps to take into account the length of the lights when buying your tree – you don't want to run out of lights halfway up. Put the tinsel on, if you have it, looping it round the branches. An elegant alternative to tinsel is a pretty red ribbon, which you can either drape over the branches or cut into pieces and tie into bows.

Next, hang your decorations. Put the larger ones on first, spacing them evenly around the tree. Fill in the gaps with the smaller decorations, saving the prettiest ones for the top branches. If you have delicate baubles, put these near the top; things tend to fall off more if they're at the bottom of the tree. Finally, place the star or angel at the top of the tree – and switch on the lights.

TWIG CHRISTMAS TREE

If you don't have the space for a real Christmas tree, or are spending Christmas away from home but still want to create a festive feel, this is a cheap yet magical solution. You will need:

* twiggy branches
* can of silver or gold metallic spray paint
* string of fairy lights

* Find a fallen twiggy branch, or several large, nicely shaped twigs. Spray them all over in silver or gold metallic spray paint (it's always best to do this outdoors). When dry, arrange the branches and twigs in a large pot or vase. Add fairy lights – and decorate with some of the decorations overleaf.

Christmas Decorations

PAPER LANTERNS

* gummed coloured paper squares
  (you can buy packets in craft shops)
* scissors
* small damp sponge

* Fold a square of gummed paper in half. Cut slits across the folded edge of the gummed square up to about 1.5 centimetres from the top and edge of the paper. Unfold the square, and turn it so the slits are running vertically, then roll it to form a lantern shape and lick or use the sponge to gum the edge. Cut a long strip from a square and gum this to the top of the lantern to form a handle.

  When you have made enough different coloured lanterns, thread the handles through a long piece of string and hang them across the room or individually on the Christmas tree.

EGG BOX BELLS

* empty cardboard egg cartons
* scissors
* pencil or toothpick
* poster paints
* masking tape
* glue
* glitter
* gold embroidery thread,
  fine ribbon, wool or tinsel

* Cut the egg box into its segments. Trim round the bottoms to make them neat and even to form 'bells'. Use a pencil or toothpick to pierce a hole at the top of each bell. Paint the insides and let them dry. Then put small dabs of glue on the outside, and sprinkle all over with glitter. Cut lengths of embroidery thread, ribbon or tinsel to form loops. Pass the loop ends through the hole at the top of the bell and secure them on the inside with masking tape. To make the chimes for the bells, cut lengths of tinsel about a centimetre longer than the bells, and tape the end inside the top of the bell.

SALT DOUGH DECORATIONS

* 2 cups plain flour
* 1 cup salt
* 1 cup water
* rolling pin
* pastry cutters or card cut to different shapes
* cocktail stick or skewer
* baking sheet
* greaseproof paper
* paints
* glitter or glitter glue
* ribbon

Mix the flour and salt in a bowl and add the water gradually, mixing until it forms a firm dough. Turn the dough onto a lightly floured surface and knead until it is smooth and stretchy. If the dough gets sticky, sprinkle on a little more flour until it is workable. Put the dough back in the bowl, cover with a cloth and leave it for half an hour.

Roll the dough with a lightly floured rolling pin until it's about ½ centimetre thick. Use pastry cutters in star, angel or tree shapes to cut out the dough, or draw shapes on some card and use them as templates to cut round the dough with a sharp knife. Make a hole with the cocktail stick or skewer at the top of each shape, big enough to take a piece of ribbon

Put the shapes on a baking sheet lined with greaseproof paper and bake at 120ºC/gas mark ½ for about six hours. The dough should be hard and dry. Allow the shapes to cool completely before handling.

To decorate, paint and then dust with a light sprinkling of glitter or use glitter glue. Thread a length of ribbon through each shape and tie.

MAKE YOUR OWN CHRISTMAS STOCKING

A long, long time ago, before he lived at the North Pole, Father Christmas is believed to have lived in Turkey. And while he was there, he gave three daughters some money in secret, dropping it down the chimney. The money fell into their stockings hanging to dry by the fire, and that is why we hang our stockings by the chimney on Christmas Eve.

It's perfectly OK to use an old sock or a pillowcase, but it's even better to have your very own special Christmas stocking to hang up. This one is very easy to make and fun to decorate. Add a new decoration each year, then when you have children of your own, you can pass it on to them. You will need:

* paper or card and pencil
* 1 metre of felt
* scissors
* embroidery thread
* scraps of felt in different colours
* sequins
* ribbon

* Draw a large stocking shape on a piece of paper or some light card (use a shop-bought stocking as a model, if you have one). Fold the felt double, pin the stocking pattern to it and cut it out so you have two identical sides.

If you want to personalize your stocking, use embroidery thread in a contrasting colour to the felt, and sew your name or initials in chain stitch on the front. You could cut out a small Christmas-tree shape in green felt and sew some sequins onto the tree, then stitch the tree to the stocking. Or, if the stocking is going to be a present, cut out a square in felt, tie a ribbon into a bow and stitch it onto the felt and then onto the stocking.

Sew all round the edges of the stocking using blanket stitch (see page 11) and coloured embroidery thread. Sew a small loop of ribbon inside one top corner so you can hang it up.

PRETEND CHRISTMAS CRACKERS

These crackers won't make a bang when you pull them, but they're a fun way to wrap up small presents or for use as decorations on the Christmas tree. You will need:

* small gifts or sweets
* empty toilet rolls
* tissue or crêpe paper
* glue
* ribbon or tinsel
* glitter glue
* images cut from old Christmas cards

* Place your small gift (along with a joke written on a slip of paper if you like) in the toilet roll (diagram A). This is the inside of your cracker. Measure out a square of tissue or crêpe paper wide enough to cover the roll with at least 15 centimetres spare at each end. Cover the toilet roll with the paper and glue it down. Cut lengths of ribbon or tinsel and tie them round the paper at each end of the roll, knot them, then tie in a bow.

To decorate the cracker, add a dash of glitter glue, or stick on small images cut from old Christmas cards – robins, Father Christmas, snowmen, angels, for example (diagram B).

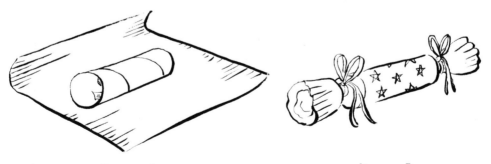

diagram A   *diagram B*

ORANGE POMANDER BALLS

The spicy clove and orange smell as you make these pomander decorations adds a deliciously Christmassy touch to the whole house. In Victorian times pomanders were used to disguise bad odours. After Christmas, store your pomander at the back of your sock drawer or hang it in your wardrobe to help keep moths at bay. You will need:

* an orange
* 60cm length of fine ribbon
* cloves
* thimble, cocktail stick, knitting needle (optional)

Tie the ribbon tightly round the orange, as if you were making a present, and knot the ribbon securely at the top. Tie the ends of the ribbon in a bow, or a loop from which to hang the finished pomander. The orange will now be divided into four equal sections by the ribbon.

Working on one section at a time, cover the whole orange with cloves, pressing them in pointed end first. (If your thumb begins to hurt, you can use a thimble or pierce a small hole first with a cocktail stick or fine knitting needle, then push the clove in.) With practice, you can make different patterns with the cloves – circles, stripes, waves – in each of the four sections. Hang the finished pomanders from the tree or use them to decorate a festive mantelpiece.

WRITING TO FATHER CHRISTMAS

When you write your Christmas list to Father Christmas you can either put it up the chimney, or send your letter in the post. Letters addressed to Toyland or Snowland will get sent to Edinburgh, letters addressed to the North Pole really do go all the way to the North Pole.

HOW TO LAY OUT SUPPER FOR FATHER CHRISTMAS AND HIS REINDEER

* a slice of Christmas cake
* 1 or 2 mince pies
* tumbler of whisky
* cup of coffee
* a carrot

It's customary and polite to give Father Christmas a snack on Christmas Eve – after all he has a lot of work to do and will be hungry. Find a nice plate, and lay out some or all of the suggestions above, along with a clean napkin. Don't forget the reindeer – a carrot each should be plenty.* Add a thank you note, folded in the napkin, for good measure and leave the meal in a place where he will find it – by the stockings or near the fireplace.

* The reindeer are called Rudolph (the one with the red nose), Dasher, Dancer, Prancer, Vixen, Donner, Blitzen, Cupid and Comet.

HOW TO EAT MINCE PIES

Mince pies should be eaten in silence. For each pie you eat, make a silent wish.

TWELFTH NIGHT

The evening of 5 January, Twelfth Night, is when all the Christmas decorations should be taken down – if they're not it brings bad luck to the house and you will have to leave them up all through the year. When you take down your Christmas cards, don't throw them away. Keep them in a box until the following year and recycle the fronts. Cut out pictures of robins, stars, angels, Father Christmas, etc. and use them as gift tags, or to make new collage Christmas cards for next year.

FORTUNE-TELLING

Next time you have friends round for tea, why not treat them to a proper cup of tea made in a pot using tea leaves and served in dainty little china cups with saucers – and then dabble in a bit of fortune-telling? Remember not to use a tea strainer!

While your guests are devouring their last biscuit, slip away and transform yourself into Gypsy Rose Lee, the famous fortune-teller extraordinaire.

The best fortune-tellers look very mysterious and exotic, so change into a long flouncy skirt (borrow one from your mum) and a white blouse. Tie a silk headscarf round your head and put on as many jangly bangles and rings as you can lay your hands on.

Before you can start reading fortunes and predicting the future, your guests must cross your palm with silver. In other words, persuade them that you can't possibly tell them if they are going to meet and fall in love with a tall dark man, or be rich, or become an astronaut, unless they come up with ten pence and put it in your hand.

Tea-Leaf Reading for Beginners

Ask the person whose fortune you are telling to place her almost empty cup upside down in the saucer. Then, with her left hand, she must turn the cup, anti-clockwise, three times in the saucer; she should use her right hand if she is left-handed.

Now, take the cup from her and turn it upright, making sure the handle is facing you. Gaze into the cup and start to 'read' the tea-leaf patterns.

Explain to your guests, in a low and mystical voice, that the teacup is divided into sections for readings:

* **The handle.** Tea leaves close to the handle have a very direct meaning. To the left of the handle they tell the past and things which are to be left behind, while to the right reveals the immediate future and present.

* **The rim and upper third of the tea cup.** This shows the present and the very near future i.e. the next few days.

* **The middle third of the cup.** This shows what will happen in the next couple of weeks.

* **The bottom of the cup.** This shows the distant future.

* Look at the patterns the tea leaves have made in the empty cup and interpret any shapes you see. Having many leaves in the teacup is said to indicate a full life. Here are some of the shapes they might have made and what these stand for:

* **apple**: achievement
* **bird**: you will take a journey soon, but alone
* **cat**: untrustworthiness, a false friend
* **clouds**: trouble and problems
* **cross**: warning sign
* **dog**: a good friend
* **egg**: good omen
* **elephant**: good health
* **eye**: be careful
* **fire**: artistic achievement

* **gun or pistol**: danger
* **heart**: things look rosy for love and romance; cracked or broken – true love won't run smoothly
* **horse**: galloping – good news
* **kite**: a wish will come true
* **ladder**: success
* **leaf**: good fortune
* **pig**: prosperity, greed
* **question mark**: caution
* **rainbow**: a wish that will come true
* **spider**: money
* **star**: health and happiness

Paper Fortune-Teller

These paper fortune-tellers are made using a traditional origami fold and are sometimes called cootie catchers. In Germany they call them nose pinchers – in Ireland they're called snicker snackers.

* Fold down one corner of a piece of A4 paper and then cut off the bottom so you have an exact square of paper.

Open out the square and fold again from the opposite diagonally.

Open the square paper, then take one corner and fold carefully into the centre of the square. Repeat with the three other corners (diagram A).

Turn the paper over and again, take one corner and turn it into the centre of the square, then repeat with all the corners (diagram B).

Now fold it in half across the middle.

Push the thumbs and index fingers of both hands into the outer flaps made by the corners.

Fold it flat again and colour each of the four outside squares in which you put your fingers and thumbs a different colour.

Turn the fortune-teller over, and write the numbers 1 to 8 on each of the triangles (diagram C).

Open up the flaps and write the words 'Yes' or 'No', comments or predictions under each of the eight numbers.

diagram A   *diagram B*   *diagram C*

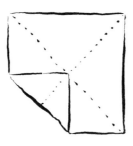
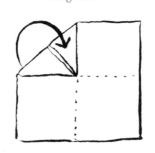

HOW TO USE YOUR FORTUNE-TELLER

* Ask a friend to think of a simple question which can be answered by 'Yes,' 'No,' 'Maybe' or 'You will have to wait,' for example.

She then chooses one of the four colours from the fortune-teller, for example, orange. Open the fortune-teller with your fingers and thumbs alternately in each direction for each letter in the word 'orange'.

Now she chooses one of the four numbers now visible – for example five.

Open and close the fortune-teller alternately in one direction, then the other, five times for the number five.

Now, for the last time, your friend chooses one of the numbers on the inside of the fortune-teller. She then lifts that flap and reads the magical answer to her question underneath.

NOTE: *There are endless variations to the fortune-teller game. Draw pictures, flowers or symbols instead of colours. Or write predictions instead of 'Yes' or 'No' answers: 'You will marry an astronaut', 'You will have twins', 'You will be a famous film star'.*

Palm Reading

Did you know that the shape and size of our hands, along with the lines and bumps (mounts) on the palms, can be 'read' to interpret our personality and predict our fate?

Practise on your own hands until you are familiar with the main lines and bumps and their meanings, then use your palm-reading skills to tell your friends what destiny has in store for them.

What your fingers say about you:

* **Your index finger is longer than your ring finger.** You are a natural leader who will achieve much. But you may also have a fiery temper!

* **Your ring finger is longer than your index finger.** You are probably very creative with lots of original ideas.

* **Your thumb is very flexible.** You are an easy-going person who adapts well to change.

* **You have stiff thumbs.** You are probably stubborn and like things to stay just as they are.

* **You have long thumbs.** The longer your thumb, the more likely you are to have a strong personality; you are also very faithful to those you love.

READING THE PALM

A real expert palm reader would look at both your hands and be able to discern subtle differences between the two. Amateurs, however, can get most of the important information they need by reading only the left hand. The bumps in the palm represent different things.

1. **Venus:** love, tenderness and sympathy. A soft and overly full mount of Venus however suggests an overindulgent personality.

2. **Mars:** this is the double symbol of courage and resistance. It denotes great determination, competitiveness and drive, but when overdeveloped may indicate an overly aggressive, quarrelsome personality.

3. **Jupiter:** self-confidence and ambition. A small mount of Jupiter points to shyness and lack of drive. If the mount is too prominent, conceit and selfishness could be your downfall.

4. **Apollo:** creativity and artistic flair. Too pronounced – you are likely to be superficial and pretentious. A flat or underdeveloped mount – a dull personality, more at home in business than the arts.

5. **Saturn:** concern for others, sensitivity and quietness. Overdeveloped – beware of loneliness. A small or no mount of Saturn – a tendency to be too frivolous.

6. **Mercury:** this mount relates to business and efficiency as well as change. If you have a well-developed mount of Mercury, you are sharp-witted and likeable, well-suited to the acting profession.

7. **Luna:** creativity, curiosity and imagination. But a too-prominent mount could mean a tendency to fantasize or err on the side of untruthfulness.

THE LINES OF THE HAND

1. **Life line**: also known as the line of vitality; a good indicator of physical health, approach to life and energy. A long, clearly defined life line with a deep curve into the palm denotes a vigorous and generous personality. A break in the life line represents an illness or a major upheaval and change.

2. **Fate line**: reveals career and destiny. A smooth, unbroken line represents a fulfilling and successful career. A hand with no fate line indicates a life of luxury and blissful happiness!

3. **Head line**: shows our abilities and potential. A straight, well-defined line across the palm denotes a practical, level-headed person. A sloping head line indicates a more creative and imaginative personality. A thin, weak line points to lack of perseverance and concentration.

4. **Heart line**: the 'perfect' heart line runs across the palm in a clear, unbroken curve, indicating lovingness and loyalty. Breaks in the heart line may point to disappointments or inconstancy in love, while a heart line that looks like a chain means flirtatiousness. A very long line running full across the palm – beware of the green-eyed monster.

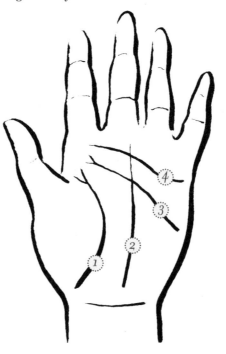

The Zodiac

There are twelve signs of the zodiac; each corresponds to a constellation in the night sky. A person's star sign is determined by the constellation the sun is moving through on the day she is born. Each star sign belongs to one of the four elements – earth, air, fire and water.

ARIES, THE RAM
21 March–20 April

* **Element:** fire
* **Gemstones:** diamond, amethyst
* **Famous Arians:** Houdini, Elton John

Aries is the first sign of the zodiac, and as a result Arians can be a little naive. They are also very exciting, energetic, likeable and optimistic. At worst, they can be overbearing, selfish, tactless and hot-tempered. Arians are likely to fall in love at first sight.

TAURUS, THE BULL
21 April–21 May

* **Element:** earth
* **Gemstones:** emerald, jade
* **Famous Taureans:** Shakespeare, Florence Nightingale

Taureans are reliable types and can be kind, loving, dedicated and loyal. At worst, they are stubborn and lazy. In romance, Taureans are devoted and faithful but may be possessive.

GEMINI, THE TWINS
22 May–21 June

* **Element:** air
* **Gemstones:** beryl, agate
* **Famous Geminis:** Paul McCartney, Marilyn Monroe, Queen Victoria

Geminis can turn on a sixpence. One minute they are charming, talented and outward-going, the next they are shallow, sneaky and heartless. In love, Geminis tend to be flirtatious and a little selfish.

CANCER, THE CRAB
22 June–22 July

* **Element:** water
* **Gemstones:** ruby, moonstone
* **Famous Cancerians:** Tom Cruise, Princess Diana

Cancerians are hard-working, witty and kind-hearted – and they tend to be very fond of their mothers. They can also be moody, insecure, untruthful and short-tempered. In love, Cancerians are devoted and very romantic.

LEO, THE LION
23 July–23 August

* **Element:** fire
* **Gemstones:** ruby, peridot, topaz
* **Famous Leos:** Napoleon, Mick Jagger, Beatrix Potter

Noble Leos are generous, tireless, optimistic, witty and creative. When vexed, they can become big-headed, bossy, vain and opinionated. In love, Leos can be affectionate, passionate and caring, but sometimes jealous.

VIRGO, THE VIRGIN
24 August–23 September

* **Element:** earth
* **Gemstones:** sapphire, agate
* **Famous Virgos:** Agatha Christie, Elisabeth I, Greta Garbo

Virgos are more likely to have a neat and tidy sock drawer – they are perfectionists. They are gentle, shy, often articulate and wise. But they can also be fussy, gloomy and interfering. Virgos are very choosy, loving and loyal.

LIBRA, THE SCALES
24 September–23 October

* **Element:** air
* **Gemstones:** opal, sapphire, diamond
* **Famous Librans:** Margaret Thatcher, John Lennon, Bob Geldof

Level-headed Librans are likeable, artistic, cautious and graceful. But they can also be indecisive, vain, and overindulgent. Librans fall in love easily and are very romantic but also flirtatious.

SCORPIO, THE SCORPION
24 October–22 November

* **Element:** water
* **Gemstones:** onyx, topaz
* **Famous Scorpios:** Marie Antoinette, Pablo Picasso, Julia Roberts

Scorpios are trustworthy, genuine, sharp-witted and brave. Get on the wrong side of them and they can be spiteful, suspicious and jealous. Scorpios are passionate and devoted, but their moods and hidden feelings can lead to misunderstandings.

SAGITTARIUS, THE ARCHER
23 November–21 December

* **Element:** fire
* **Gemstones:** turquoise, topaz, amethyst
* **Famous Sagittarians:** Jane Austen, Walt Disney, Steven Spielberg

Fun-loving Sagittarians are gifted, talented and exciting – but they can sometimes let things get out of hand and can be reckless. Sagittarians are passionate but take a while to settle down.

CAPRICORN, THE GOAT
22 December–20 January

* **Element:** earth
* **Gemstones:** garnet, tourmaline
* **Famous Capricorns:** Elvis Presley Kate Moss, Orlando Bloom

Capricorns can come across as quiet, but when you get to know them they are fun-loving and very amusing. They are hard-working, responsible and loyal. At their worst, they can be greedy, gloomy and shy. Capricorns tend to hide their feelings but are very faithful and steadfast.

AQUARIUS, THE WATER CARRIER
21 January–19 February

* **Element:** air
* **Gemstones:** aquamarine, sapphire
* **Famous Aquarians:** Jennifer Aniston, Charles Darwin, Charles Dickens

Aquarians are honest, creative, original and thoughtful. They can also be a little forgetful, rebellious, oversensitive and eccentric. When Aquarians fall in love it will be with someone like them.

PISCES, THE FISH
20 February–20 March

* **Element:** water
* **Gemstones:** turquoise, amethyst
* **Famous Pisceans:** Albert Einstein, Rudolph Nureyev, Michelangelo

At best, Pisceans are unselfish, spiritual, romantic and loving. At worst, they can be overemotional, talkative, weak and timid. In love, Pisceans are loving and sensuous and tend to settle with someone they can rely on.

Rhymes and Things

Sneezing

Sneeze on Monday, sneeze for danger;
Sneeze on Tuesday, kiss a stranger;
Sneeze on Wednesday, get a letter;
Sneeze on Thursday, something better;
Sneeze on Friday, sneeze for sorrow;
Sneeze on Saturday, see your sweetheart tomorrow;
Sneeze on Sunday, safety seek.

Monday's Child

Monday's child is fair of face,
Tuesday's child is full of grace,
Wednesday's child is full of woe,
Thursday's child has far to go,
Friday's child is loving and giving,
Saturday's child works hard for a living,
And the child that is born on the Sabbath day
Is bonny and blithe, and good and gay.

Magpies

Single magpies are supposed to be bad luck:

One for sorrow, two for joy
Three for a girl and four for a boy
Five for silver, six for gold
Seven for a secret never to be told.

If you spot a magpie on its own, you can counteract the bad luck by saying, 'Good morning, Mr Magpie, how is Mrs Magpie?' or by nodding seven times in its direction.

Elizabeth I (1533–1603)

* *As the daughter of Henry VIII and his second wife, Anne Boleyn, Elizabeth Tudor survived a rotten beginning (her father had her mother executed) to become the great and glorious Good Queen Bess. Initially, her chances of ascending to the throne of England seemed slim, especially given the birth of her brother Edward in 1537. But after his death and that of her half-sister, Mary (also known as Bloody Mary, and not to be confused with Mary, Queen of Scots), she was crowned in 1558. She inherited a nation crippled by debt, divided by religious rivalry and under constant threat from the French and Spanish; she left behind a powerful, rich, trading nation.*

  She had a fiery temper and was impulsive but also shrewd, intelligent, highly educated – she spoke six languages – and politically astute. She also had a flair for making the most of a dramatic opportunity, famously sending her fleet off to face the Armada with the words: 'I know I have the body of a weak and feeble woman, but I have the heart and stomach of a king.' And then, of course, there were those frocks, the ruffs, the jewels and the fact that she never married, declaring herself married to her country; but there were rumours about a love affair with Robert Dudley, which added to the romantic aura surrounding her. She was so good at doing her job that people subsequently said she must have been a man in disguise. Men often say that about women they cannot control.

Marie Curie (1867–1934)

* *Born Maria Sklodowska in Poland, Marie Curie moved to Paris in 1891 to study at the Sorbonne. It was there that she met and married Pierre Curie, professor of physics at the university. Together they made a number of ground-breaking discoveries, including isolating polonium (named after her country of origin) and radium. She was awarded the Nobel prize twice, once jointly with her husband in 1903 and then on her own in 1911.*

  She was remarkable as a unique example of a successful female in a world dominated by men. She inspired huge respect in her peers, and after the sudden death of her husband in 1906 she succeeded him at the Sorbonne.

BOREDOM BUSTERS

If you're bored, you're not trying hard enough. Snap out of it. Do something. Anything – it doesn't have to be edifying, complicated or even useful. The important thing is to occupy your mind and, if possible, body. Before you know it time will have flown past.

Games to Play During Break

CLAPPING GAMES

Clapping games are usually played in pairs. Stand opposite your partner, not too far apart so you can easily reach each other's hands.

* Start by simply clapping your own hands together once, then clap your right hand against your partner's left hand and your left against her right. Make up the clapping pattern and rhythm as you go along. You can cross hands, for example, with your right hand clapping her right hand; you can use double claps; you could turn your hands round so you clap against the backs of your hands. It's easiest if you intersperse each clap between the two of you with one on your own – this will help keep the rhythm going. Start slowly, then go as fast as you can. You can introduce different actions such as clapping against your own thighs, shoulders or hands, or turning around and bumping bottoms or hips together.

Here are some rhymes and chants to clap to:

Sailor Went to Sea

A sailor went to sea, sea, sea,
To see what he could see, see, see,
But all that he could see, see, see,
Was the bottom of the deep blue
Sea, sea, sea.

My Mummy is a Baker

My mummy is a baker, yummy yummy, fat tummy,
My daddy is a dustman, pooey pooey, pooey pooey,
My sister is a show-off, na-na-na-na, na-na-na-na,
My brother is a cowboy, bang, bang,
Fifty bullets in your head, turn around, touch the ground,
YOU'RE DEAD!

SKIPPING GAMES AND SONGS

You'll need a long rope and two people at either end to turn the rope. In most of these games and songs, the skippers take turns to run in and jump the rope. If you stumble and stop the rope as you jump, you're out, and it's your turn to turn the rope. If there are only two of you, you can still play; just tie one end of the rope to a tree or post.

Here are some of our favourite chants:

Teddy bear, teddy bear,
turn around.

Teddy bear, teddy bear,
touch the ground.

Teddy bear, teddy bear,
show your shoe.

Teddy bear, teddy bear,
that will do!

Teddy bear, teddy bear,
go upstairs.

Teddy bear, teddy bear,
say your prayers,

Teddy bear, teddy bear,
turn out the lights.

Teddy bear, teddy bear,
say goodnight!

The skipper performs the actions as they are chanted – turning around, touching the floor, etc.

Alternatively . . .

Jelly on the plate, jelly on the plate
Wibble, wobble, wibble wobble
Jelly on the plate.

Sausage in the pan, sausage in the pan
Turn it over, turn it over
Sausage in the pan.

Baby on the floor, baby on the floor
Pick him up, pick him up
Baby on the floor.

Robber at the door, robber at the door
Kick him out, kick him out!
Robber at the door.

Again, the skipper must wobble like a jelly and turn around and around like the sausage and so on, without stopping the turning rope.

Another variation . . .

Cinderella, dressed in yellow

Went upstairs to kiss a fellow.

By mistake

She kissed a snake.

How many doctors did it take?

1 . . . 2 . . . 3 . . . 4 . . . 5 . . .

The skipper keeps skipping as others count until she misses a jump or trips on the rope.

FRENCH SKIPPING (ALSO KNOWN AS CHINESE SKIPPING OR ELASTICS)

* To make an elastic, get roughly 3 metres of knicker elastic (about 5 centimetres wide) and tie the ends together.

Ask two people to be the 'enders'; they stand inside the loop, the elastic at ankle height to begin with and their feet slightly apart so it is stretched into a rectangle.

The jumper jumps over the left elastic, then the right elastic, into the middle, then wide so both feet are outside the elastic. Then, catching the elastic round her ankles, she jumps again so that the elastic crosses, then jumps back into the middle releasing the elastic as she does so. Lastly she must land on the elastic with both feet. If she stumbles or fails to complete the sequence in the right order, she is out, and someone else takes a turn.

Each time you successfully complete a round, the elastic gets raised higher — to the calves, then knees, thighs, then the waist. You can invent your own variations on these moves, and make up your own rules too.

HOPSCOTCH

Hopscotch can be played on paving stones if they are laid out in the right pattern, or you can mark the hopscotch grid out on the ground with chalk. Draw squares big enough to hold both your feet in the pattern as shown in the diagram.

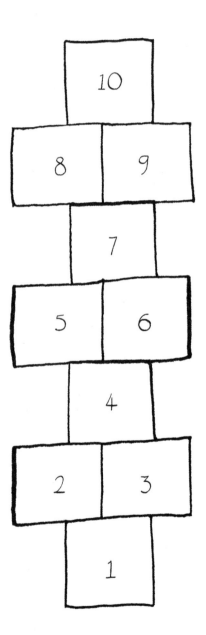

*   Each player finds a small flat stone. The first player stands at a chosen point in front of square one, and throws their stone to land in this first square. The stone must land well within the square – if it lands in another square or even on the line, that player has missed and must wait until all the others have had their turn before having another go. If the stone lands in the square, the player hops and jumps up the grid and back down again, only placing one foot in each square at any given time. On the way back, the player must scoop up their stone without touching the ground with the other foot or using their free hand to balance. If you land on a line, you are out. And you must not touch or hop into the square where your stone is. Continue to throw the stone into the squares in sequence. Once a player completes all the numbers, she writes her name in any square she chooses. From then on, only she may step in it. As the game continues, and more players write their names in the squares, it gets harder to hop from square to square without making a mistake.

CAT'S CRADLE

* To play cat's cradle you need to find a length of string roughly 60 centimetres long and a friend to play with.

Tie the two ends together to form a loop. Place the string on your hands as shown. Follow the diagrams, pulling the string from one hand to the other with the middle finger, first on one hand, then the other. You should have made a criss-cross pattern in the string. Now your partner takes the string between her thumb and index finger, then pulls the string outwards, down, inwards and up through the middle of your string criss-cross, and lifts the string from your hands. You now grasp the string at the intersection, and repeat the movements above, lifting the string off your friend's hands.

Your partner hooks her little fingers around the two middle strings on each side, and repeats as above. She pulls the string outwards, down, inwards and up through the middle of your string criss-cross, and again lifts the string from your hands.

There are lots of much more complicated cat's cradle games to play once you have mastered these basic steps.

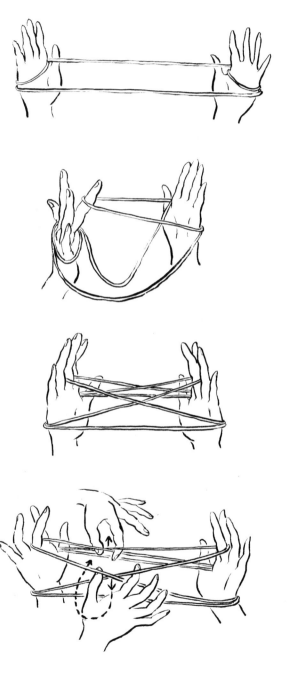

Games for Rainy Days
and When Stuck in the Car

ARM WRESTLING

First, find someone to wrestle with – preferably someone who is neither bigger nor stronger than you – and ask a friend or relative to be the referee.

*   Sit opposite your opponent at a table and place one elbow on the table. Use your strongest arm, and make sure you are relaxed and sitting comfortably before the struggle begins.

Grasp your opponent's hand. On the word 'go' from the referee, flex your muscles and use all your strength to try to force the opponent's arm down to the table. You are not allowed to use your other arm or hand as leverage.

If your hands get sweaty after a few bouts, dust them lightly with talcum powder.

FOOT FIGHTS

*   Lie opposite your opponent, either on the bed or on the floor (both players' knees should be slightly bent). Place the soles of your feet against your partner's, and push. The aim of the game is to force your legs straight so that the opponent's knees buckle and bend.

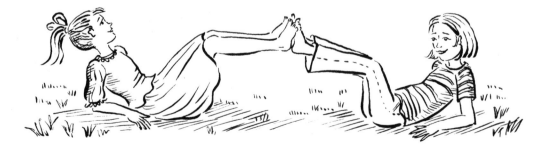

SARDINES

This is a good hide-and-seek game to play indoors on a dark, wet day.

* One player is chosen to hide and runs off to find a hiding place – a wardrobe, for example. All the other players are the seekers. When someone finds the hiding spot, that player joins the hidden person in the wardrobe. The game continues with players cramming themselves into the hiding place until they are all tightly packed like sardines. The last person to find the hidden sardines is the person to hide first in the next game.

YELLOW CAR

This is a game to relieve the boredom of long car journeys with or without traffic jams. Everyone in the car can play. The first person to see a yellow car shouts 'yellow car' and wins a point. The person with the most points at the end of the journey wins.

* Degrees of difficulty and variations on the scoring system may be introduced, if desired. A yellow car scores ten points, for example, while a yellow van only five points, and a yellow lorry, a measly one point.

STARING COMPETITIONS

The staring competition is a battle of will and wits rather than strength, which can be played anywhere, any time. Ask someone to be the referee, in case of disputes.

* Sit opposite your opponent. Relax and close your eyes for a moment and clear your mind of all amusing thoughts. On the word 'go', players open their eyes and must stare straight into each other's eyes. Blinking, smiling, snorting, laughing and talking are not allowed and you must not take your eyes away from your opponent's. Ear-waggling, as far as we know, is allowed. The first person to give in to the giggles wins.

Clubs and Secret Societies

Clubs and secret societies can be a lot of fun, but they are not an excuse to be horrid or nasty to people who don't belong. That's not fun, that's bullying.

SECRET LANGUAGE

* Eggy-peggy is a favourite. Add the word 'egg' before each vowel. Thus 'Mary had a little lamb' becomes 'Meggary heggad egga leggittle leggamb.' Infuriating for those not in the know.

INVISIBLE INK

* a lemon
* writing paper
* cotton bud or fine paintbrush

* Squeeze the juice from a lemon. Dip a cotton bud or a fine paintbrush in the juice, write your message on the paper, leave it to dry and it will have become invisible. To read the message, just hold the paper up to a heat source – a light bulb will do. Not too close, or the secret message will go up in flames!

LAUREL LEAVES

* Another good way to transmit top-secret messages is to write on a laurel leaf. Laurel bushes are often found in garden hedges and the leaves have a slightly bitter-almond smell when you break them.

To send a secret message on the leaf, use a sharp stone, a small stick or even a safety pin to scratch out the word. You might need to write the message on several leaves if it's a long one.

Give the leaf to the chosen society member. She must push the leaf securely up her sleeve. The heat of her arm will cause the leaf to change colour where you marked it, revealing the message.

Parlour Games

If you think parlour games are the stuff of stiff Victorian drawing rooms, think again. These will have everyone shouting at the top of their voice, and may even lead to family feuds.

CHARADES

The aim of charades is to use your theatrical skills to communicate the title of a famous work of art without saying a word.

* Divide into two teams. Appoint someone responsible to keep score. Decide on the number of rounds to play, grab some paper and a pen and move to separate rooms to plot your rivals' demise.

  Each team chooses the titles that a member of the opposing team will have to enact. These can be a book, play, TV show, film or song title. Try not to be too obvious – on the other hand you shouldn't be too hard. If it's too difficult, it just gets boring. Write all the titles down on individual slips of paper and put them in a bowl or basket.

To play, the first player from team A takes a slip from team B's basket. They have about 10 seconds to think up a way to portray the title. They then have three minutes to act it out, silently, using only gestures. If at the end of the three minutes no one from their team has guessed it, then they've lost that turn, and the title is revealed. The winning team jeer accordingly, and then it's their turn.

The game continues until every player has had a chance to 'act'. The score-keeper must keep a record of the amount of time it takes each team to guess the correct answers and the team with the smallest score wins the game.

Here are a few tips and conventions in charades.

To indicate:

* **a book title**: open your hands like a book

* **a movie title**: pretend to crank an old-fashioned camera

* **a play title**: sweep open the theatre curtains

* **a song title**: pretend to sing

* **a TV show**: draw a square in the air

* **the number of words in the title**: hold up the number of fingers

* **which word you're working on**: hold up the number of fingers again

* **number of syllables**: lay the number of fingers on your forearm

* **which syllable you're working on**: lay the number of fingers on your arm again.

* **length of word**: make a small or large gesture, as though you were measuring a fish

* **correct guess**: if someone makes a correct guess, put one finger on your nose and point at the person with your other hand

* **sounds like**: pull your earlobe

THE HAT GAME

The hat game is a simpler, faster and, to be honest, rather more fun version of charades. You can play the hat game with just a few friends or a whole crowd – the more the merrier.

* Each person is given five slips of paper and writes down the name of a famous person on each one. All the slips are put into a hat and shaken up. The players are divided into two teams and appoint a referee. The teams take it in turns to pick out a name from the hat. The player's aim is to communicate the name on the slip of paper to members of their own team without using:

  * any part of that person's actual name

  * any 'sounds likes'

  * any titles; you couldn't say about Shakespeare that he wrote *Romeo and Juliet*

As soon as a name is correctly identified, the player takes another name out of the hat until their time limit, which is one minute, expires. If they are in the middle of a name when the limit expires, that name goes back in the hat. It is not permitted to put names back that are too difficult. Even if it's hopeless, the player must struggle on, giving the opposing team many opportunities for jeering and heckling.

The winning team is the one that has guessed the most names correctly.

FIRST AID

Accidents can happen, and they can happen to anyone, anywhere, at any time, no matter how careful we are. When Rosemary was little, for example, the following accidents befell her . . .

* Her big sister twisted her arm when she was asleep in her pram and dislocated her shoulder.

* She got her finger caught in a door which slammed shut and then couldn't be opened.

* A bee and her left eye collided when she was freewheeling at great speed down a hill on her bicycle. It didn't sting her, but Rosemary and the bee were both badly bruised.

Most accidents and injuries happen in the home and most happen in the kitchen. Minor cuts from the slip of a chopping knife, or a burn from a hot grill, can be quickly and safely treated at home with a little basic first aid knowledge. But with a bit of care and simple common sense, most accidents in the home can be avoided.

Emergency Numbers

In the case of a serious injury or emergency, dial 999 or 112 (this number works everywhere in the European Union). Make sure you know where to find the telephone numbers of your local doctor, hospital and chemist – write them at the front of your address book or keep them near the phone where you can find them quickly.

IN THE KITCHEN

* Never have a saucepan on the stove with the handle turned outwards.

* Keep kettles with their cords and plugs pushed well back on work surfaces.

* Be extremely careful and sensible when using sharp knives and scissors.

* Put away all knives and scissors carefully after use – store knives with the blade down in a knife block or a drawer which toddlers and babies can't reach.

IN THE BATHROOM

* Be careful when getting in and out of the bath.

* Don't run or lark about if the floor is wet and slippery.

* Don't fall asleep in the bath.

* Don't drop anything electrical in water.

ON THE STAIRS

* Avoid running up (or down) stairs in slippers or socks – one slip and . . . thump, thump, thud!

Minor Injuries and Mishaps

MINOR CUTS AND GRAZES

* If the wound is dirty, clean it with an alcohol-free wipe or rinse it under slowly running cold water. Usually you will only need to put a plaster over the wound but if the bleeding doesn't stop, lift the injured part above the level of the heart and apply pressure – don't touch the wound with your hand – and then cover it.

BLACK EYE AND BRUISES

Bruising is due to bleeding into the tissues, which causes swelling and black and blue marks on the skin. Use a cold compress, either a cloth soaked in very cold water and then wrung out or a packet of frozen peas or some ice cubes in a plastic bag – wrap the plastic in a clean cloth – and apply to the bruise with gentle pressure for about 10 minutes.

* If someone is bruised all over and a little shaken, perhaps from a fall, a hot bath is very soothing.

  The traditional remedy for a black eye is to cover it with a steak from the fridge – we wouldn't recommend it, though. Witch hazel is another traditional remedy for bruising and is meant to reduce swelling and help prevent discolouration. Arnica is a homeopathic remedy which can have a remarkable healing effect on wounds and bruising; it can be applied as a cream or taken in tablet form.

TOOTHACHE

* For temporary relief before treatment at the dentist, a hot-water bottle held against the face relieves the pain as does a pad of cotton wool soaked in oil of cloves against the tooth.

BLISTERS ON THE FEET

You can try to prevent these, if you are planning on a hike or walking weekend, by bathing the feet with surgical spirit and then dusting them with talcum powder daily for several weeks, and/or wearing woollen socks, soaped at the toe, heel and ball of the foot.

* If you have a blister, treat it either by swabbing it with surgical spirit or cover it with an ordinary plaster or use a blister plaster, which is padded and helps protect the blister from being rubbed and draws the moisture out of it. Do not remove the loose skin on the blister as this acts as a further protective layer.

MINOR BURNS AND SCALDS

Burns are caused by dry heat, friction or electricity. Scalds are caused by moist heat such as steam or boiling water. Burns are classified by the depth of damage to the skin. There are three depths: superficial, partial thickness and full thickness.

* For minor or superficial burns which have caused little more than reddening of the skin, hold the affected area under slowly running cold water for at least 10 minutes to calm the burn and sooth the pain. If water isn't available you can use milk instead. Cover the burn with a sterile dressing or a non-fluffy pad and bandage loosely. If a blister does form NEVER burst it or you could make it infected. Cover it with a non-stick dressing and leave it in place till the blister reduces of its own accord.

  Rosemary's grandmother always insisted on rubbing butter on a burn. This is NOT RECOMMENDED as it increases the risk of infection!

  Aloe vera gel is an excellent natural remedy for minor burns and sunburn.

SUNBURN AND SUNSTROKE

Avoid sunburn by keeping well covered in the sun — always wear sunblock and a hat and sunglasses. It is important in hot sun to keep the back and spine covered.

* In case of sunburn or sunstroke get the person out of the sun and into the shade, or if you can't do this cover their skin with light clothing or a towel. Bathe in a cool, but not ice-cold, bath, with the water covering all the burnt areas. Do not rub the skin to dry it. Get the patient to have frequent sips of cold water.

  Aloe vera gel and calamine lotion are excellent for mildly sunburnt skin. But be aware that sunburn can be severe enough to warrant medical attention.

FAINTING

Fainting is a brief loss of consciousness caused by reduced blood flow to the brain. If someone thinks they are going to faint, lay them down and raise their feet — prop them up on a chair or pile lots of cushions under them. If someone has fainted try to get them onto the floor and make sure their feet are higher than their head. Loosen any tight clothes such as a collar and make sure there's plenty of air. A casualty should recover from a faint very rapidly; help them to sit up gradually and if they feel faint again lay them down and raise the legs.

* Smelling salts, made from ammonium carbonate, are a traditional remedy to revive someone from a faint, but few people these days carry them round with them as a matter of course.

  If the patient does not regain consciousness quickly, this is not a faint and you should call an ambulance.

CHOKING

If a person is choking, your priority is to try to unblock their airway.

∗ In an adult or a child encourage them to cough and remove any obvious obstruction from the mouth. If this doesn't work get the casualty to bend forwards and give them up to five slaps between the shoulder blades. Stop if the obstruction clears and check the mouth.

If the obstruction hasn't gone, call for an adult who may need to telephone for an ambulance.

NOSE BLEEDS

∗ Get the patient to breathe through their mouth and sit down and lean forwards to prevent the blood going down their throat. Pinch the end of the nostrils. After 10 minutes release the pressure. If necessary repeat for two further periods of 10 minutes. Tell the patient not to blow their nose and avoid exertion for a few hours.

FOREIGN BODY IN THE EYE

NEVER touch anything that is sticking to the eye, which penetrates the eyeball or which rests on the iris or pupil – you could easily damage the eye. Usually dust or grit floats on the white of the eye and can be easily rinsed off.

∗ Stand behind the patient, tilt her head back against your chest, holding the affected eye open gently with your first and second fingers, and clean the eye by pouring clean water or sterile eyewash across it. If this doesn't work, gently try to lift the object off with a clean moist handkerchief.

If something is caught under the upper eyelid, get the casualty to grasp the lashes of the upper lid and pull the lid down over the lower lashes. Or ask them to try blinking underwater to get the object to float away.

HICCUPS

* To stop hiccups, drink water backwards. This is not as easy as it sounds, but is done by placing the lips on the far side of the glass and bending the head forward until you can swallow some water.

  Sucking a lump of sugar sprinkled with a few drops of peppermint essence is also meant to work, as is dropping a cold spoon down the back of the sufferer's shirt, or surprising them with a shout or a funny face.

NAUSEA AND TRAVEL SICKNESS

Ginger in all its forms is very good at helping relieve nausea.

* For ginger tea, roughly chop a 2-centimetre piece of fresh ginger and let it steep for 5 minutes in boiling water. For car sickness, nibble on a small piece of peeled fresh ginger. To prevent car sickness, put some crushed angelica leaves in the car before a journey. These freshen the air and can help ward off nausea. For seasickness, marjoram tea is recommended; put a few sprigs of fresh or a teaspoon of dried marjoram in a cup and cover with boiling water. Let it infuse for 5 minutes.

SPRAINED ANKLE

Sprains and strains occur when the soft tissues – muscles, ligaments, tendons – have been overstretched or torn. Remove the shoe before the foot becomes too swollen.

* RICE is the remedy – rest, ice, compression, elevation. Support the ankle in a comfortable position and apply an ice pack or cold compress to reduce swelling and bruising. Apply gentle pressure by padding all around the foot and ankle with cotton wool and secure it with a firm figure-of-eight bandage. Check it's not too tight by feeling for good circulation every 10 minutes or so. Keep the foot elevated to reduce blood flow and minimize bruising.

STINGS AND INSECT BITES

* **Bee:** If you can see the sting get rid of it by brushing it sideways with your fingernail – don't use tweezers as more poison might enter the wound. Then apply an ice pack or cold compress.

* **Wasp:** A wasp doesn't leave its sting in the wound, otherwise the treatment is the same as for a bee sting.

* **Nettle:** The traditional remedy is to rub the sting as soon as possible with a dock leaf. Where there are nettles there are usually dock leaves. Aloe vera gel is excellent for soothing the sting.

* **Mosquito, midge or flea:** Calamine lotion, lavender oil, onion juice or a poultice of parsley leaves can help calm the itching. If the reaction is severe, a chemist will recommend a good antihistamine cream.

Bites or stings in the mouth are potentially dangerous because they cause swelling and may block the airway. Pesky wasps and bees love sweet drinks. Be careful in the summer when they can find their way into an unattended can. The best way to avoid this is to always use a straw or cup. Some people experience anaphylactic shock after a bite or sting and their tongue and throat can swell. Call an ambulance immediately if this happens.

SNAKE BITE

The only poisonous snake in Britain is the adder, which can be recognized by the black zigzag on its back.

* As in all cases of poisoning, speed is of the essence. The patient should be taken immediately to hospital or an ambulance should be called. Calming and treating the patient appropriately for shock is therefore crucial.

Wash the bite thoroughly and immobilize the bitten body part with a firm bandage – do not use a tourniquet, do not cut the wound. To prevent the venom from spreading throughout the body, do not allow the patient to attempt to walk if the bite is on the leg.

THINGS EVERY GIRL
SHOULD KNOW

A funny little chapter, full of essential hints and tips from how to get out of the most awkward of situations to what to do when the boy you like ignores you in front of his friends. It does exactly what it says on the tin.

WHAT TO DO WHEN INTRODUCED TO ELDERLY RELATIVES OR PARENTS' FRIENDS

This method works for pretty much anyone, except perhaps the Queen. Offer your hand firmly and confidently, and say, 'How do you do.' Do not simper or glower. The adult in question will then probably say something patronizing or obvious, such as 'Ooh, hasn't she grown!' or 'Gosh, doesn't she look like her father!' If the person does decide to address you directly, try not to be monosyllabic in your answers. They may attempt to kiss you, in which case steel yourself for whiskers or bad breath, possibly both, and conceal your revulsion. Your ordeal will probably not last more than five minutes.

HOW NOT TO BE FAZED BY OTHER PEOPLE'S STRANGE HABITS

All families have peculiar habits – indeed your family might seem odd to a stranger. If you are invited to stay in someone else's house, it's very important you prepare yourself mentally. Here are just a few examples of unsettling conduct we have encountered in our time:

* not locking the bathroom door
* mothers who sunbathe topless
* cats/dogs sleeping in their owners' beds and/or eating on the table
* having all the windows wide open even though it is freezing outside
* going for picnics in the rain
* eating very undercooked meat
* having the television on all day as background noise

You can add your own things to the list. Do not let on that you think they are MAD, and remember this useful adage, 'Each to each is what we preach.'

HOW TO ASK FOR THE LOO...

* **In French:** *Excusez-moi, où sont les toilettes?*
  (Exoosai-mooah, oo son lay twalets?)

* **In Italian:** *Mi scusi, dov'e il bagno?*
  (Me skoosi, dovey eel banyo?)

* **In Spanish:** *Perdoname, dónde está el baño?*
  (Purrdonamay, adonday esta el banyo?)

* **In German:** *Entschuldigen Sie bitte, wo sind die Toiletten?*
  (Enshooldigen zee bitter, vo zind dee toyletten?)

HOW TO EAT BREAD AT THE TABLE

* Don't be fooled by side plates with knives. Bread must always be broken using your hands, never cut or sliced using a knife. The knife is for spreading butter on the bread.

HOW TO EAT SOUP WITHOUT SLURPING

* Firstly, do not overfill your spoon. Secondly, don't so much suck the liquid in as pour it in. It may sound strange, but an ability not to slurp soup will get you a long way in certain circles.

HOW TO EAT SPAGHETTI LIKE AN ITALIAN

* Tuck your napkin into the neck of your top. Never, ever cut your spaghetti. And never use a spoon – no self-respecting Italian would be caught using a spoon. Instead, twirl the strands of spaghetti (about 10 or 15 at a time) around your fork using just one hand. Now move your mouth towards your plate. Move it a bit further. Pop the spaghetti in. Swiftly suck in any stray ends. Repeat until the plate is empty. If you have bread to hand, use it to mop up what remains of the sauce. *Buon appetito!*

HOW TO TELL IF AN EGG IS FRESH

* Put the egg in a bowl of cold water. If it sinks to the bottom it's fresh; if it floats, it's rotten.

HOW TO SET YOUR INNER ALARM CLOCK

* Turn off the light and lie down in your bed. Relax. Now, bang your head against your pillow according to the hour you wish to awake – if you want to wake up at six a.m., bang six times. If you like you can add an internal chant: 'I want to wake up at six,' for example. Try it. It works.

HOW TO DEAL WITH BOYS

The main difference between boys and girls is that boys like doing things – driving cars, playing football, throwing stuff, eating, farting, etc. – and girls like feeling things – love, friendship, happiness, excitement, etc. Boys are very physical; girls are very emotional. Of course this is a gross generalization, but it helps to remember that when you ask a boy 'How are you feeling?' he will probably answer 'Hungry' or 'Cold' and not 'Deliriously happy because I am with you'. To begin with this can be disappointing, but it can't really be helped, since expressing emotion comes as naturally to a boy as ballet does to an elephant.

* If you are friends with a boy, bear in mind the following: boys worry a great deal about what other boys think of them. Therefore, even if a boy really likes you, he will be weird about showing this in front of other boys. If he's very immature, he may ignore you completely when he's with his friends. This means he's probably too much of a baby to bother with, although you may wish to give him a second chance if he apologizes and promises never to do it again. If he's actively rude to you in front of his mates, forget about him. He is not just immature, he is an idiot.

* Boys are often spoilt by their mothers so they have a tendency to think girls should do all the boring things in life, like cleaning, cooking and ironing their favourite T-shirt, while they get to do all the exciting things, like jet-skiing, playing in rock bands and being spies. Don't indulge this belief; the sooner they get re-educated the better.

Boys don't always say what they mean, and very often they don't mean what they say. Communication is not their strong point. They're not terribly sensitive to other people's moods either, so if you are upset about something, you will have to spell it out to a boy. It's unlikely he'll work it out for himself, no matter how much sulking or moody hints you drop. Just tell him what's bothering you – and he'll probably be genuinely surprised and sorry he's upset you.

Although boys go to great pains to show the world a confident front, underneath it all they are just as insecure as the rest of us. Sometimes, when it's obvious they are feeling sad (and you will know this through your superior powers of intuition), a bit of encouragement or a compliment can help them feel better. One of the nicest things you can say to a boy is that they are good at something, e.g. skateboarding, running, building a tree house, solving quadratic equations.

If you remember these few basic rules, boys can be among the best friends you'll ever have. And they'll carry your books for you too.

HOW TO HAVE A BEST FRIEND

Your best friend is the one who loves you no matter what. You don't have to explain anything to her because she just gets it. You laugh at exactly the same things. You share secrets, clothes, hours of fun. Because you know she is out in the world, you never have to feel alone.

* You don't exactly choose a best friend – you both sort of choose one another. Once you have found her, you must never take her for granted. The trick to all great friendships is a very important thing called empathy: this means putting yourself in her shoes, so you can understand how she might feel in any given circumstance. You must take care of her tender feelings, not laugh at her when she makes a fool of herself, and understand that sometimes she has grumpy days.

* Best friends are fiercely loyal to one another and trust each other completely. They are not too shy to pay each other compliments, and they often give each other silly presents when it is not a birthday or Christmas, but just because. They always know how to say they are sorry. And they know that friendship is one of the very best things in the whole wide world.

Occasionally, sad as we are to admit it, friendships go wrong, and so you also have to know . . .

HOW TO COPE WHEN YOUR BEST FRIEND GETS A NEW BEST FRIEND

Let her go. This is so important you should read it again. Let her go.

* You may want to have hysterics, plot some fiendish revenge or make her sorry. None of this will work. You have to take an incredibly deep breath, and realize that some things just do not last for ever. This does not mean you are not allowed to be sad. Crying will help; as will writing everything down in a diary. Talk to your mum, who will understand because it has certainly happened to her too.

The key thing to remember is that your best friend not being your best friend any more does not mean there is anything wrong with you. It is not because of something you did, and there was nothing you could have done to stop it.

The best approach is to put on a smiling public face. Be charming, be polite. Soon the horrible feelings of rejection will pass and you will be able to look back with gratitude that you behaved with dignity.

The truth is you will soon find another best friend, much better than the first, who may easily have had the same experience, and you will feel happy that you did not waste any more time on someone who was faithless.

HOW TO KEEP A DIARY

Keeping a diary is one of the great pleasures of life. It means that nothing is lost, and you can look back and see all the crucial moments, remember all the great jokes and fun times. It is where you can safely write down all the thoughts you don't want made public and it is where you can be yourself.

* It is also one of life's mysterious rules that writing things down always makes you feel better about them. If, when you are feeling sad and confused, you write it all down and read it back to yourself you will often think: Well, it's not so bad really, what was I making such a fuss about? This is because when random thoughts whirl around in your head they get all tangled and muddled, but once they are down on the page they make a whole lot more sense.

You may find an actual diary with a page for each day does not allow you enough room, so a simple fat notebook is best – you can just make a note of the dates as you go along. It also means that if you miss writing in your diary for a few days, there aren't horrible gaping holes; you will also not be obliged to write on days when you don't feel like it. Keeping a diary isn't a chore; it should be something you do because you want to.

Keep your diary somewhere safe. A locked box is ideal. But a clever ruse is to take the dust cover of a similar-sized book and slip it over the cover of your diary. That way you can keep it on your bookshelves along with all the other books, and no one will be any the wiser.

HOW TO KEEP A SECRET

This is a vital skill, and sometimes extremely difficult. A secret can be so delicious that you itch to share it. Don't. However much you are tempted, resist. Any short-term thrill you get from telling the secret will pass quickly. But the friend who told you the secret will feel betrayed. She may never tell you a secret again. You may get a reputation as a blabbermouth.

There are various techniques for keeping a secret:

* Try to forget it, as if it never existed (when you grow old and forgetful, you will find this quite easy).

* Write it down in your diary, providing this is kept in a safe place.

* Make a little ceremony of your secret-keeping by writing the secret down on a piece of paper, and then tearing it into tiny scraps and throwing it away.

* Tell the dog or a very young baby.

HOW TO SULK

Sulking is of course pointless, counterproductive and extremely silly. It is also occasionally irresistible. So, since you will almost certainly find yourself doing it at some time in your life, you might as well know how to do it properly and with style.

* The crucial thing to remember about sulking is that it almost never has the desired result. Instead of giving you the attention you crave, people will do incredibly annoying things such as ignoring you, laughing at you or, most maddening of all, not even noticing you're in a sulk.

Even a really good sulk will almost certainly not get you whatever it was you wanted in the first place, so the only reason for doing it is as an end in itself. So make it a great theatrical production. Excellent elements of sulking are the Black Look, the Deep Sigh and the No One Ever Understands a Single Thing I'm Going Through Shrug.

A sulk should be short and intense. Don't try doing it for a whole day, because you will exhaust yourself. You could wear black if you want to go for a real existential sulk, listen ostentatiously to your most gloomy records, and even read a little poetry (this is known as the Continental Sulk). You may want to write deep thoughts in your diary. Obviously, there is no eating involved, which is another very good reason why it should not last for long.

HOW TO HAVE A CRUSH

The thing to understand about a crush is that it is a fantasy. Fantasies are beautiful things, as long as you do not make the error of confusing them with anything that actually happens in real life – Johnny Depp is not suddenly going to arrive in Hemel Hempstead (or wherever you happen to live) and declare that you are the love of his life.

* You may collect pictures of your crush, and plaster your walls with them. The gathering of impossible amounts of obscure information about the crush is also very satisfying. Obviously, you will go to all his films, concerts, plays, etc. However, the writing of a fan letter is often a let-down – you will only get a standard letter back, probably not even signed by the crush himself.

  A particularly satisfying crush is the obscure crush. It's easy and obvious to develop a passion for Brad Pitt or a member of the newest boy band. But if you want to follow a road less travelled and have your crush all to yourself, it's worth making a bit of an effort to find some barely known boy with a guitar and the voice of an angel who will never make it into the top forty, or an actor who can bring Shakespeare to vivid glittering life but is never going to sell out to Hollywood.

  The most important rule is never meet your crush. You have built him up, in your own crazy fantastic world, to be the dream boy to end them all. In life, there is a very real danger that he has bad hair days, gets spinach caught in his teeth and has absolutely no conversation.

HOW TO BE COOL

There is only one sure-fire way to be completely absolutely beyond any argument cool, which is: never, ever, try to be cool.

* Think about the coolest person you know. It will not be someone who only listens to the hippest most obscure bands, or pretends they don't care about anything, or has the very latest trainers. It will not be anyone who is a slave to fashion, however cutting edge. It will not, in fact, be the person who adopts

* the newest buzzword and sneers at anyone who is still using yesterday's expressions. It will be the person who is completely, unquestionably themself.

The essence of cool goes right deep down to the core of a person. A cool girl can turn up with the wrong hair, the wrong shoes, the wrong clothes and get away with it, because that's what she likes and she really doesn't mind what anyone else has to say about it. A cool girl is not afraid to laugh at silly jokes, or hang around with the computer geeks. A cool girl will happily own up to liking Shakespeare sonnets, or old black and white films, or maths.

So just follow your own goofy little star, and one day you will wake up and find that you have become drop-dead, drag-out cool.

HOW TO FIX A LADDER IN YOUR TIGHTS

* There you are, all dressed up and fabulous, and you look down and see the beginning of a ladder in your tights. It's going to run and spread, and within ten minutes your legs will look as if the cat has been at them. This is why a small bottle of clear nail varnish is an essential tool to carry with you whenever you are wearing hosiery. Simply apply a touch of varnish to either end of the ladder to stop the pesky little beggar in its tracks.

HOW TO UNBLOCK A TOILET

A blocked toilet can be embarrassing as well as unpleasant, but there's no need to call the plumber right away.

* Take a large bucket of water, and pour it quickly from as high as you can in one long, smooth flow. The force of the water should dislodge the blockage immediately – then flush as normal. If the blockage is not cleared after the first bucket, try again with another, taking care not to flood the toilet.

FURTHER READING

* *The Anchor Book of Needlecraft Techniques*, Carroll & Brown Ltd, 2003

* *The Art of Tea-Leaf Reading*, Jane Struthers, Godsfield Press Ltd, 2006

* *The Boys Book of Conjuring*, Eugene Stone (ed.), Ward, Lock & Co, 1953

* *The Boys and Girls Handbook*, Octopus Books, 1985

* *Colour Paper Decoration*, Frederick T. Day, C. Arthur Pearson Ltd, 1948

* *Culpeper's Colour Herbal*, Nicholas Culpeper, Foulsham, 2002

* *The Complete Illustrated Holistic Herbal*, David Hoffmann, Element, 1996

* *Darina Allen's Ballymaloe Cookery Course*, Darina Allen, Kyle Cathie, 2001

* *The Everyday Games Book*, V. C. Alexander, Evans Brothers, 1939

* *Games for Parties*, Kate Stevens, Ward, Lock & Co, 1939

* *Gardens from Garbage*, Judith F. Handlesman, Milbrook Press, 1993

* *Giant Gift Book for Girls and Boys*, Geo W. Blow, Associated Newspapers, *c.* 1936

* *Girl Annual*, Hulton Publications

* *Heaven on Earth, An Astrological Entertainer with Slides, Wheels and Changing Pictures*, Emma Curzon and Fritz Wegner, Bulfinch Press, 1992

* *How to Make Things for Fun*, Ladybird, 1978

* *The Illustrated Language of Flowers*, Jena Marsh, illustrations Kate Greenaway, Holt, Rinehart and Winston, 1978

* *Jekka's Complete Herb Book*, Jekka McVicar and Penelope Hobhouse, Kyle Cathie, 1994

* *The Jolly Play Book*, Collins, 1956

* *The Junior Weekend Book*, Victor Gollancz, 1939

* *'Mandy' For Girls*, D. C. Thomson, 1979

* *My First Ballet Book*, Kate Castle, Kingfisher Books Ltd, 2006

* *The Outdoor Book*, Jack Cox, Lutterworth Press, 1955

* *The Prediction Book of Palmistry*, Jo Logan, Cassell, 1985

* *The Times Cookbook*, Frances Bissell, Chatto & Windus, 1993

* *The Young Gardener*, Clare Bradley, Metro Books, 1999

USEFUL ADDRESSES

BOOKS

www.abebooks.com
www.abebooks.co.uk
To search for old and out-of-print books, the best place to start is at Abe Books on the internet, where you can often find rare and unusual books at very reasonable prices.

COOKING

www.cakescookiesandcraftsshop.co.uk
Vast range of cooking and baking accessories including cookie cutters, baking tins, chocolate-making moulds and party supplies.

www.splatcooking.co.uk
Baking accessories, cookie kits, aprons, chefs' hats and workshops.

CRAFT MATERIALS

www.craftikids.co.uk
Good selection of craft materials and kits to buy online.

www.crafts4kids.co.uk
Arts and crafts materials, kits, books and more.

www.ziggyart.co.uk
Online art supplier with good range of children's craft and art materials as well as face paints.

www.etsy.com
American online shop selling handicrafts, kits, yarns and more – inspiring and fun.

www.littlebirds.typepad.com
Very cute website with photographs of hand-made craft items. Good for ideas and inspiration.

ESSENTIAL OILS, SKINCARE AND BATH PRODUCTS

www.theorganicpharmacy.com
Organic essential oils and natural bath and beauty products.

www.nealsyardremedies.com
Essential oils, bath, body and skincare products.

www.culpeper.co.uk
Natural herbal bath products, herbal teas and tinctures.

www.mariposa.co.uk
Organic and natural bath and beauty products.

www.speziaorganics.com
Organic essential oils, bath and beauty products.

GARDENING

www.jekkasherbfarm.com

Wonderful supplier of organic herb plants and seeds – order seeds and plants online or request a catalogue to browse before ordering.

www.thomasetty.co.uk

Lovely selection of wild flower, herb and vegetable seeds and bulbs to order online.

www.growersorganics.com

Organic plants, vegetables, herbs, flowers and compost bins.

www.wigglywigglers.co.uk

Suppliers of wormeries, composters, bird boxes and pest control.

www.wildlifetrusts.org

Helpful advice and suggestions for attracting wildlife to your garden.

www.english-nature.org.uk

Informative site giving advice on wildlife-friendly gardening and details of guided nature walks and events across the UK.

www.organiccatalog.com

Flower and vegetable seeds, seeds for sprouting, sprouting jars and lots of other things to help you in the garden.

GENERAL

www.girlguiding.org.uk/brownies

The official website of the Brownies in the UK. Competitions, games, advice, bookclub and information on badges.

www.girlguiding.org.uk

The official site of the Guide Association, home of Guiding and Girl Scouting in the United Kingdom. Programme information for Rainbows, Brownies, Guides, how to join the Guides, activities and advice.

NATURE

www.bbc.co.uk/nature

Useful and informative site with details of what to look for in nature throughout the year and bird-feeding tips and advice.

www.rspb.org.uk

The Royal Society for the Protection of Birds offers good advice on wildlife care, events and an online shop with bird feeders and seed, bird baths and nesting boxes.

PERFUME

www.olfattorio.it

L'Olfattorio – Bar à Parfums,
34 Via di Ripetta, Rome

The ultimate olfactory experience – not to be missed if you are in Rome.

PETS

www.rspca.org.uk

The Royal Society for the Prevention of Cruelty to Animals website provides information on where and how to find a pet at one of its animal rescue centres.

www.dogshome.org

The Battersea Dog and Cat Home is one of the oldest and most famous dog and cat rescue centres in the world. A good place to find the dog or cat of your dreams.

www.pcuk.org

Established in 1928, the Pony Club organizes activities for and educates young people who love ponies and riding.

SEWING PATTERNS, FABRICS AND TRIMMINGS

www.fitzpatterns.com

Fun and fashionable sewing patterns to download including some free patterns.

www.betsyrosspatterns.com

Easy patterns for skirts, tops, bags and more to order online.

www.sewessential.co.uk

Needlework kits, fabrics, felts, soft toy kits and trimmings.

www.kleins.co.uk

Buttons, trimmings and more to buy online.

WOOL AND YARNS

www.loop.gb.com

Loop, 41 Cross Street, London N1

Beautiful wool shop which offers lunchtime knitting classes. Wools and patterns can also be ordered online.

www.yarnsmith.co.uk

Good range of wools, yarns and kits to order online.

www.getknitted.com

Yarns, knitting needles, patterns and accessories to buy online.

ACKNOWLEDGEMENTS

We would like to thank everyone at Janklow & Nesbit for putting up with us, and Venetia Butterfield, Sarah Fraser, John Hamilton, Tom Weldon, Keith Taylor, Eleo Gordon, Jenny Dean, Georgina Atsiaris, Karol Davies, Sophie Mitchell and everyone at Penguin for making it happen, and Liz Davis for her brilliant copy-editing. Also: Tania Kindersley for her infinite wisdom, Claire Paterson for her endless encouragement and tips on falling, Kirsty Gordon and Michelle Henery for their invaluable contributions. Sarah would like to thank her husband Michael for being generally brilliant and her own dear mother for … well, for just being a great mother in the face of considerable adversity. Rosemary would like to thank Sarah Jane Lovett, Liz Calder, Arzu Tahsin, Rachel Cugnoni, Anna Hart, Lilias Wallace — and all her sisters.

And finally, Natacha Ledwidge, who did the beautiful illustrations.